Social Work and Research

SOCIAL WORK AND RESEARCH

Dr. K.K. Saran

CENTRUM PRESS
NEW DELHI-110002 (INDIA)

CENTRUM PRESS

H.O.: 4360/4, Ansari Road, Daryaganj,
New Delhi-110002 (India)
Tel: 23278000, 23261597, 23255577, 2328[illegible]375

B.O.: No. 1015, Ist Main Road, BSK IIIrd Stage,
IIIrd Phase, IIIrd Block, Bengaluru-560085 (INDIA)
Tel: 080-41723429

Email: centrumpress@gmail.com
Visit us at: www.centrumpress.com

Social Work and Research

First Edition, 2012

ISBN 978-93-81293-67-6

PRINTED IN INDIA

Printed at Tarun Offset, Delhi

Contents

Preface

The process of social work practice starts with identification of problem. Once a problem is identified we need to specify the precise problem with which we are concerned, what factors might contribute to the problem, and which aspects of the problem will be given priority. In problem assessment, one has to decide which behavioural systems are involved in a problem-individual, group, or societal-and whether effective intervention is possible.

It must be borne in mind that the process of social work research is not that of social research. There are many similarities between social work research process and the social research process. However, the process of social work research has some additional steps designed to suit the objectives of social work practice. By following the process social work researchers are in a position to know precisely what intervention was applied and how much effect was produced. The process links research and practice. Social work research starts with problem identification and setting up of objectives. This is followed by the process of need assessment of the clients' problems. During these initial stages, the researcher strives to obtain a clear and specific understanding of the problem, using assessment tools such as interviewing, observation etc..

Social work being a scientific profession, higher professional standard calls for improving the knowledge base for social work education and practice and delivering more effective services to the clients. As such, social work practice has to be a scientific practice or data guided practice. To meet the challenging task of higher professional standards and accountability, social work profession has to depend more and more on empirical evidences showing relationship between interventions and its effects. In a sense, the profession as to prepare itself to accept the client's right to equity. In this context, research has multifaceted roles to play. Research can provide scientific support to the social work practice methodology right from scientific assessment of the problem to the evaluation of the intervention outcome. For this, conscious efforts have to be made to restructure the social work curriculum and integrate research, theory and practice.

There are some special areas of social work practice in which social research has direct linkage. The areas are: understanding human behaviour in social environments needs assessment, assessment of client functioning, programme evaluation, and practice effectiveness. List of areas is not exhaustive. These five areas, however, will serve as a helpful aid as we analyse the linkages of social research with the social work practice.

This book re-examines the concept of Social Work and Research in the Indian and abroad context and attempts to integrate participatory.

—Editor

1

Integration of Social Work Research

Social work has a challenging task ahead of it to meet the demands of accountability and higher professional standards. The accountability on the part of social work-empirical evidences of intervention outcome pertaining to client's goal-is *sine* qua non for social work to be recognized as a profession. In other words, the profession has to prepase itself to accept the clients' right to demand that social workers justify their actions and recommendations on specific and demonstrable grounds.

Social work being a scientific profession, higher professional standard calls for improving the knowledge base for social work education and practice and delivering more effective services to the clients. As such, social work practice has to be a scientific practice or data guided practice. To meet the challenging task of higher professional standards and accountability, social work profession has to depend more and more on empirical evidences showing relationship between interventions and its effects. In a sense, the profession as to prepare itself to accept the client's right to equity. In this context, research has multifaceted roles to play. Research can provide scientific support to the social work practice methodology right from scientific assessment of the problem to the evaluation of the intervention outcome. For this, conscious efforts have to be made to restructure the social work curriculum and integrate research, theory and practice.

The greatest drawback of social work education has been the lack of fit between theory, research and practice. According to Haworth (1984), social work requires a theoretical base that comes basically from observation, understanding and experiencing the reality of knowledge, values and action. The role of various theories in social work profession has not been given due importance; rather, they are given peripheral position. It has been ignored that theories provide a framework of reference, which justifies the process of social work.

Moreover, theories serve, guide and direct research and practice. They focus attention on certain phenomena as being relevant to the profession. If theories are ignored then it could be rather difficult to study and analyse problem and adopt an appropriate intervention strategy. In comprehending theories and the role they play, it is being realised that though many social workers use theories in their research-and practice settings but are not conscious of using them and they do not consider them theories.

Practice courses in social work education draw more from practice wisdom than from research, while research courses are not necessarily practice oriented. Consequently, practice and research are treated independently at the training level and the approach, therefore, continues in the post-training careers of social workers. The gulf between researchers and practitioners, over the years, has widened. Researchers frequently complain that practitioners ignore this pertinent and important findings, Practitioners consider much of the university stimulated research irrelevant and express their inability to use it. Such gaps have been widened by the belief that the sane person cannot be both a good researcher and a practitioner. Such beliefs have been substantiated by the facts that social work researchers hardly find time to practice. Conversely, the practitioners, due to their preoccupation with service delivery systems, are least concerned about research. Both the contentions underscore the need to Integration of Social solidify the relationship between schools of social work and agencies by integrating Work Practice and research and practice (Reid, 1978).

The purpose of this paper is to assess the current status of social work practice and research, and identify the ways and means to integrate them for achieving higher professional standards and accountability.

CURRENT STATUS OF SOCIAL WORK PRACTICE

By and large, social work practice has been following problem-solving model to address key intervention approaches. These approaches are primarily based on theoretical assumptions' and seldom require empirical support. The practice models, in general, focus on assessment, treatment, planning and evaluation and emphasise use of practice wisdom and skills rather than scientific assessment of the problem and evaluation of outcome, Mostly the practitioners rely on visual significance of intervention outcome. As such, these outcomes neither contribute to the theories nor to the practice of social work.

Social work is a practice profession. As such, it follows a number of practice paradigms like psycho-social, functionalists, problem-solving, cognitive-behavioural, task-oriented, case management, crisis intervention, ecological perspective, eclectic and others, These paradigms are not mutually exclusive. Each paradigm, if evaluated critically, appears to omit one or other important aspects of practice or overemphasizes things that are not applicable to many problems or clients. Certain paradigms are sometimes criticised for dealing only with superficial aspects of client's problems or dealing only with symptoms without resolving underlying issues that will perpetuate the problem in other forms.

SOCIAL WORK PRACTICE: THE PROCESS

The process of social work practice starts with identification of problem. Once a problem is identified we need to specify the precise problem with which we are concerned, what factors might contribute to the problem, and which aspects of the problem will be given priority. In problem assessment, one has to decide which behavioural systems are involved in a problem-individual, group, or societal-and whether effective intervention is possible.

Formulation of Intervention Strategy

We develop a strategy for intervention that will be effective in alleviating the problem specified in the assessment stage. We choose an appropriate intervention strategy from among numerous intervention strategies, such as crisis intervention, behaviour modification, vocational training etc.

Implementation

The intervention strategy selected in the preceding stage is then implemented. We collect information data as a part of intervention stage and attempt to change the people we are studying, Here, we are primarily concerned with the effectiveness of the intervention strategy in creating some change in clients or the systems in which they, interact.

Evaluation

Then we evaluate the effectiveness of the intervention strategy implemented at the preceding stage. In this stage we try to get answers to a set of questions, such as: Were the goals of the plan achieved? What was the cost of strategy? Were there any undesirable side effects of the changes brought about by the intervention? Which aspects of the intervention process seemed to be most important in producing the change that resulted? The final stage is 'closure to the intervention effort'. The extent to which the intervention has been effective must be determined and also the degree to which the goals of the intervention cannot be, and possibly never will be achieved. We might suggest other sources of help that the client could utilize to cope with problems still unresolved by the intervention.

SOCIAL WORK RESEARCH

It must be borne in mind that the process of social work research is not that of social research. There are many similarities between social work research process and the social research process. However, the process of social work research has some additional steps designed to suit the objectives cf social work practice. By following the process social work researchers are in a position to know precisely what intervention was applied and how much effect was produced. The process links research and practice.

Problem Identification and Need Assessment

Social work research starts with problem identification and setting up of objectives. This is followed by the process of need assessment of the clients' problems. During these initial stages, the researcher strives to obtain a clear and specific understanding of the problem, using assessment tools such as interviewing, observation etc..

Setting up Goals

After the problem is identified and needs are assessed, the next step is to set up goals to be achieved. The goals arc required to be specific, precisely defined and measurable in some way.

Pre-Intervention Measurement

The third step in the process is to have a pre-intervention measurement, that is the measurement prior to intervention; the pre-intervention measurement is used as basis from which to compare the client's condition after the intervention is introduced.

Intervention Phase

Next stage in the process is to introduce intervention. It is important here to note that only a single, coherent intervention be applied during any intervention phase.

Data Analysis

Following the intervention we assess the effects of intervention by occuparing the measurements, that is, pre-intervention measurement and measurements during intervention. Data are analysed in order to determine the intervention effects.

Drawing of Conclusions

Final step in social work research is to draw conclusions from the analysis of data. Linkages between Social Work Practice and Social Work Research The intent of this paper is to highlight the ways and means of integrating social work practice with social research. We do this by emphasising the parallels and linkages between practice and research. The processes discussed above show the parallels and linkages between research and social work practice. Social work research provides the means for understanding the problems with which students of social work encounter and the means for evaluating change. Students of social work need to understand, apply, and in some cases, conduct research while practising social work. It also shows the parallels between social work practice and research and the benefits students of social work will get if they incorporate into practice some of the research techniques.

Both research and practice are based on observation, but the observations of students of social work are under constructed and intuitive. Thus, students of social work cafc benefit from using structured observations-a technique of research-in their practice.

Single-subject design of social work research is, in fact, a combination of social work practice and research. The research methodology of single-subject research design involves pre-intervention data, intervention and post-intervention data to examine the effectiveness of social work practice, that parallels the scientific practice.

Application of Research in Social Work Practice

There are some special areas of social work practice in which social research has direct linkage. The areas are: understanding human behaviour in social environments needs assessment, assessment of client functioning, programme evaluation, and practice effectiveness. List of areas is not exhaustive. These five areas, however, will serve as a helpful aid as we analyse the linkages of social research with the social work practice.

Behaviour and Social Environments

Social work students link people to resources they can use, enhance people's coping abilities, improve the operation of social systems, and participate in the development of social policy, to name a few. All these activities rest on an understanding of the people to whom services are provided and a comprehension of the social environments in which they function.

Social work research can provide much of this knowledge. An agency providing services to street children, for example, can turn to research on street children for a better understanding of the problems facing their clients. Studies of changing values among children could help the agency assess the stigma their particular clients might face. Social research on how families react to EIIWAIDS might aid in understanding how the families of HIVIAIDS might cope with the crisis they comfront. In other words, there is a wide range of behavioural research, much of it basic research, that is only indirectly linked to practice but that can inform intervention. Social work students need to be able to understand and assess this research in terms of whether it is sufficiently important to practice.

Need Assessment

Social work research can be used to make an accurate assessment of the need for various forms of service and suggest alternative strategies from meeting those needs. The purpose of this research is to determine whether a problem exists, to indicate the severity of the problem, and to estimate the number and characteristics of people adversely affected by the problem.

Need assessment research is often descriptive rather than focusing explanation or prediction. Through research we can collect information fram individuals and households in order to discover the extent of unmet economic needs and the nature of those needs. The researchers determine how those needs varied in terms of income levels, size of households, expenditure patterns, etc. They can also determine if there were seasonal variations in economic needs. Another goal of the research is to analyse the way in which people respond to changing levels of income and to the limits of welfare. This descriptive data would then be available to administrative and political decision makers as they develop long-term public policy.

Assessment of Client Functioning

In social work practice, it is often necessary to assess the level of functioning of clients. What fund of communication problem exists in a family? How capable is parent of dealing with the delinquent children? How skilled is a person in negotiating a job interview? Though social work students make such assessments often, there is a danger that they will be made unsystematicaly. Observational techniques used in social research can sometimes be incorporated into practice in order to make more valid and reliable assessments. This is illustrated as follows:

In a study a researcher developed a procedure for the systematic observation and classification of mannerisms among blind children. Such children often exhibit repetitive and stereotypical movements, but there is lunch variation among individuals in the specific form of mannerisms. The researchers set out to develop a coding scheme that took into account such variables as the intensity, direction, syncronisation, and order of the body movements. This tool not only helped to understand the causes and type of manneristic behaviour but also enabled clinicians and Counsellors who work with the blind to measure more precisely the performance of their clients and establish intervention plans.

Programme Evaluation

In the past few decades, we have seen many ambitious and extensive programmes intended to cope with social problems and provide services to individuals. Along with the growth of these programmes has emerged an increasing concern over their results: Do they achieve their intended goals? These programmes are costly, and some evaluation is needed to assess whether resources are being effectively utilized. Programme evaluation is the utilisation of scientific research techniques to assess the results of a programme and evaluate whether the programme currently designed achieves its stated goals.

Practice Effectiveness

In recent years there have been major advances in the

capacity of research to answer professionals' questions about the efficacy of intervention efforts on specific clients. One form of such research is called single-subject design, where social work researchers devise a way to measure the occurrence of a problem and to monitor the behaviour of a client for a baseline period. Then intervention begins, and the behaviour is again monitored. Comparison between the baseline and intervention periods permits the practitioners to make more accurate assessments of progress than the informal assessments on which practitioners have traditionally relied. Though the procedure is quite elaborate and requires expertise, but even a final year MSW students can readily apply the basic model.

Through such careful monitoring of behaviour and measuring of intervention effects, it is possible for professionals not only to enhance his or her own effectiveness, but also to contribute to the development of an intervention technology that others can successfully apply.

The Framework for Integrating Research

Social work is emerging as a multidimensional and multi-theoretical profession, therefore, the lack of fit between research, theory and practice cannot be ignored. Research provides appropriate theoretical base to the social work profession. A conceptual framework, well-defined' procedure and scientific attitude are essential and they cannot be achieved without integrating research, theory and practice of social work. At this point question arises about the diversity of various theories. Do we really need so many and highly diverse theories? The answer is simple; we should not forget the large canvas which social work covers. Right from the problem of nail biting among children to the problem of communal tension social work is required for providing Integration of Social a helping hand. In this situation many conceptual dimension and philosophical Work Practice and Research consideration are needed for social work practice.

Although research is different in many respects from practice, there are significant similarities between the two, which if integrated can help practitioners have better understanding of the problem and provide services accordingly. Research begins with problem formulation. Having formulated a researchable problem, researchers develop a research design. Next stage in research is data collection, and the final step is to draw conclusions by analysing the data. In much the same way practitioners first assess the problem to decide effective intervention is possible. After that, practitioners develop a strategy for intervention that will be effective in alleviating the problem specified in the assessment stage. This is followed by implementation of the intervention strategies. Finally, the practitioners evaluate the effectiveness of the intervention strategies implemented.

SCIENTIFIC ATTITUDE

Scientific attitude is really a composite of a number of mental habits, or of tendencies to react consistently in certain ways to a novel or problematic situation. These habits or tendencies include accuracy, intellectual honesty, open-mindedness, suspended judgment, criticalness, and a habit of looking for true cause and effect relationships. It is a cognitive concept; scientific attitudes are normally associated with the mental processes of scientists.

Challenges in Measurement of Scientific Attitude

Development of scientific attitude is considered as an important objective of science learning all over the world. Many teaching techniques are evolved and suggested to develop scientific attitude. Some out of them are the outcome of elaborate efforts of researchers. The challenge remains with the measurement of effects of these techniques. In other words it is a challenge of measurement of learning of scientific attitude, which is discussed at length in this write up. During the course of my work in the area of scientific attitude for the last 25 years, I have come across these challenges and tried to face them. This paper is aimed at making teacher educators, teachers, research students and also NGOs in the field aware of these challenges.

Following are some of the major challenges in measurement of scientific attitude

1) Conceptualizing
2) Domain decision
3) Content validity
4) Selection of right type of measuring instrument
5) Objectivity
6) Teachers training.

The Challenge of Conceptualizing

Scientific attitude comprises of many complex factors. Only some of them are listed below after detailed study of related literature.

a) Belief on cause and effect relationship.
b) Suspend the judgment till enough data is gathered.
c) Emphasis on empirical evidence.
d) Open mindedness.
e) Accuracy in thought and action.
f) Intellectual honesty.
g) Objectivity.
h) Criticality.
i) Unbiased decision making ability.
j) Ability to identify difference between hypothesis and facts.
k) Habit of reviewing the data.
l) To keep away oneself from blind beliefs.
m) Curiosity.
n) Ability to think logically.
o) Faith in development.
p) Faith in problem solving.
q) Ability to recognize self limitations.
r) Interest in newness.

Apart from above sub-factors of scientific attitude, scientific temper and scientific outlook are the concepts having a very close relationship with scientific attitude. Under such circumstances, it is mandatory for test constructor –

- To understand and define each factor of the above list by dictionary meaning and also by some examples.
- To identify some similarities and differences in these factors.
- To classify them into sub-categories.
- To limit to some of these factors for the purpose of measurement so as to make the measuring instrument usable.
- To make operational definition of scientific attitude.

In the process of limiting to few factors and converting those into operational definitions, the totality of the concept and as a consequence the totality of measuring instrument is likely to be threatened.

Apart from this, the selected factors (which will define scientific attitude) may not be easily convertible in the test items in spite of best efforts of defining them operationally.

The Challenge of Domain Decision

Psychological variables are generally categorized into three domains. These are cognitive, affective and psychomotor. The domain of the variable which is to be measured needs to be fixed for two reasons.

a) It helps in deciding right type of measuring instrument.

b) It also helps in writing appropriate test items.

The test constructor faces the challenge in making this decision as attitude is generally categorized as a factor of the affective domain. But if we look at the factors given above, which comprise scientific attitude, we realize that only one single domain is not sufficient to encompass all the factors. Categorization of each factor under some single domain will also be artificial.

Still if tried, factors like objectivity, criticality, unbiased decision making ability, ability to identify difference between hypothesis and facts will have to be categorized under cognitive domain. Where as factors like intellectual honesty, habit of reviewing the data, faith in development, faith in problem solving will occupy space in affective domain. A factor like accuracy in action will go under the psychomotor domain.

The Challenge of Content Validity

A decision of content validity is the next challenge for the test constructor. The development of scientific attitude starts from learning of science. But later on, it is expected to exhibit its presence in all walks of life. So the content is too vast for the test or it can be said that it will not be limited to the specific content. To select the sample content for construction of scientific attitude test items from general experiences is not an easy task.

Another issue in this is how one can guarantee transfer of scientific attitude from one area to another, i.e. the person having scientific attitude in health related issues may not have it in issues related to religion.

Type of Measuring Instrument

Witnessing concrete evidence of scientific attitude through objective measuring instrument is extremely difficult. Attitude is defined as a stable predisposition to respond. This stability is understood either

(a) As a consistency across modes of responding to an attitude object.

(b) As a consistency in individual responses across time.

Such an analysis suggests the inadequacy of the usual procedure of measuring attitude at a single time by attitude scales and calling these responses attitude. Scientific attitude cannot involve only a measure of final product. The process also becomes important with the use of word scientific, as this word refers to the way attitude is developed. If an attitude scale is constructed and the test item asks to give favourable or unfavourable response to the statements then this response alone may not provide enough information about scientific attitude because the process involved in reaching to this response cannot be revealed.

The test items for measuring scientific attitude need to measure cognitive, psychomotor and affective aspects. So varied types of test items need to be constructed. A routine type of attitude scale will not serve the purpose. Multiple types of tests and test items need to be thought.

Challenge of Objectivity

Whichever is the tool chosen for measurement of scientific attitude, it will carry along with it numerous problems of objective measurement because of the complexity of the phenomenon. It is observed that experts in the field hardly come to a unanimous opinion about scientific attitude as a procedure and also as a product. It affects adversely on inter-examiners' objectivity.

Challenge of Teacher Training

Teachers hardly get any training of construction of scientific attitude measurement test at pre-service or in-service training programs. This training is essential as the standardized tools are rarely available and even if they are available they may not serve local purposes. Teachers training institutes need to think in this direction. It is seen that this major objective of science teaching is neglected in evaluation, measurement process and so as a consequence of this it is neglected in teaching too. At S.N.D.T. Women's University, we have done some efforts at pre-service teachers training programs, at M.Ed. and at doctoral research level to orient and to provide some experiences to our students regarding measurement of scientific attitude and have tried to over come some of the above said challenges.

DIFFERENT SCOPE OF SOCIAL WORK

Social work we mean work for the society. Social work is a work by which a social worker can aware individual about their problems, identify their worth & dignity & give a satisfactory and independent life which they can't get by their own effort. The first school of social work was set-up in Bombay in 1936. According to Prof. Friedlander," Social work is a professional service based upon scientific knowledge & skill in human relations which assists individuals alone or in groups to obtain social & professional satisfaction & independence."

SCOPE OF SOCIAL WORK

Child Development

Children are the most vital part of our Nation. They are the foundation of any nation. For progress of any country their development is necessary. Their mental, physical, emotional, psychological, social development is important. The following services has been organized by the Central Social Welfare Board for welfare of child in India. They are:

- Right to education
- Right against exploitation
- Right for rehabilitation
- Right to speech & expression.

Government policy :

- Institutions for their protection, education & rehabilitation of the socially handicapped children
- Temporary homes for the sick children suffering from TB & skin disease
- Children home, infant home, Balbadi, Nursery, Pre-primary school, day care centre, recreation & cultural centres
- Holiday homes for the children of the family of economic weaker sections
- Child Health Centre
- Child Guidance Clinic
- Schools for Mentally retarded children.

Social workers work in this institutions & tries their level best to solve their problems and strengthen the path forth development of their personality. He also develop the abilities & capabilities of the child.

Medical Social Work

The medical social work provide assistance to patient &

their family who are coping with many problems A social worker have the potentiality to aware the Doctor about the problem and collect & analyse patient's detail information to help other health professions to understand the needs of the patients & their family In fact when a doctor come into any conclusion in a minute, a social worker diagnosis a problem thoroughly.

Clinical Social Work

The clinical social work provides a full range of Mental Health Services including assessment, diagnosis & treatment. It provide referral service to individuals, couples, families & groups. Assist clients in adjusting to measure life style changes due to death of loved one, disability, divorce or loss of a job.

Social Work Administration & Management

To manage a programme planning is most important. The important of social worker related to Fund raising & making grants :

- Budget management
- Monitoring & evaluation of public & social policy
- Co-ordinate activities to achieve the agencies goal
- Staff co-ordination.

International Social Work

The role of social work is to :

- Counsel & aid refugees to ensure a smooth transition into a new environment
- Facilitate international adoption
- Provide disaster relief in the time of crisis
- Counsel families to find better solution to their problems. Remove children from abusive situation & place it to care homes
- Find employment & housing for homeless families
- Assist pregnant women, adoptive parents & adoptive children in crisis

- Provide assessment, support, counselling
- Provide assistants to women & their children who are victims of domestic violence.

Acute Psychiatric Hospital

A social worker can help to a psycho patient very trick fully because of her/his professional quality. She/he can provide-

- Complete Intake
- Psycho-social assessment
- Participate in the treatment plan
- Provide patient & family education & support
- Provide individual treatment family & group therapy
- Provide discharge & after planning.

Community Organizer

- Assist the community in defining a school problem
- Provide direction & guidance to the community in-order to mobilize & identified cause by case work, group work & community organization
- Assist in establishing new programmes to meet the needs of individuals, groups and families.

Other Scopes

- Addiction Treatment
- Child abuse, adoption & welfare
- Criminal justice
- Crisis Intervention
- Developmental disabilities
- Disaster relief
- Domestic Relief
- Domestic Violence
- HIV/AIDS
- Military social work
- Political development

- Rural development
- Industrial development
- Women welfare.

PROBLEM FORMULATION

So how do researchers come up with the idea for a research project? Probably one of the most common sources of research ideas is the experience of practical problems in the field. Many researchers are directly engaged in social, health or human service program implementation and come up with their ideas based on what they see happening around them. Others aren't directly involved in service contexts, but work with (or survey) people who are in order to learn what needs to be better understood. Many of the ideas would strike the outsider as silly or worse. For instance, in health services areas, there is great interest in the problem of back injuries among nursing staff. It's not necessarily the thing that comes first to mind when we think about the health care field. But if you reflect on it for a minute longer, it should be obvious that nurses and nursing staff do an awful lot of lifting in performing their jobs. They lift and push heavy equipment, and they lift and push often times heavy patients! If 5 or 10 out of every hundred nursing staff were to strain their backs on average over the period of one year, the costs would be enormous — and that's pretty much what's happening. Even minor injuries can result in increased absenteeism. Major ones can result in lost jobs and expensive medical bills. The nursing industry figures that this is a problem that costs tens of millions of dollars annually in increased health care. And, the health care industry has developed a number of approaches, many of them educational, to try to reduce the scope and cost of the problem. So, even though it might seem silly at first, many of these practical problems that arise in practice can lead to extensive research efforts.

Another source for research ideas is the literature in your specific field. Certainly, many researchers get ideas for research by reading the literature and thinking of ways to extend or refine previous research. Another type of literature that acts as a source of good research ideas is the Requests For Proposals (RFPs) that are published by government agencies and some companies. These RFPs describe some problem that the agency would like researchers to address — they are virtually handing the researcher an idea! Typically, the RFP describes the problem that needs addressing, the contexts in which it operates, the approach they would like you to take to investigate to address the problem, and the amount they would be willing to pay for such research. Clearly, there's nothing like potential research funding to get researchers to focus on a particular research topic.

And let's not forget the fact that many researchers simply think up their research topic on their own. Of course, no one lives in a vacuum, so we would expect that the ideas you come up with on your own are influenced by your background, culture, education and experiences.

Very soon after you get an idea for a study reality begins to kick in and you begin to think about whether the study is feasible at all. There are several major considerations that come into play. Many of these involve making tradeoffs between rigor and practicality. To do a study well from a scientific point of view may force you to do things you wouldn't do normally. You may have to control the implementation of your program more carefully than you otherwise might. Or, you may have to ask program participants lots of questions that you usually wouldn't if you weren't doing research. If you had unlimited resources and unbridled control over the circumstances, you would always be able to do the best quality research. But those ideal circumstances seldom exist, and researchers are almost always forced to look for the best tradeoffs they can find in order to get the rigor they desire.

There are several practical considerations that almost always need to be considered when deciding on the *feasibility* of a research project. First, you have to think about how long the research will take to accomplish. Second, you have to question whether there are important ethical constraints that need consideration. Third, can you achieve the needed cooperation to take the project to its successful conclusion. And fourth, how significant are the costs of conducting the research. Failure to consider any of these factors can mean disaster later.

The Literature Review

One of the most important early steps in a research project is the conducting of the literature review. This is also one of the most humbling experiences you're likely to have. Why? Because you're likely to find out that just about any worthwhile idea you will have has been thought of before, at least to some degree. Every time I teach a research methods course, I have at least one student come to me complaining that they couldn't find anything in the literature that was related to their topic. And virtually every time they have said that, I was able to show them that was only true because they only looked for articles that were *exactly* the same as their research topic. A literature review is designed to identify related research, to set the current research project within a conceptual and theoretical context. When looked at that way, there is almost no topic that is so new or unique that we can't locate relevant and informative related research.

Some tips about conducting the literature review. First, concentrate your efforts on the *scientific* literature. Try to determine what the most credible research journals are in your topical area and start with those. Put the greatest emphasis on research journals that use a blind review system. In a blind review, authors submit potential articles to a journal editor who solicits several reviewers who agree to give a critical review of the paper.

The paper is sent to these reviewers with no identification of the author so that there will be no personal bias (either for or against the author). Based on the reviewers' recommendations, the editor can accept the article, reject it, or recommend that the author revise and resubmit it. Articles in journals with blind review processes can be expected to have a fairly high level of credibility. Second, do the review early in the research process. You are likely to learn a lot in the literature review that will help you in making the tradeoffs you'll need to face. After all, previous researchers also had to face tradeoff decisions. What should you look for in the literature review?

First, you might be able to find a study that is quite similar to the one you are thinking of doing. Since all credible research studies have to review the literature themselves, you can check their literature review to get a quick-start on your own. Second, prior research will help assure that you include all of the major relevant constructs in your study. You may find that other similar studies routinely look at an outcome that you might not have included.

If you did your study without that construct, it would not be judged credible if it ignored a major construct. Third, the literature review will help you to find and select appropriate measurement instruments. You will readily see what measurement instruments researchers use themselves in contexts similar to yours. Finally, the literature review will help you to anticipate common problems in your research context. You can use the prior experiences of other to avoid common traps and pitfalls.

DESIGN OF SOCIOLOGICAL RESEARCH

"Design of Sociological Research" or Research Design is a broad plan of a piece of empirical research specifying the manner in which data are to be collected and analysed in order to test Research Design derived from theory, or to develop insights into the problem being investigated. It combines relevance of the problem with economy in procedure. The design stage is most crucial phase of the research process. A particular design may specify whether experiment, social survey, participant observation, other methods, or a combination of more than one method will be used.

Nowadays it has became imperative to chart out the research design before starting any work, Modern research in sociology thus specifies the probable method to be used for date collection analysis, etc. keeping in view, time money and, of course, the topic of research. Generally, a research design includes the following steps:

a) Universe of Study (whether a tribe, or a village, or an urban areas, or a particular group, etc.)

b) Subject of Study (whether it focuses on the whole society, or any specific institution or a part of it).

c) Tentative relationship between certain variables (Formulating a Research Design but it is not obligatory to start with a Research Design; certain research designs lack Research Design).

d) Sets of selected methods (whether participant observation, Interview, Questionnaire, or some other methods of data collection would be used).

e) Analytical categories (by which the empirical data is subjected to analysis and interpretation).

Although the steps for formulating a research design remain common the designs differ, depending on the research purpose. The latter may be to report an unknown tribe, or to investigate the intricacies of an institution, or to test a specific Research Design in field situation, or to test a well-designed Research Design in controlled situations.

Depending on the research purpose, one delineates an appropriate research design. However, validity of the steps for forming the design will always have to be there. Every study has its own purpose, but all the research purposes can be conceptualized as falling in one of the following categories. Each category refers to a type of research design. Thus, generally, social scientists identify three types of research design on the basis of different research purposes.

These are:

Explanatory research Design

When the purpose of the study is to explore a new universe, one that has not been studied earlier, the research design, is called explanatory. The research purpose in this case is to gain familiarity in unknown areas. Often explanatory research design is used to formulate a problem for precise investigation, or aims at formulating Research Design. Thus, often when the universe of study is an unknown community, explanatory design forms the first step of research, after which other types of research designs can be used.

Two very good examples of explanatory designs are:

(i) Malinowski's study of Trobriand society; and

(ii) Whyte's study of the Street Corner Society.

Both these studies for the collection of data have relied on the special method of participant observation. Both researchers had an explanatory objective. Rather than aiming to test a limited set of specific Research Design, Malinowski and Whyte present in advance only the out line a conceptual model and provide a wide range of detail from which a number of other Research Design can be derived. Instead of concentrating on just unspecific areas and selecting a few aspects for consideration (as may be the case in descriptive research design), researchers gather such a great variety of data that they are able to see the actors in their total life situation. Explanatory studies are not to be confused with raw empiricism, with fact gathering that is unrelated to sociological theory. The explanatory study always carries with it a set of concepts that guide the researcher to look for the facts.

Descriptive research Design

Generally, if a researcher is studying a community which is familiar and his research purpose is to depict accurately and in detail the characteristics of a particular institution, group or an event in the community, the appropriate research design is called Descriptive research Design. Sometimes, descriptive design forms a second step of research, the first step being explanatory design. Thus some times, research Research Design is formulated through explanatory design and to test the Research Design, descriptive design is formulated.

Experimental research Design

The research design that is used to test a Research Design of causal relationship under controlled situation is called experimental design. The essence of the experimental design lies in its testing Research Design derived from a theory. The experimentation in sociology observes the following aspects:

a. In an experimental design, the investigator controls or manipulates an independent variable or stimulus (X),

b. And observes the effects on the dependent variable (Y), and

c. The effect of the independent variable on the dependent variable is observed by minimizing the effects of extraneous variables that might confound the result.

e. These propositions are tested off on the sample, generally called the experimental sample (E).

Experimentation in sociology raises certain important questions, viz. ethical question, difficulties in forming a control sample and retaining it over time; the difficulties encountered in controlling the extraneous environment, etc. Realizing these problems, in some of the 'experiments' carried out by sociologists, the experimental sample is used as the control sample. It is debatable whether the absence of a control means a non-experimental study. This actually is a modification of the classic experimental design.

The theoretical propositions followed here are the following.

i. Experimental sample is also the control sample.

ii. The experimental sample is measured in the given respect before introducing the independent variable,

iii. After it has been measured, the stimulus for independent variable is introduced.

iv. The experimental sample is measured after stimulus and the change is calculated.

This modification of the experimental design in generally accepted in sociology and is called before and after research. The best example of this type of research design is the Hawthorne study carried out by E. Mayo, F. Roethlisberger, W. Disckson and G. Homans. In this study, the relationship between physical conditions of world (independent variable) and the productivity of the worker (dependent variable) is examined.

FOUNDATIONS OF SOCIAL RESEARCH

The origin of the survey can be traced back at least early as the Domesday Book in 1086, whilst some scholars pinpoint the origin of demography to 1663 with the publication of John Graunt's *Natural and Political Observations upon the Bills of Mortality*. Social research began most intentionally, however, with the positivist philosophy of science in the early 19th century.

Auguste Comte (1798–1857) first described the epistemological perspective of positivism in *The Course in Positive Philosophy*, a series of texts published between 1830 and 1842. These texts were followed by the 1844 work, *A General View of Positivism* (published in English in 1865). The first three volumes of the *Course* dealt chiefly with the physical sciences already in existence (mathematics, astronomy, physics, chemistry, biology), whereas the latter two emphasized the inevitable coming of social science. Observing the circular dependence of theory and observation in science, and classifying the sciences in this way, Comte may be regarded as the first philosopher of science in the modern sense of the term. For him, the physical sciences had necessarily to arrive first, before humanity could adequately channel its efforts into the most challenging and complex "Queen science" of human society itself.

Modern social research, and indeed the formal academic discipline of sociology, began with the work of Émile Durkheim (1858–1917). While Durkheim rejected much of the detail of Comte's philosophy, he retained and refined its method, maintaining that the social sciences are a logical continuation of the natural ones into the realm of human activity, and insisting that they may retain the same objectivity, rationalism, and approach to causality. Durkheim set up the first European department of sociology at the University of Bordeaux in 1895, publishing his Rules of the Sociological Method (1895). In this text he argued: "[o]ur main goal is to extend scientific rationalism to human conduct... What has been called our positivism is but a consequence of this rationalism."

Durkheim's seminal monograph, *Suicide* (1897), a case study of suicide rates amongst Catholic and Protestant populations, distinguished sociological analysis from psychology or philosophy.

By carefully examining suicide statistics in different police districts, he attempted to demonstrate that Catholic communities have a lower suicide rate than that of Protestants, something he attributed to social (as opposed to individual or psychological) causes. He developed the notion of objective *suis generis* "social facts" to delineate a unique empirical object for the science of sociology to study. Through such studies he posited that sociology would be able to determine whether any given society is 'healthy' or 'pathological', and seek social reform to negate organic breakdown or "social anomie". For Durkheim, sociology could be described as the "science of institutions, their genesis and their functioning".

Methodological Assumptions

Social research is based on logic and empirical observations. Charles C. Ragin writes in his *Constructing Social Research* book that "Social research involved the interaction between ideas and evidence. Ideas help social researchers make sense of evidence, and researchers use evidence to extend, revise and test ideas". Social research thus attempts to create or validate theories through data collection and data analysis, and its goal is exploration, description and explanation. It should never lead or be mistaken with philosophy or belief. Social research aims to find social patterns of regularity in social life and usually deals with social groups (aggregates of individuals), not individuals themselves (although science of psychology is an exception here). Research can also be divided into pure research and applied research. Pure research has no application on real life, whereas applied research attempts to influence the real world.

There are no laws in social science that parallel the laws in the natural science. A law in social science is a universal generalization about a class of facts. A fact is an observed phenomenon, and observation means it has been seen, heard or otherwise experienced by researcher. A theory is a systematic explanation for the observations that relate to a particular aspect of social life. Concepts are the basic building blocks of theory and are abstract elements representing classes of phenomena. Axioms or postulates are basic assertions assumed to be true. Propositions are conclusions drawn about the relationships among concepts, based on analysis of axioms. Hypotheses are specified expectations about empirical reality which are derived from propositions. Social research involves testing these hypotheses to see if they are true.

Social research involves creating a theory, operationalization (measurement of variables) and observation (actual collection of data to test hypothesized relationship). Social theories are written in the language of variables, in other words, theories describe logical relationships between variables. Variables are logical sets of attributes, with people being the 'carriers' of those variables (for example, gender can be a variable with two attributes: male and female). Variables are also divided into independent variables (data) that influences the dependent variables (which scientists are trying to explain). For example, in a study of how different dosages of a drug are related to the severity of symptoms of a disease, a measure of the severity of the symptoms of the disease is a dependent variable and the administration of the drug in specified doses is the independent variable. Researchers will compare the different values of the dependent variable (severity of the symptoms) and attempt to draw conclusions.

Rules for Social Research

Although there are no laws in social science that parallel laws in the natural sciences, there is consensus about fundamental rules or principles about how to do social research. When social scientists speak of "good research" the focus is on how the research is done – whether the research is methodologically sound – rather than on whether the results of the research are consistent with personal biases or preconceptions. Glenn Firebaugh summarizes the principles for good research in his book *Seven Rules for Social Research.* The first rule is that "There should be the possibility of surprise in social research." As Firebaugh (p. 1) elaborates: "Rule 1 is intended to warn that you don't want to be blinded by preconceived ideas so that you fail to look for contrary evidence, or you fail to recognize contrary evidence when you do encounter it, or you recognize contrary evidence but suppress it and refuse to accept your findings for what they appear to say." In addition, good research will "look for differences that make a difference" (Rule 2) and "build in reality checks" (Rule 3). Rule 4 advises researchers to replicate, that is, "to see if identical analyses yield similar results for different samples of people". The next two rules urge researchers to "compare like with like" (Rule 5) and to "study change" (Rule 6); these two rules are especially important when researchers want to estimate the effect of one variable on another (e.g. how much does college education actually matter for wages?). The final rule, "Let method be the servant, not the master," reminds researchers that methods are the means, not the end, of social research; it is critical from the outset to fit the research design to the research issue, rather than the other way around.

2

Scientific Attitude and Method of Social Work

THE SCIENTIFIC METHOD

Science is the process of observing nature (and performing and observing experiments) and deducing natural laws. But there are traps, which lead to false deductions. And so a general method has evolved which more or less prevents scientists from falling into these traps. This general method is called the Scientific Method:

1. Information (data) is gathered by observation of the phenomenon being studied.
2. A hypothesis (preliminary generalization) is formed to perhaps explain the data.
3. Deductions and implications from the hypothesis suggest further observations and experiments to test the hypothesis.
4. Based on these tests, the hypothesis is either rejected or accepted.

This is an ongoing process. The results may suggest further observations and experiments, or they may suggest an alternative hypothesis. Along with this method, a scientific attitude is also important:

1. The scientist tries to be impartial.
2. Measurements are more reliable than subjective results.

3. Experiments are designed to test (disprove), not just confirm.
4. Data are recorded so they can be studied, and so the experiments can be replicated.
5. Certain common errors (like contamination or experimenter bias) are guarded against.
6. Statistical analysis is used to study the data.

The Scientific Method is not a checklist that scientists consciously follow. It is implied in the way they do science. Sometimes it may seem that errors occur, as a false hypothesis survives for a long time. Sometimes there actually are errors, and even fraud. But mostly, the false paths are natural, and are corrected eventually, merely by further testing. Sometimes, this may involve looking at the situation from an entirely different perspective.

SCIENTIFIC METHOD

An approach to research that relies on observation and data collection, hypothesis testing, and the falsifiability of ideas. The scientific method involves a wide array of approaches and is better seen as an overall perspective rather than a single, specific method. The scientific method that has been adopted was initially based on the concept of positivism, which involved the search for general descriptive laws that could be used to predict natural phenomena. Once predictions were possible, scientists could attempt to control the occurrence of those phenomena. Subsequently, scientists developed underlying explanations and theories. In the case of psychology, the goal would be to describe, to predict, then to control behavior, with knowledge based on underlying theory.

Although the positivist approach to science has undergone change and scientists are continually redefining the philosophy of science, the premises on which it was based continue to be the mainstream of current research. One of the prime requisites of a scientific approach is falsifiability; that is, a theory is seen as scientific if it makes predictions that can be demonstrated as true or false. Another critical element of the scientific method is that it relies on empiricism, that is, observation and data collection.

Research often involves the hypothetico-inductive method. The scientist starts with a hypothesis based on observation, insight, or theory. A hypothesis is a tentative statement of belief based on the expert judgment of the researcher. This hypothesis must be subject to falsification; that is, the research needs to be set up in such a way that the scientist is able to conclude logically either that the hypothesis is correct or incorrect. In many cases, a research project may allow the scientist to accept or reject a hypothesis and will lead to more research questions.

Psychologists employ a diversity of scientific approaches. These include controlled experiments that allow the researcher to determine cause and effect relationships; correlation methods that reveal predictable relations among variables; case studies involving in-depth study of single individuals; archival approaches that make novel use of records, documents, and other existing information; and surveys and questionnaires about opinions and attitudes.

Because the scientific method deals with the approach to research rather than the content of the research, disciplines are not regarded as scientific because of their content, but rather because of their reliance on data and observation, hypothesis testing, and the falsifiability of their ideas. Thus, scientific research legitimately includes the study of attitudes, intelligence, and other complicated human behaviours. Although the tools that psychologists use to measure human behavior may not lead to the same degree of precision as those in some other sciences, it is not the precision that determines the scientific status of a discipline, but rather the means by which ideas are generated and tested.

ELEMENTS OF SCIENTIFIC METHODS

Knowledge based on sensory observation has a paradoxical character. The following statement seeks to convey this paradox in a simple way. In order to gain knowledge about anything we should know something about it. If we know nothing at all about the object of our enquiry we shall never be able to know anything about it. In case we are totally ignorant about something and yet want to acquire knowledge about it through sensory observation, we make certain assumptions about it, and start our enquiry with the belief that these assumptions are true. Of course if these assumptions are not supported by facts gathered through sensory observations, we should be ready to abandon them. The significance of these assumptions is that they tell us what to look for or where to direct our sensory observation.

If a Doctor trained in modern medicine wants to find out the reasons for the symptoms like headache, giddiness, and general weakness, he might examine the digestive systems, the food taken by his patient or he might monitor the heart beats and blood pressure or enquire about his sleeping patterns and also take in to account the weather conditions. He may find his answer from these conditions.

A shaman in a tribal village also tries to cure a patient with similar symptoms. He may explore the possibility of a spell caused by a witch or disenchantment of the super natural power with the person concerned due to some act of omission or commission on his part.

In the case of the doctor trained in modern medicine his search for the cause is governed by a set of assumptions namely: human body is unified whole though it has specialized parts. These parts tend to be interdependent and malfunctioning of one lead to malfunctioning of the other. Basing himself on such assumption he is likely to see interrelationship between headache and digestion failure etc.

On the other hand the shaman by means of assumption that world is governed by super natural forces that need to be propitiated. Failure to do so might invite divine retribution. Thus from the above illustrations one can see how underlying assumptions shape one's enquiry. A set of mutually consistent assumptions which underlie our approach to things we want to explore is called a perspective. All systematized enquiries need perspective. So it is required for sociology as well.

Concepts

Language is a system of symbols that forms the medium through which we comprehend the world around and inside us and it is the basis of our thought processes. It also acts as a means of communication with others without which social life would be impossible. Language has been termed as a system of symbols because linguistic terms are abstractions i.e they are mentally created and to them certain meanings are imputed by which they come to stand for the real phenomena. All languages are made up of concepts. Only difference being that concept in scientific language is more precisely and unambiguously defined. Concepts help in comprehending the reality that a science is engaged in studying. They act as mediums of short cut communication among those associated with the enquiry. In sociology most of the concepts are terms taken from day to day language which is given precise meaning.

Theory and Facts

The popular understanding of this relationship obscures more than it illuminates. They are generally conceived as direct opposites. Theory is confused with speculation and theory remains speculation until it is proved. When this proof is made, theory becomes fact. Facts are thought to be definite, certain, without question and their meaning to be self-evident. Science is thought to be concerned with facts alone. Theory is supposed to be realm of philosophers. Scientific theory is therefore thought to be merely summation of facts that have been accumulated upon a given subject. However if we observe the way scientists actually do research, it becomes clear

1. Theory and fact are not diametrically opposed but inextricably intertwined.
2. Theory is not speculation.
3. Scientists are very much concerned with both theory and facts.

A fact is regarded as an empirically verifiable observation. A theory refers to the relationship between facts or to the ordering of them in some meaningful way. Facts of science are the product of observations that are not random but meaningful, i.e., theoretically relevant. Therefore we cannot think of facts and theory as being opposed rather they are interrelated in many complex ways. The development of science can be considered as a constant interplay between theory and fact.

Theory is a tool of science in these ways:

1. it defines the major orientation of a science, by defining the kinds of data that are to be abstracted.
2. it offers a conceptual scheme by which the relevant phenomena are systematized, classified and interrelated.
3. it summarizes facts into empirical generalizations and systems of generalizations.
4. It predicts facts and
5. It points to gaps in our knowledge.

On the other hand facts are also productive of theory in these ways:

(1) Facts help to initiate theories.

(2) They lead to the reformulation of existing theory.

(3) They cause rejection of theories that do not fit the facts.

(4) They change the focus and orientation of theory and

(5) They clarify and redefine theory.

SCIENTIFIC PROCESS

There is interplay between theory and fact. Although popular opinion thinks of theory as being opposed to fact since theory is mere speculation, observation of what scientists actually do suggests that fact and theory stimulate each other. The growth of science is seen is seen in new facts and new theory. Facts take their ultimate meaning from the theories which summarize them, classify them, predict them, point them out and define them. However theory may direct the scientific process, facts in turn play a significant role in the development of theory. New and anomalous facts may initiate new theories. New observations lead to the rejection and reformulation of existing theory or may demand that we redefine our theories. Concepts which had seemed definite in meaning are clarified by the specific facts relating to them.

The sociologist must accept the responsibilities of the scientists who must see fact in theory and theory in fact. This is more difficult than philosophic speculation about reality or the collection of superficial certainties but it leads more surely to the achievement of scientific truth about social behavior.

Gathering information and constructing Explanations

The basic procedural steps involved in gathering information and construction of explanation are:

Observation

Scientific knowledge is based on sensory observation of reality. Those aspects of reality that are definite certain self-evident and have independent existence are called "Facts". Since they have an independent existence of their own so they are amendable to sensory observation. However scientific investigation is not a search for isolated and random facts rather it is a guided enquiry to test the authenticity of definite propositions that form the starting point of gathering information. They are called "hypothesis".

A hypothesis states what we are looking for. It formulates the logical relationship between different aspects of reality expressed in terms of scientific concepts. A good hypothesis should be scientific, simple and presented in a testable form. Sociology also makes use of hypothesis in carrying our sociological research but this practice is not always strictly adhered to. Especially when a sociologist is trying to explore society, about which he knows very little, it would not be possible to begin the research with hypothesis. Some example of hypothesis which may be used in sociological enquiry can be.

(a) Crime rates are higher in urban areas than in rural areas.

(b) Pace of urbanization increases with that of industrialization.

Sometimes hypothesis may be tested under experimental conditions. Most of the established sciences do use experimental method quite successfully. However, in Sociology, experimental method is only rarely possible due to both practical and ethical reason: so observation is carried out mostly under non-experimental conditions. Sources of data include social survey, observational and interview methods etc.

SCOPE OF SOCIAL WORK IN INDIA AND ITS ORGANISATIONAL SET-UP

In 1948 an ad-hoc committee for considering the establishment of an All India Council of Social Service and an institute was appointed and representatives of various institutions were invited to attend the meeting. The Committee recommended that the All India Council of Social Service should be set up as an Advisory Body with the following aims and objects :

(i) to collect and disseminate data concerning Social Service and to act as a clearing house of information for Social Service Units, Associations and Organisations;

(ii) to provide opportunities Ad facilities to social Welfare Workers to come together for discussion of their problems and for suggestions on the lines of Social Service;

(iii) to devise methods and means of Social Welfare Services;

(iv) to recognise Social Welfare societies;

(v) to consider applications and to recommend disbursement of grants-in-aid to Social Welfare Societies, Organizations and Institutes;

(vi) to advise Government on matters relating to Social Welfare;

(vii) to recommend to the Government of India names of representatives for International Conferences, such as UNESCO.

On the recommendation of the Committee a Council consisting of representatives of the Provincial Governments and certain Social Service Institutions has been set up.

At the present moment Social Welfare Work is being conducted by certain societies and organizations such as the Indian Conference of Social Work, Bombay, the United Council for Relief, Delhi and other agencies. The Government of India have been taking active interest in the work of these organizations and have in certain cases given grants-in-aid to them. There are also four important schools which impart training in Social Welfare Work. These are:- (i) Tata Institute of Social Sciences, Bombay; (ii) The National YWCA. School of Social Work, Delhi; (iii) Department of Social Welfare, Calcutta University; and (iv) Institute of Social Service, Kashi Vidyapith, Banaras. These institutions have their degree and diploma courses. The Ministry of Education in consultation with the Ministries of Labour, Health and Rehabilitation, has recently undertaken to co-ordinate the courses of these institutions and have suggested the allocation of fundamental and specialized courses among them.

India stressed the need for establishing a Social Service Unit in India under the aegis of the Government in 1940, a sub-Committee appointed by the Central Advisory Board of Education recommended that a central body called the All-India Council of Social Service with an Institute for research and training school for social workers should be brought into existence. On account of the War, no action could be taken on the recommendation. The Central Advisory Board has again considered this question and recommended that these recommendations should now be implemented. The Chairman pointed out that the AdHoc Committee would have to consider two questions:-

1. The desirability of establishing an All-India Council of Social Service to stimulate and co-ordinate the activities of the existing Social Service Organisations, official and voluntary.
2. The necessity for a Research Institute to undertake enquiry and research into the problems of Social Welfare and coordinate the functions and activities of those Departments of the Government of India which are concerned with Social Welfare. This Institute should,

have a Department or a School for training of Social Welfare Workers.

The Chairman pointed out that in every Province there are a number of organisations which are doing useful welfare work, e.g., Y.M.C.A.'s, Y.W.C.A.'s, the Seva Samiti, the Ramkrishna Mission and other Institutions. The present Council would aim at the coordination of the work of these organisations and societies scattered all over India.

As for the Institute for Social Service, the Central Advisory Board had suggested that it should do the kind of work which the London School of Economics does. The Chairman pointed out that it was difficult to decide the relations between the Council and the Institute. Should it be a Social Welfare Department or an Institute for investigation and research ?

After the speech of the Chairman a general discussion ensued The Committee came to the conclusion that the All-India Council of Social Service should be an advisory body. It should bring together the representatives of the various Institutions and organisations doing Social Service in different areas so that they would gain by one another's experience. It would also act as an incentive to workers in the Provinces and serve as a guiding and advisory body for Institutions which are already in the field. The Committee expressed the hope that it would also lead to the formation of Social Service Organisations in areas where at present they did not exist.

SOCIAL WORK IN INDIA

Starting with one institute offering a programme in Social Work in 1946, we have today a hoard of such institutes functioning from all across the country. But in India, social work as a profession has failed to take roots One Discipline, borrowed from America, taught in India at the university level is the discipline of Social Work. We have graduate, post graduate, MPhil and PhD degrees awarded in this discipline, as is in the case of most other disciplines. But Social Work is a professional course. It can earn a living directly.

Starting with one institute offering a programme in Social Work in 1946, we have today a hoard of such institutes functioning from all across the country. The earliest graduates in Social Work migrated to the United States of America or Europe because Social Work is a recognised profession there. A degree in Social Work offered good employment opportunities as well as scope for private practice. In India Social Work never got established as an independent profession. The government social welfare departments, hospitals largely employed trained social workers against lower middle rung posts. When Indian labour laws made it compulsory to appoint welfare officers in the factories, Social Work degree became a passport to appointment against these posts. With time, welfare officers saw themselves becoming personnel officers and later human resource development (HRD) managers. People with Social Work background thus got higher status in society.

When management education came to India (also from the USA), HRD became a preferred area of specialisation and management graduates soon replaced Social Work graduates from HRD jobs. A new attractive field opened for the Social Work graduates when some non-government organisations (NGOs) adopted corporate culture under the influence of its foreign donors. But these employment opportunities were limited in numbers because how many NGOs in India would find foreign funds? High profile jobs for Social Work graduates were therefore ruled out. The scope for practising Social Work as private profession in India is next to nil. Petty political party workers who also call themselves social workers appear to be doing better. The image of a social worker amongst the general public is such that if a trained social worker were to introduce himself/herself the response coming from the opposite person most likely is to be: I am a social worker too.

It is difficult for the Indian people to conceive that there could be professionals around called social workers to be approached when facing personal or family problems. The reason is not far to see. Helping each other in the Indian traditions is a noble cause. Every body therefore shows eagerness to help every body else. Why in that case someone pay a social worker? Since the very concept of professional social work is missing from the Indian minds, trained social workers are going to find it very difficult to establish roots in this country. It is also to remember that profession wise it is the clients who approach the professionals and not the other way round.

If we look at the methods of professional social work, they talk of (1) helping people individually (Social Case Work Method) (2) helping people in groups (Social Group Work Method) and (3) helping people's communities (Community Development Method). It may be seen that of these, the last two methods can not be practiced by trained social workers in private practice since these require a larger setting.

Only organised bodies such government, corporate houses, NGOs can afford it. Trained social workers therefore have to be necessarily employed to be able to practice these two methods. This leaves Social Case Work method as the only method that can be employed by trained social workers to earn an independent living.

In Social Case Work method, the trained social worker interviews his/her client, in private and takes down the personal history. Through this he/she makes an assessment of the likely cause for the problem faced by the client. The process of interviewing is simple chitchatting. The client may not even know if he/she is being helped or having a street corner talk. One interview with the client is not sufficient; more have to be arranged.

Some clients may not be prepared for repeat visits. Even if the cause is discovered successfully, the solution that is offered to the client may not be out of the ordinary. It consists of plain suggestions and motivational talks. Unlike doctors and psychiatrists who prescribe medicines, professional social workers prescribe no such thing. This leaves the clients a bit disappointed. In fact, many people (the household social workers) have been giving advises to them.

Experience shows that people in India are happier discussing their personal problems with astrologers, tantrics, priests and saddhus for they offer mantras, tabeej (locket), bhasma (ashes), flowers, etc said to be containing charismatic powers or ask to perform certain rituals such as feeding the fish, donating mustard oil, performing puja etc that heal all the problems. People have no hesitation in paying them; sometimes even paying big money. It appears that people are more interested in purchasing hope than getting rid of the problem.

From the discussion so far it is clear that professional Social Work is a big failure in India; it can neither provide you decent employment nor earn an independent living. Students of Social Work at the universities, colleges and departments are therefore heading for a disaster. The government should take steps to weed out such unnecessary disciplines from our education system or consider modifying these to suit our conditions. Employing trained social workers in rural areas where community organisation is a big challenge also appears to be an attractive option. Is any body listening?

3

Research and Design: Definition and Importance

ETHICS IN RESEARCH

We are going through a time of profound change in our understanding of the ethics of applied social research. From the time immediately after World War II until the early 1990s, there was a gradually developing consensus about the key ethical principles that should underlie the research endeavour. Two marker events stand out (among many others) as symbolic of this consensus. The Nuremberg War Crimes Trial following World War II brought to public view the ways German scientists had used captive human subjects as subjects in often times gruesome experiments. In the 1950s and 1960s, the Tuskegee Syphilis Study involved the withholding of known effective treatment for syphilis from African-American participants who were infected. Events like these forced the reexamination of ethical standards and the gradual development of a consensus that potential human subjects needed to be protected from being used as 'guinea pigs' in scientific research.

By the 1990s, the dynamics of the situation changed. Cancer patients and persons with AIDS fought publicly with the medical research establishment about the long time needed to get approval for and complete research into potential cures for fatal diseases. In many cases, it is the ethical assumptions of the previous thirty years that drive this 'go-slow' mentality. After all, we would rather risk denying treatment for a while until we achieve enough confidence in a treatment, rather than run the risk of harming innocent people (as in the Nuremberg and Tuskegee events). But now, those who were threatened with fatal illness were saying to the research establishment that they *wanted* to be test subjects, even under experimental conditions of considerable risk. You had several very vocal and articulate patient groups who wanted to be experimented on coming up against an ethical review system that was designed to protect them from being experimented on.

Although the last few years in the ethics of research have been tumultuous ones, it is beginning to appear that a new consensus is evolving that involves the stakeholder groups most affected by a problem participating more actively in the formulation of guidelines for research. While it's not entirely clear, at present, what the new consensus will be, it is almost certain that it will not fall at either extreme: protecting against human experimentation at all costs vs. allowing anyone who is willing to be experimented on.

Ethical Issues

There are a number of key phrases that describe the system of ethical protections that the contemporary social and medical research establishment have created to try to protect better the rights of their research participants. The principle of *voluntary participation* requires that people not be coerced into participating in research. This is especially relevant where researchers had previously relied on 'captive audiences' for their subjects — prisons, universities, and places like that. Closely related to the notion of voluntary participation is the requirement of *informed consent*. Essentially, this means that prospective research participants must be fully informed about the procedures and risks involved in research and must give their consent to participate. Ethical standards also require that researchers not put participants in a situation where they might be at *risk of harm* as a result of their participation. Harm can be defined as both physical and psychological. There are two standards that are applied in order to help protect the privacy of research participants. Almost all research guarantees the participants *confidentiality* — they are assured that identifying information will not be made available to anyone who is not directly involved in the study. The stricter standard is the principle of *anonymity* which essentially means that the participant will remain anonymous throughout the study — even to the researchers themselves. Clearly, the anonymity standard is a stronger guarantee of privacy, but it is sometimes difficult to accomplish, especially in situations where participants have to be measured at multiple time points (e.g., a pre-post study). Increasingly, researchers have had to deal with the ethical issue of a person's *right to service*. Good research practice often requires the use of a no-treatment control group — a group of participants who do *not* get the treatment or program that is being studied. But when that treatment or program may have beneficial effects, persons assigned to the no-treatment control may feel their rights to equal access to services are being curtailed.

Even when clear ethical standards and principles exist, there will be times when the need to do accurate research runs up against the rights of potential participants. No set of standards can possibly anticipate every ethical circumstance. Furthermore, there needs to be a procedure that assures that researchers will consider all relevant ethical issues in formulating research plans. To address such needs most institutions and organizations have formulated an *Institutional Review Board (IRB)*, a panel of persons who reviews grant proposals with respect to ethical implications and decides whether additional actions need to be taken to assure the safety and rights of participants. By reviewing proposals for research, IRBs also help to protect both the organization and the researcher against potential legal implications of neglecting to address important ethical issues of participants.

Sampling

Sampling is the process of selecting units (e.g., people, organizations) from a population of interest so that by studying the sample we may fairly generalize our results back to the population from which they were chosen. Let's begin by covering some of the key terms in sampling like "population" and "sampling frame." Then, because some types of sampling rely upon quantitative models, we'll talk about some of the statistical terms used in sampling. Finally, we'll discuss the major distinction between probability and Nonprobability sampling methods and work through the major types in each.

External Validity

External validity is related to generalizing. That's the major thing you need to keep in mind. Recall that validity refers to the approximate truth of propositions, inferences, or conclusions. So, *external* validity refers to the approximate truth of conclusions the involve generalizations. Put in more pedestrian terms, external validity is the degree to which the conclusions in your study would hold for other persons in other places and at other times.

In science there are two major approaches to how we provide evidence for a generalization. I'll call the first approach the Sampling Model. In the sampling model, you start by identifying the population you would like to generalize to. Then, you draw a fair sample from that population and conduct your research with the sample. Finally, because the sample is representative of the population, you can automatically generalize your results back to the population. There are several problems with this approach. First, perhaps you don't know at the time of your study who you might ultimately like to generalize to. Second, you may not be easily able to draw a fair or representative sample. Third, it's impossible to sample across all times that you might like to generalize to (like next year).

Threats to External Validity

A threat to external validity is an explanation of how you might be wrong in making a generalization. For instance, you conclude that the results of your study (which was done in a specific place, with certain types of people, and at a specific time) can be generalized to another context (for instance, another place, with slightly different people, at a slightly later time). There are three major threats to external validity because there are three ways you could be wrong — people, places or times. Your critics could come along, for example, and argue that the results of your study are due to the unusual type of people who were in the study. Or, they could argue that it might only work because of the unusual place you did the study in (perhaps you did your educational study in a college town with lots of high-achieving educationally-oriented kids). Or, they might suggest that you did your study in a peculiar time. For instance, if you did your smoking cessation study the week after the Surgeon General issues the well-publicized results of the latest smoking and cancer studies, you might get different results than if you had done it the week before.

Improving External Validity

How can we improve external validity? One way, based on the sampling model, suggests that you do a good job of drawing a sample from a population. For instance, you should use random selection, if possible, rather than a nonrandom procedure. And, once selected, you should try to assure that the respondents participate in your study and that you keep your dropout rates low. A second approach would be to use the theory of proximal similarity more effectively. How? Perhaps you could do a better job of describing the ways your contexts and others differ, providing lots of data about the degree of similarity between various groups of people, places, and even times. You might even be able to map out the degree of proximal similarity among various contexts with a methodology like concept mapping. Perhaps the best approach to criticisms of generalizations is simply to show them that they're wrong — do your study in a variety of places, with different people and at different times. That is, your external validity (ability to generalize) will be stronger the more you replicate your study.

SAMPLING TERMINOLOGY

As with anything else in life you have to learn the language of an area if you're going to ever hope to use it. Here, I want to introduce several different terms for the major groups that are involved in a sampling process and the role that each group plays in the logic of sampling.

The major question that motivates sampling in the first place is: "Who do you want to generalize to?" Or should it be: "To whom do you want to generalize?" In most social research we are interested in more than just the people who directly participate in our study. We would like to be able to talk in general terms and not be confined only to the people who are in our study. Now, there are times when we aren't very concerned about generalizing. Maybe we're just evaluating a program in a local agency and we don't care whether the program would work with other people in other places and at other times. In that case, sampling and generalizing might not be of interest. In other cases, we would really like to be able to generalize almost universally. When psychologists do research, they are often interested in developing theories that would hold for all humans. But in most applied social research, we are interested in generalizing to specific groups. The group you wish to generalize to is often called the population in your study. This is the group you would like to sample from because this is the group you are interested in generalizing to. Let's imagine that you wish to generalize to urban homeless males between the ages of 30 and 50 in the United States. If that is the population of interest, you are likely to have a very hard time developing a reasonable sampling plan. You are probably not going to find an accurate listing of this population, and even if you did, you would almost certainly not be able to mount a national sample across hundreds of urban areas. So we probably should make a distinction between the population you would like to generalize to, and the population that will be accessible to you. We'll call the former the theoretical population and the latter the accessible population. In this example, the accessible population might be homeless males between the ages of 30 and 50 in six selected urban areas across the U.S.

Once you've identified the theoretical and accessible populations, you have to do one more thing before you can actually draw a sample — you have to get a list of the members of the accessible population. (Or, you have to spell out in detail how you will contact them to assure representativeness). The listing of the accessible population from which you'll draw your sample is called the sampling frame. If you were doing a phone survey and selecting names from the telephone book, the book would be your sampling frame. That wouldn't be a great way to sample because significant subportions of the population either don't have a phone or have moved in or out of the area since the last book was printed. Notice that in this case, you might identify the area code and all three-digit prefixes within that area code and draw a sample simply by randomly dialing numbers (cleverly known as *random-digit-dialing*). In this case, the sampling frame is not a list *per se*, but is rather a procedure that you follow as the actual basis for sampling. Finally, you actually draw your sample (using one of the many sampling procedures). The sample is the group of people who you select to be in your study. Notice that I didn't say that the sample was the group of people who are actually *in* your study. You may not be able to contact or recruit all of the people you actually sample, or some could drop out over the course of the study. The group that actually completes your study is a subsample of the sample — it doesn't include nonrespondents or dropouts. The problem of nonresponse and its effects on a study will be addressed when discussing "mortality" threats to internal validity.

People often confuse what is meant by random selection with the idea of random assignment. You should make sure that you understand the distinction between random selection and random assignment. At this point, you should appreciate that sampling is a difficult multi-step process and that there are lots of places you can go wrong. In fact, as we move from each step to the next in identifying a sample, there is the possibility of introducing systematic error or bias. For instance, even if you are able to identify perfectly the population of interest, you may not have access to all of them. And even if you do, you may not have a complete and accurate enumeration or sampling frame from which to select. And, even if you do, you may not draw the sample correctly or accurately. And, even if you do, they may not all come and they may not all stay. Depressed yet? This is a very difficult business indeed.

STATISTICAL TERMS IN SAMPLING

Let's begin by defining some very simple terms that are relevant here. First, let's look at the results of our sampling efforts. When we sample, the units that we sample — usually people — supply us with one or more responses. In this sense, a response is a specific measurement value that a sampling unit supplies. In the figure, the person is responding to a survey instrument and gives a response of '4'. When we look across the responses that we get for our entire sample, we use a statistic. There are a wide variety of statistics we can use — mean, median, mode, and so on. In this example, we see that the mean or average for the sample is 3.75. But the reason we sample is so that we might get an estimate for the population we sampled from. If we could, we would much prefer to measure the entire population. If you measure the entire population and calculate a value like a mean or average, we don't refer to this as a statistic, we call it a parameter of the population.

The Sampling Distribution

So how do we get from our sample statistic to an estimate of the population parameter? A crucial midway concept you need to understand is the sampling distribution. In order to understand it, you have to be able and willing to do a thought experiment. Imagine that instead of just taking a single sample like we do in a typical study, you took three independent samples of the same population. And furthermore, imagine that for each of your three samples, you collected a single response and computed a single statistic, say, the mean of the response. Even though all three samples came from the same population, you wouldn't expect to get the exact same statistic from each. They would differ slightly just due to the random "luck of the draw" or to the natural fluctuations or vagaries of drawing a sample. But you would expect that all three samples would yield a similar statistical estimate because they were drawn from the same population. Now, for the leap of imagination! Imagine that you did an *infinite* number of samples from the same population and computed the average for each one. If you plotted them on a histogram or bar graph you should find that most of them converge on the same central value and that you get fewer and fewer samples that have averages farther away up or down from that central value. In other words, the bar graph would be well described by the *bell curve* shape that is an indication of a "normal" distribution in statistics. The distribution of an infinite number of samples of the same size as the sample in your study is known as the sampling distribution. We don't ever actually construct a sampling distribution. Why not? You're not paying attention! Because to construct it we would have to take an *infinite* number of samples and at least the last time I checked, on this planet infinite is not a number we know how to reach. So why do we even talk about a sampling distribution? Now that's a good question! Because we need to realize that our sample is just one of a potentially infinite number of samples that we could have taken. When we keep the sampling distribution in mind, we realize that while the statistic we got from our sample is probably near the center of the sampling distribution (because most of the samples would be there) we could have gotten one of the extreme samples just by the luck of the draw. If we take the average of the sampling distribution — the average of the averages of an infinite number of samples — we would be much closer to the true population average — the parameter of interest. So the average of the sampling distribution is essentially equivalent to the parameter. But what is the standard deviation of the sampling distribution (OK, never had statistics? There are any number of places on the web where you can learn about them or even just brush up if you've gotten rusty. This isn't one of them. I'm going to assume that you at least know what a standard deviation is, or that you're capable of finding out relatively quickly). The standard deviation of the sampling distribution tells us something about how different samples would be distributed. In statistics it is referred to as the standard error (so we can keep it separate in our minds from standard deviations. Getting confused? Go get a cup of coffee and come back in ten minutes...OK, let's try once more... A standard deviation is the spread of the scores around the average in a single sample. The standard error is the spread of the averages around the average of averages in a sampling distribution.

Sampling Error

In sampling contexts, the standard error is called sampling error. Sampling error gives us some idea of the precision of our statistical estimate. A low sampling error means that we had relatively less variability or range in the sampling distribution. But here we go again — we never actually see the sampling distribution! So how do we calculate sampling error? We base our calculation *on the standard deviation of our sample.* The greater the sample standard deviation, the greater the standard error (and the sampling error). The standard error is also related to the sample size. The greater your sample size, the smaller the standard error. Why? Because the greater the sample size, the closer your sample is to the actual population itself. If you take a sample that consists of the entire population you actually have no sampling error because you don't have a sample, you have the entire population. In that case, the mean you estimate is the parameter.

The 68, 95, 99 Percent Rule

You've probably heard this one before, but it's so important that it's always worth repeating... There is a general rule that applies whenever we have a normal or bell-shaped distribution. Start with the average — the center of the distribution. If you go up and down (i.e., left and right) one standard unit, you will include approximately 68% of the cases in the distribution (i.e., 68% of the area under the curve). If you go up and down two standard units, you will include approximately 95% of the cases. And if you go plus-and-minus three standard units, you will include about 99% of the cases. Notice that I didn't specify in the previous few sentences whether I was talking about standard deviation units or standard error units. That's because the same rule holds for both types of distributions (i.e., the raw data and sampling distributions). For instance, in the figure, the mean of the distribution is 3.75 and the standard unit is.25 (If this was a distribution of raw data, we would be talking in standard deviation units. If it's a sampling distribution, we'd be talking in standard error units). If we go up and down one standard unit from the mean, we would be going up and down.25 from the mean of 3.75. Within this range — 3.5 to 4.0 — we would expect to see approximately 68% of the cases. This section is marked in red on the figure. I leave to you to figure out the other ranges. But what does this all mean you ask? If we are dealing with raw data and we know the mean and standard deviation of a sample, we can *predict* the intervals within which 68, 95 and 99% of our cases would be expected to fall. We call these intervals the — guess what — 68, 95 and 99% confidence intervals.

Now, here's where everything should come together in one great aha! experience if you've been following along. If we had a *sampling distribution*, we would be able to predict the 68, 95 and 99% confidence intervals for where the population parameter should be! And isn't that why we sampled in the first place? So that we could predict where the population is on that variable? There's only one hitch. We don't actually have the sampling distribution (now this is the third time I've said this in this essay)!

But we do have the distribution for the sample itself. And we can from that distribution estimate the standard error (the sampling error) because it is based on the standard deviation and we have that. And, of course, we don't actually know the population parameter value — we're trying to find that out — but we can use our best estimate for that — the sample statistic. Now, if we have the mean of the sampling distribution (or set it to the mean from our sample) and we have an estimate of the standard error (we calculate that from our sample) then we have the two key ingredients that we need for our sampling distribution in order to estimate confidence intervals for the population parameter.

Perhaps an example will help. Let's assume we did a study and drew a single sample from the population. Furthermore, let's assume that the average for the sample was 3.75 and the standard deviation was.25. This is the raw data distribution depicted above. now, what would the sampling distribution be in this case? Well, we don't actually construct it (because we would need to take an infinite number of samples) but we *can* estimate it. For starters, we assume that the mean of the sampling distribution is the mean of the sample, which is 3.75. Then, we calculate the standard error. To do this, we use the standard deviation for our sample and the sample size (in this case N=100) and we come up with a standard error of.025 (just trust me on this). Now we have everything we need to estimate a confidence interval for the population parameter. We would estimate that the probability is 68% that the true parameter value falls between 3.725 and 3.775 (i.e., 3.75 plus and minus.025); that the 95% confidence interval is 3.700 to 3.800; and that we can say with 99% confidence that the population value is between 3.675 and 3.825. The real value (in this fictitious example) was 3.72 and so we have correctly estimated that value with our sample.

PROBABILITY SAMPLING

A probability sampling method is any method of sampling that utilizes some form of *random selection*. In order to have a random selection method, you must set up some process or procedure that assures that the different units in your population have equal probabilities of being chosen. Humans have long practiced various forms of random selection, such as picking a name out of a hat, or choosing the short straw. These days, we tend to use computers as the mechanism for generating random numbers as the basis for random selection.

Some Definitions

Before I can explain the various probability methods we have to define some basic terms. These are:

- N = the number of cases in the sampling frame
- n = the number of cases in the sample
- ${}_{N}C_{n}$ = the number of combinations (subsets) of n from N
- f = n/N = the sampling fraction

That's it. With those terms defined we can begin to define the different probability sampling methods.

Simple Random Sampling

The simplest form of random sampling is called simple random sampling. Pretty tricky, huh? Here's the quick description of simple random sampling:

- Objective: To select n units out of N such that each ${}_{N}C_{n}$ has an equal chance of being selected.

- Procedure: Use a table of random numbers, a computer random number generator, or a mechanical device to select the sample.

A somewhat stilted, if accurate, definition. Let's see if we can make it a little more real. How do we select a simple random sample? Let's assume that we are doing some research with a small service agency that wishes to assess client's views of quality of service over the past year. First, we have to get the sampling frame organized. To accomplish this, we'll go through agency records to identify every client over the past 12 months. If we're lucky, the agency has good accurate computerized records and can quickly produce such a list. Then, we have to actually draw the sample. Decide on the number of clients you would like to have in the final sample. For the sake of the example, let's say you want to select 100 clients to survey and that there were 1000 clients over the past 12 months. Then, the sampling fraction is $f = n/N = 100/1000 = .10$ or 10%. Now, to actually draw the sample, you have several options. You could print off the list of 1000 clients, tear then into separate strips, put the strips in a hat, mix them up real good, close your eyes and pull out the first 100. But this mechanical procedure would be tedious and the quality of the sample would depend on how thoroughly you mixed them up and how randomly you reached in. Perhaps a better procedure would be to use the kind of ball machine that is popular with many of the state lotteries. You would need three sets of balls numbered 0 to 9, one set for each of the digits from 000 to 999 (if we select 000 we'll call that 1000). Number the list of names from 1 to 1000 and then use the ball machine to select the three digits that selects each person. The obvious disadvantage here is that you need to get the ball machines. (Where do they make those things, anyway? Is there a ball machine industry?).

Neither of these mechanical procedures is very feasible and, with the development of inexpensive computers there is a much easier way. Here's a simple procedure that's especially useful if you have the names of the clients already on the computer. Many computer programs can generate a series of random numbers. Let's assume you can copy and paste the list of client names into a column in an EXCEL spreadsheet. Then, in the column right next to it paste the function =RAND() which is EXCEL's way of putting a random number between 0 and 1 in the cells. Then, sort both columns — the list of names and the random number — by the random numbers. This rearranges the list in random order from the lowest to the highest random number. Then, all you have to do is take the first hundred names in this sorted list. pretty simple. You could probably accomplish the whole thing in under a minute.

Simple random sampling is simple to accomplish and is easy to explain to others. Because simple random sampling is a fair way to select a sample, it is reasonable to generalize the results from the sample back to the population. Simple random sampling is not the most statistically efficient method of sampling and you may, just because of the luck of the draw, not get good representation of subgroups in a population. To deal with these issues, we have to turn to other sampling methods.

Stratified Random Sampling

Stratified Random Sampling, also sometimes called *proportional* or *quota* random sampling, involves dividing your population into homogeneous subgroups and then taking a simple random sample in each subgroup. In more formal terms:

Objective: Divide the population into non-overlapping groups (i.e., *strata*) N_1, N_2, N_3,... N_i, such that $N_1 + N_2 + N_3 + ... + N_i = N$. Then do a simple random sample of $f = n/N$ in each strata.

There are several major reasons why you might prefer stratified sampling over simple random sampling. First, it assures that you will be able to represent not only the overall population, but also key subgroups of the population, especially small minority groups. If you want to be able to talk about subgroups, this may be the only way to effectively assure you'll be able to. If the subgroup is extremely small, you can use different sampling fractions (f) within the different strata to randomly over-sample the small group (although you'll then have to weight the within-group estimates using the sampling fraction whenever you want overall population estimates). When we use the same sampling fraction within strata we are conducting *proportionate* stratified random sampling. When we use different sampling fractions in the strata, we call this *disproportionate* stratified random sampling. Second, stratified random sampling will generally have more statistical precision than simple random sampling. This will only be true if the strata or groups are homogeneous. If they are, we expect that the variability within-groups is lower than the variability for the population as a whole. Stratified sampling capitalizes on that fact.

For example, let's say that the population of clients for our agency can be divided into three groups: Caucasian, African-American and Hispanic-American. Furthermore, let's assume that both the African-Americans and Hispanic-Americans are relatively small minorities of the clientele (10% and 5% respectively). If we just did a simple random sample of n=100 with a sampling fraction of 10%, we would expect by chance alone that we would only get 10 and 5 persons from each of our two smaller groups. And, by chance, we could get fewer than that! If we stratify, we can do better.

First, let's determine how many people we want to have in each group. Let's say we still want to take a sample of 100 from the population of 1000 clients over the past year. But we think that in order to say anything about subgroups we will need at least 25 cases in each group. So, let's sample 50 Caucasians, 25 African-Americans, and 25 Hispanic-Americans. We know that 10% of the population, or 100 clients, are African-American. If we randomly sample 25 of these, we have a within-stratum sampling fraction of 25/100 = 25%. Similarly, we know that 5% or 50 clients are Hispanic-American. So our within-stratum sampling fraction will be 25/50 = 50%. Finally, by subtraction we know that there are 850 Caucasian clients. Our within-stratum sampling fraction for them is 50/850 = about 5.88%. Because the groups are more homogeneous within-group than across the population as a whole, we can expect greater statistical precision (less variance). And, because we stratified, we know we will have enough cases from each group to make meaningful subgroup inferences.

Systematic Random Sampling

Here are the steps you need to follow in order to achieve a systematic random sample:

- number the units in the population from 1 to N
- decide on the n (sample size) that you want or need
- k = N/n = the interval size
- randomly select an integer between 1 to k
- then take every kth unit

All of this will be much clearer with an example. Let's assume that we have a population that only has N=100 people in it and that you want to take a sample of n=20. To use systematic sampling, the population must be listed in a random order. The sampling fraction would be f = 20/100 = 20%. in this case, the interval size, k, is equal to N/n = 100/20 = 5. Now, select a random integer from 1 to 5. In our example, imagine that you chose 4. Now, to select the sample, start with the 4th unit in the list and take every k-th unit (every 5th, because k=5). You would be sampling units 4, 9, 14, 19, and so on to 100 and you would wind up with 20 units in your sample.

For this to work, it is essential that the units in the population are randomly ordered, at least with respect to the characteristics you are measuring. Why would you ever want to use systematic random sampling? For one thing, it is fairly easy to do. You only have to select a single random number to start things off. It may also be more precise than simple random sampling. Finally, in some situations there is simply no easier way to do random sampling. For instance, I once had to do a study that involved sampling from all the books in a library. Once selected, I would have to go to the shelf, locate the book, and record when it last circulated. I knew that I had a fairly good sampling frame in the form of the shelf list (which is a card catalogue where the entries are arranged in the order they occur on the shelf). To do a simple random sample, I could have estimated the total number of books and generated random numbers to draw the sample; but how would I find book #74,329 easily if that is the number I selected? I couldn't very well count the cards until I came to 74,329! Stratifying wouldn't solve that problem either. For instance, I could have stratified by card catalogue drawer and drawn a simple random sample within each drawer. But I'd still be stuck counting cards. Instead, I did a systematic random sample. I estimated the number of books in the entire collection. Let's imagine it was 100,000. I decided that I wanted to take a sample of 1000 for a sampling fraction of 1000/100,000 = 1%.

To get the sampling interval k, I divided N/n = 100,000/ 1000 = 100. Then I selected a random integer between 1 and 100. Let's say I got 57. Next I did a little side study to determine how thick a thousand cards are in the card catalogue (taking into account the varying ages of the cards). Let's say that on average I found that two cards that were separated by 100 cards were about.75 inches apart in the catalogue drawer. That information gave me everything I needed to draw the sample. I counted to the 57th by hand and recorded the book information. Then, I took a compass. (Remember those from your high-school math class? They're the funny little metal instruments with a sharp pin on one end and a pencil on the other that you used to draw circles in geometry class.)

Then I set the compass at.75", stuck the pin end in at the 57th card and pointed with the pencil end to the next card (approximately 100 books away). In this way, I approximated selecting the 157th, 257th, 357th, and so on. I was able to accomplish the entire selection procedure in very little time using this systematic random sampling approach. I'd probably still be there counting cards if I'd tried another random sampling method.

Cluster (Area) Random Sampling

The problem with random sampling methods when we have to sample a population that's disbursed across a wide geographic region is that you will have to cover a lot of ground geographically in order to get to each of the units you sampled. Imagine taking a simple random sample of all the residents of New York State in order to conduct personal interviews. By the luck of the draw you will wind up with respondents who come from all over the state. Your interviewers are going to have a lot of travelling to do. It is for precisely this problem that cluster or area random sampling was invented.

In cluster sampling, we follow these steps:

- divide population into clusters (usually along geographic boundaries)
- randomly sample clusters
- measure all units within sampled clusters.

Let's say that we have to do a survey of town governments that will require us going to the towns personally. If we do a simple random sample state-wide we'll have to cover the entire state geographically. Instead, we decide to do a cluster sampling of five counties. Once these are selected, we go to *every* town government in the five areas. Clearly this strategy will help us to economize on our mileage. Cluster or area sampling, then, is useful in situations like this, and is done primarily for efficiency of administration. Note also, that we probably don't have to worry about using this approach if we are conducting a mail or telephone survey because it doesn't matter as much (or cost more or raise inefficiency) where we call or send letters to.

Multi-Stage Sampling

The four methods we've covered so far — simple, stratified, systematic and cluster — are the simplest random sampling strategies. In most real applied social research, we would use sampling methods that are considerably more complex than these simple variations. The most important principle here is that we can combine the simple methods described earlier in a variety of useful ways that help us address our sampling needs in the most efficient and effective manner possible. When we combine sampling methods, we call this multi-stage sampling.

For example, consider the idea of sampling New York State residents for face-to-face interviews. Clearly we would want to do some type of cluster sampling as the first stage of the process. We might sample townships or census tracts throughout the state. But in cluster sampling we would then go on to measure everyone in the clusters we select. Even if we are sampling census tracts we may not be able to measure *everyone* who is in the census tract. So, we might set up a stratified sampling process within the clusters. In this case, we would have a two-stage sampling process with stratified samples within cluster samples. Or, consider the problem of sampling students in grade schools. We might begin with a national sample of school districts stratified by economics and educational level. Within selected districts, we might do a simple random sample of schools. Within schools, we might do a simple random sample of classes or grades. And, within classes, we might even do a simple random sample of students. In this case, we have three or four stages in the sampling process and we use both stratified and simple random sampling. By combining different sampling methods we are able to achieve a rich variety of probabilistic sampling methods that can be used in a wide range of social research contexts.

NONPROBABILITY SAMPLING

The difference between nonprobability and probability sampling is that nonprobability sampling does not involve *random* selection and probability sampling does. Does that mean that nonprobability samples aren't representative of the population? Not necessarily. But it does mean that nonprobability samples cannot depend upon the rationale of probability theory.

At least with a probabilistic sample, we know the odds or probability that we have represented the population well. We are able to estimate confidence intervals for the statistic. With nonprobability samples, we may or may not represent the population well, and it will often be hard for us to know how well we've done so. In general, researchers prefer probabilistic or random sampling methods over nonprobabilistic ones, and consider them to be more accurate and rigorous. However, in applied social research there may be circumstances where it is not feasible, practical or theoretically sensible to do random sampling. Here, we consider a wide range of nonprobabilistic alternatives.

We can divide nonprobability sampling methods into two broad types: *accidental* or *purposive*. Most sampling methods are purposive in nature because we usually approach the sampling problem with a specific plan in mind. The most important distinctions among these types of sampling methods are the ones between the different types of purposive sampling approaches.

Accidental, Haphazard or Convenience Sampling

One of the most common methods of sampling goes under the various titles listed here. I would include in this category the traditional "man on the street" (of course, now it's probably the "person on the street") interviews conducted frequently by television news programs to get a quick (although nonrepresentative) reading of public opinion. I would also argue that the typical use of college students in much psychological research is primarily a matter of convenience. (You don't really believe that psychologists use college students because they believe they're representative of the population at large, do you?). In clinical practice, we might use clients who are available to us as our sample. In many research contexts, we sample simply by asking for volunteers. Clearly, the problem with all of these types of samples is that we have no evidence that they are representative of the populations we're interested in generalizing to — and in many cases we would clearly suspect that they are not.

Purposive Sampling

In purposive sampling, we sample with a *purpose* in mind. We usually would have one or more specific predefined groups we are seeking. For instance, have you ever run into people in a mall or on the street who are carrying a clipboard and who are stopping various people and asking if they could interview them? Most likely they are conducting a purposive sample (and most likely they are engaged in market research). They might be looking for Caucasian females between 30-40 years old. They size up the people passing by and anyone who looks to be in that category they stop to ask if they will participate. One of the first things they're likely to do is verify that the respondent does in fact meet the criteria for being in the sample. Purposive sampling can be very useful for situations where you need to reach a targeted sample quickly and where sampling for proportionality is not the primary concern. With a purposive sample, you are likely to get the opinions of your target population, but you are also likely to overweight subgroups in your population that are more readily accessible.

All of the methods that follow can be considered subcategories of purposive sampling methods. We might sample for specific groups or types of people as in modal instance, expert, or quota sampling. We might sample for diversity as in heterogeneity sampling. Or, we might capitalize on informal social networks to identify specific respondents who are hard to locate otherwise, as in snowball sampling. In all of these methods we know what we want — we are sampling with a purpose.

Modal Instance Sampling

In statistics, the *mode* is the most frequently occurring value in a distribution. In sampling, when we do a modal instance sample, we are sampling the most frequent case, or the "typical" case. In a lot of informal public opinion polls, for instance, they interview a "typical" voter. There are a number of problems with this sampling approach. First, how do we know what the "typical" or "modal" case is? We could say that the modal voter is a person who is of average age, educational level, and income in the population. But, it's not clear that using the averages of these is the fairest (consider the skewed distribution of income, for instance). And, how do you know that those three variables — age, education, income — are the only or even the most relevant for classifying the typical voter? What if religion or ethnicity is an important discriminator? Clearly, modal instance sampling is only sensible for informal sampling contexts.

Expert Sampling

Expert sampling involves the assembling of a sample of persons with known or demonstrable experience and expertise in some area. Often, we convene such a sample under the auspices of a "panel of experts." There are actually two reasons you might do expert sampling. First, because it would be the best way to elicit the views of persons who have specific expertise. In this case, expert sampling is essentially just a specific subcase of purposive sampling. But the other reason you might use expert sampling is to provide evidence for the validity of another sampling approach you've chosen. For instance, let's say you do modal instance sampling and are concerned that the criteria you used for defining the modal instance are subject to criticism. You might convene an expert panel consisting of persons with acknowledged experience and insight into that field or topic and ask them to examine your modal definitions and comment on their appropriateness and validity. The advantage of doing this is that you aren't out on your own trying to defend your decisions — you have some acknowledged experts to back you. The disadvantage is that even the experts can be, and often are, wrong.

Quota Sampling

In quota sampling, you select people nonrandomly according to some fixed quota. There are two types of quota sampling: *proportional* and *non proportional*. In proportional quota sampling you want to represent the major characteristics of the population by sampling a proportional amount of each. For instance, if you know the population has 40% women and 60% men, and that you want a total sample size of 100, you will continue sampling until you get those percentages and then you will stop. So, if you've already got the 40 women for your sample, but not the sixty men, you will continue to sample men but even if legitimate women respondents come along, you will not sample them because you have already "met your quota." The problem here (as in much purposive sampling) is that you have to decide the specific characteristics on which you will base the quota. Will it be by gender, age, education race, religion, etc.?

Nonproportional quota sampling is a bit less restrictive. In this method, you specify the minimum number of sampled units you want in each category. Here, you're not concerned with having numbers that match the proportions in the population. Instead, you simply want to have enough to assure that you will be able to talk about even small groups in the population. This method is the nonprobabilistic analogue of stratified random sampling in that it is typically used to assure that smaller groups are adequately represented in your sample.

Heterogeneity Sampling

We sample for heterogeneity when we want to include all opinions or views, and we aren't concerned about representing these views proportionately. Another term for this is sampling for *diversity*. In many brainstorming or nominal group processes (including concept mapping), we would use some form of heterogeneity sampling because our primary interest is in getting broad spectrum of ideas, not identifying the "average" or "modal instance" ones.

In effect, what we would like to be sampling is not people, but ideas. We imagine that there is a universe of all possible ideas relevant to some topic and that we want to sample this population, not the population of people who have the ideas. Clearly, in order to get all of the ideas, and especially the "outlier" or unusual ones, we have to include a broad and diverse range of participants. Heterogeneity sampling is, in this sense, almost the opposite of modal instance sampling.

Snowball Sampling

In snowball sampling, you begin by identifying someone who meets the criteria for inclusion in your study. You then ask them to recommend others who they may know who also meet the criteria. Although this method would hardly lead to representative samples, there are times when it may be the best method available. Snowball sampling is especially useful when you are trying to reach populations that are inaccessible or hard to find.

For instance, if you are studying the homeless, you are not likely to be able to find good lists of homeless people within a specific geographical area. However, if you go to that area and identify one or two, you may find that they know very well who the other homeless people in their vicinity are and how you can find them.

DESIGN

Research design provides the glue that holds the research project together. A design is used to structure the research, to show how all of the major parts of the research project — the samples or groups, measures, treatments or programs, and methods of assignment — work together to try to address the central research questions. Here, after a brief introduction to research design, I'll show you how we classify the major types of designs. You'll see that a major distinction is between the experimental designs that use random assignment to groups or programs and the quasi-experimental designs that don't use random assignment. [People often confuse what is meant by random selection with the idea of random assignment. You should make sure that you understand the distinction between random selection and random assignment.] Understanding the relationships among designs is important in making design choices and thinking about the strengths and weaknesses of different designs. Then, I'll talk about the heart of the art form of designing designs for research and give you some ideas about how you can think about the design task. Finally, I'll consider some of the more recent advances in quasi-experimental thinking — an area of special importance in applied social research and program evaluation.

INTERNAL VALIDITY

Internal Validity is the approximate truth about inferences regarding cause-effect or causal relationships. Thus, internal validity is only relevant in studies that try to establish a causal relationship. It's not relevant in most observational or descriptive studies, for instance. But for studies that assess the effects of social programs or interventions, internal validity is perhaps the primary consideration. In those contexts, you would like to be able to conclude that your program or treatment made a difference — it improved test scores or reduced symptomology. But there may be lots of reasons, other than your program, why test scores may improve or symptoms may reduce. The key question in internal validity is whether observed changes can be attributed to your program or intervention (i.e., the cause) and not to other possible causes (sometimes described as "alternative explanations" for the outcome). One of the things that's most difficult to grasp about internal validity is that it is only relevant to the specific study in question.

That is, you can think of internal validity as a "zero generalizability" concern. All that internal validity means is that you have evidence that what you did in the study (i.e., the program) caused what you observed (i.e., the outcome) to happen. It doesn't tell you whether what you did for the program was what you wanted to do or whether what you observed was what you wanted to observe — those are construct validity concerns. It is possible to have internal validity in a study and not have construct validity.

For instance, imagine a study where you are looking at the effects of a new computerized tutoring program on math performance in first grade students. Imagine that the tutoring is unique in that it has a heavy computer game component and you think that's what will really work to improve math performance. Finally, imagine that you were wrong (hard, isn't it?) — it turns out that math performance did improve, and that it was because of something you did, but that it had nothing to do with the computer program. What caused the improvement was the individual attention that the adult tutor gave to the child — the computer program didn't make any difference. This study would have internal validity because something that you did affected something that you observed — you did cause *something* to happen. But the study would not have construct validity, specifically, the label "computer math program" does not accurately describe the actual cause (perhaps better described as "personal adult attention").

Since the key issue in internal validity is the causal one, we'll begin by considering what conditions need to be met in order to establish a causal relationship in your project. Then we'll consider the different threats to internal validity — the kinds of criticisms your critics will raise when you try to conclude that your program caused the outcome. For convenience, we divide the threats to validity into three categories. The first involve the single group threats — criticisms that apply when you are only studying a single group that receives your program.

The second consists of the multiple group threats — criticisms that are likely to be raised when you have several groups in your study (e.g., a program and a comparison group). Finally, we'll consider what I call the social threats to internal validity — threats that arise because social research is conducted in real-world human contexts where people will react to not only what affects them, but also to what is happening to others around them.

ESTABLISHING CAUSE & EFFECT

How do we establish a cause-effect (causal) relationship? What criteria do we have to meet? Generally, there are three criteria that you must meet before you can say that you have evidence for a causal relationship:

Temporal Precedence

First, you have to be able to show that your cause happened *before* your effect. Sounds easy, huh? Of course my cause has to happen before the effect. Did you ever hear of an effect happening before its cause? Before we get lost in the logic here, consider a classic example from economics: does inflation cause unemployment? It certainly seems plausible that as inflation increases, more employers find that in order to meet costs they have to lay off employees. So it seems that inflation could, at least partially, be a cause for unemployment. But both inflation and employment rates are occurring together on an ongoing basis. Is it possible that fluctuations in employment can affect inflation? If we have an increase in the work force (i.e., lower unemployment) we may have more demand for goods, which would tend to drive up the prices (i.e., inflate them) at least until supply can catch up. So which is the cause and which the effect, inflation or unemployment? It turns out that in this kind of cyclical situation involving ongoing processes that interact that both may cause and, in turn, be affected by the other. This makes it very hard to establish a causal relationship in this situation.

Covariation of the Cause and Effect

What does this mean? Before you can show that you have

a *causal* relationship you have to show that you have some type of relationship. For instance, consider the syllogism:

if X then Y

if not X then not Y

If you observe that whenever X is present, Y is also present, and whenever X is absent, Y is too, then you have demonstrated that there is a relationship between X and Y. I don't know about you, but sometimes I find it's not easy to think about X's and Y's. Let's put this same syllogism in program evaluation terms:

- if program then outcome
- if not program then not outcome.

Or, in colloquial terms: if you give a program you observe the outcome but if you don't give the program you don't observe the outcome. This provides evidence that the program and outcome are related. Notice, however, that this syllogism doesn't not provide evidence that the program caused the outcome — perhaps there was some other factor present with the program that caused the outcome, rather than the program. The relationships described so far are rather simple binary relationships. Sometimes we want to know whether different amounts of the program lead to different amounts of the outcome — a continuous relationship:

- if more of the program then more of the outcome
- if less of the program then less of the outcome.

No Plausible Alternative Explanations

Just because you show there's a relationship doesn't mean it's a causal one. It's possible that there is some other variable or factor that is causing the outcome. This is sometimes referred to as the "third variable" or "missing variable" problem and it's at the heart of the issue of internal validity. What are some of the possible plausible alternative explanations? Just go look at the threats to internal validity — each one describes a type of alternative explanation. In order for you to argue that you have demonstrated internal validity — that you have shown there's a causal relationship — you have to "rule out" the plausible alternative explanations. How do you do that? One of the major ways is with your research design. Let's consider a simple single group threat to internal validity, a *history* threat. Let's assume you measure your program group before they start the program (to establish a baseline), you give them the program, and then you measure their performance afterwards in a posttest. You see a marked improvement in their performance which you would like to infer is caused by your program.

One of the plausible alternative explanations is that you have a history threat — it's not your program that caused the gain but some other specific historical event. For instance, it's not your anti-smoking campaign that caused the reduction in smoking but rather the Surgeon General's latest report that happened to be issued between the time you gave your pretest and posttest. How do you rule this out with your research design? One of the simplest ways would be to incorporate the use of a control group — a group that is comparable to your program group with the only difference being that they didn't receive the program.

But they did experience the Surgeon General's latest report. If you find that they didn't show a reduction in smoking even though they did experience the same Surgeon General report you have effectively "ruled out" the Surgeon General's report as a plausible alternative explanation for why you observed the smoking reduction.

In most applied social research that involves evaluating programs, temporal precedence is not a difficult criterion to meet because you administer the program before you measure effects. And, establishing covariation is relatively simple because you have some control over the program and can set things up so that you have some people who get it and some who don't (if X and if not X). Typically the most difficult criterion to meet is the third — ruling out alternative explanations for the observed effect. That is why research design is such an important issue and why it is intimately linked to the idea of internal validity.

SINGLE GROUP THREATS

To help make this a bit more concrete, let's imagine that we are studying the effects of a compensatory education program in mathematics for first grade students on a measure of math performance such as a standardized math achievement test. In the post-only design, we would give the first graders the program and then give a math achievement posttest. We might choose not to give them a baseline measure because we have reason to believe they have no prior knowledge of the math skills we are teaching. It wouldn't make sense to pretest them if we expect they would all get a score of zero. In the pre-post design we are not willing to assume that they have no prior knowledge. We measure the baseline in order to determine where the students start out in math achievement. We might hypothesize that the change or gain from pretest to posttest is due to our special math tutoring program. This is a *compensatory* program because it is only given to students who are identified as potentially low in math ability on the basis of some screening mechanism.

The Single Group Threats

With either of these scenarios in mind, consider what would happen if you observe a certain level of posttest math achievement or a change or gain from pretest to posttest. You want to conclude that the outcome is due to your math program. How could you be wrong? Here are some of the ways, some of the threats to interval validity that your critics might raise, some of the plausible alternative explanations for your observed effect:

History Threat

It's not your math program that caused the outcome, it's something else, some historical event that occurred. For instance, we know that lot's of first graders watch the public TV program *Sesame Street*. And, we know that in every *Sesame Street* show they present some very elementary math concepts. Perhaps these shows cause the outcome and not your math program.

Maturation Threat

The children would have had the exact same outcome even if they had never had your special math training program. All you are doing is measuring normal maturation or growth in understanding that occurs as part of growing up — your math program has no effect. How is this maturation explanation different from a history threat? In general, if we're talking about a specific event or chain of events that could cause the outcome, we call it a history threat. If we're talking about all of the events that typically transpire in your life over a period of time (without being specific as to which ones are the active causal agents) we call it a maturation threat.

Testing Threat

This threat only occurs in the pre-post design. What if taking the pretest made some of the children more aware of that kind of math problem — it "primed" them for the program so that when you began the math training they were ready for it in a way that they wouldn't have been without the pretest. This is what is meant by a testing threat — taking the pretest (not getting your program) affects how participants do on the posttest.

Instrumentation Threat

Like the testing threat, this one only operates in the pretest-posttest situation. What if the change from pretest to posttest is due not to your math program but rather to a change in the test that was used? This is what's meant by an instrumentation threat. In many schools when they have to administer repeated testing they don't use the exact same test (in part because they're worried about a testing threat!) but rather give out "alternate forms" of the same tests. These alternate forms were designed to be "equivalent" in the types of questions and level of difficulty, but what if they aren't? Perhaps part or all of any pre-post gain is attributable to the change in instrument, not to your program. Instrumentation threats are especially likely when the "instrument" is a human observer. The observers may get tired over time or bored with the observations. Conversely, they might get better at making the observations as they practice more. In either event, it's the change in instrumentation, not the program, that leads to the outcome.

Mortality Threat

Mortality doesn't mean that people in your study are dying (although if they are, it would be considered a mortality threat!). Mortality is used metaphorically here. It means that people are "dying" with respect to your study. Usually, it means that they are dropping out of the study. What's wrong with that? Let's assume that in our compensatory math tutoring program we have a nontrivial dropout rate between pretest and posttest. And, assume that the kids who are dropping out are the low pretest math achievement test scorers. If you look at the average gain from pretest to posttest using all of the scores available to you at each occasion, you would include these low pretest subsequent dropouts in the pretest and not in the posttest. You'd be dropping out the potential low scorers from the posttest, or, you'd be artificially inflating the posttest average over what it would have been if no students had dropped out. And, you won't necessarily solve this problem by comparing pre-post averages for only those kids who stayed in the study. This subsample would certainly not be representative even of the original entire sample. Furthermore, we know that because of regression threats these students may appear to actually do worse on the posttest, simply as an artifact of the non-random dropout or mortality in your study. When mortality is a threat, the researcher can often gauge the degree of the threat by comparing the dropout group against the nondropout group on *pretest* measures. If there are no major differences, it may be more reasonable to assume that mortality was happening across the entire sample and is not biasing results greatly. But if the pretest differences are large, one must be concerned about the potential biasing effects of mortality.

Regression Threat

A regression threat, also known as a "regression artifact" or "regression to the mean" is a statistical phenomenon that occurs whenever you have a nonrandom sample from a population and two measures that are imperfectly correlated.

OK, I know that's gibberish. Let me try again. Assume that your two measures are a pretest and posttest (and you can certainly bet these aren't perfectly correlated with each other). Furthermore, assume that your sample consists of low pretest scorers. The regression threat means that the pretest average for the group in your study will appear to increase or improve (relatively to the overall population) even if you don't do anything to them — even if you never give them a treatment. Regression is a confusing threat to understand at first. I like to think about it as the "*you can only go up from here*" phenomenon. If you include in your program only the kids who constituted the lowest ten percent of the class on the pretest, what are the chances that they would constitute exactly the lowest ten percent on the posttest? Not likely. Most of them would score low on the posttest, but they aren't likely to be the lowest ten percent twice. For instance, maybe there were a few kids on the pretest who got lucky on a few guesses and scored at the eleventh percentile who won't get so lucky next time. No, if you choose the lowest ten percent on the pretest, they can't get any lower than being the lowest — they can only go up from there, relative to the larger population from which they were selected. This purely statistical phenomenon is what we mean by a regression threat. To see a more detailed discussion of why regression threats occur and how to estimate them, click *here*.

How do we deal with these single group threats to internal validity? While there are several ways to rule out threats, one of the most common approaches to ruling out the ones listed above is through your research design. For instance, instead of doing a single group study, you could incorporate a control group. In this scenario, you would have two groups: one receives your program and the other one doesn't. In fact, the only difference between these groups should be the program. If that's true, then the control group would experience all the same history and maturation threats, would have the same testing and instrumentation issues, and would have similar rates of mortality and regression to the mean. In other words, a good control group is one of the most effective ways to rule out the single-group threats to internal validity. Of course, when you add a control group, you no-longer have a single group design. And, you will still have to deal with threats two major types of threats to internal validity: the multiple-group threats to internal validity and the social threats to internal validity.

REGRESSION TO THE MEAN

A regression threat, also known as a "regression artifact" or "regression to the mean" is a statistical phenomenon that occurs whenever you have a nonrandom sample from a population and two measures that are imperfectly correlated. Pretest scores are "normally" distributed, the frequency distribution looks like a "bell-shaped" curve. Assume that the sample for your study was selected exclusively from the low pretest scorers. You can see on the top part of the figure where their pretest mean is — clearly, it is considerably below the population average. What would we predict the posttest to look like? First, let's assume that your program or treatment doesn't work at all (the "null" case). Our naive assumption would be that our sample would score just as badly on the posttest as they did on the pretest. In actuality, the sample's posttest mean wound up closer to the posttest population mean than their pretest mean was to the pretest population mean. In other words, the sample's mean appears to *regress toward the mean* of the population from pretest to posttest.

Why Does It Happen?

Let's start with a simple explanation and work from there. To see why regression to the mean happens, consider a concrete case. In your study you select the lowest 10% of the population based on their pretest score. What are the chances that on the posttest that exact group will once again constitute the lowest ten percent? Not likely. Most of them will probably be in the lowest ten percent on the posttest, but if even just a few are not, then their group's mean will have to be closer to the population's posttest than it was to the pretest. The same thing is true on the other end. If you select as your sample the highest ten percent pretest scorers, they aren't likely to be the highest ten percent on the posttest (even though most of them may be in the top ten percent). If even just a few score below the top ten percent on the posttest their group's posttest mean will have to be closer to the population posttest mean than to their pretest mean.

Here are a few things you need to know about the regression to the mean phenomenon:

- It is a *statistical* phenomenon. Regression toward the mean occurs for two reasons. First, it results because you asymmetrically sampled from the population. If you randomly sample from the population, you would observe (subject to random error) that the population and your sample have the same pretest average. Because the sample is already at the population mean on the pretest, it is impossible for them to regress towards the mean of the population any more!
- It is a *group* phenomenon. You cannot tell which way an individual's score will move based on the regression to the mean phenomenon. Even though the group's average will move toward the population's, some individuals in the group are likely to move in the other direction.
- It happens between *any two variables*. Here's a common research mistake. You run a program and don't find any overall group effect. So, you decide to look at those who did best on the posttest (your "success" stories!?) and see how much they gained over the pretest. You are selecting a group that is extremely high on the posttest. They won't likely all be the best on the pretest as well (although many of them will be). So, their pretest mean has to be closer to the population mean than their posttest one. You describe this nice "gain" and are almost ready to write up your results when someone suggests you look at your "failure" cases, the people who score worst on your posttest. When you check on how they were doing on the pretest you find that they weren't the worst scorers there. If they had been the worst scorers both times, you would have simply said that your program didn't have any effect on them. But now it looks worse than that — it looks like your program

actually made them worse relative to the population! What will you do? How will you ever get your grant renewed? Or your paper published? Or, heaven help you, how will you ever get tenured?

What you have to realize, is that the pattern of results I just described will happen anytime you measure two measures! It will happen forwards in time (i.e., from pretest to posttest). It will happen backwards in time (i.e., from posttest to pretest)! It will happen across measures collected at the same time (e.g., height and weight)! It will happen even if you don't give your program or treatment.

- It is a *relative* phenomenon.
- You can have regression up or down.

  If your sample consists of below-population-mean scorers, the regression to the mean will make it appear that they move *up* on the other measure. But if your sample consists of high scorers, their mean will appear to move *down* relative to the population. (Note that even if their mean increases, they could be losing ground to the population. So, if a high-pretest-scoring sample gains five points on the posttest while the overall sample gains 15, we would suspect regression to the mean as an alternative explanation [to our program] for that relatively low change).
- The more extreme the sample group, the greater the regression to the mean. If your sample differs from the population by only a little bit on the first measure, there won't be much regression to the mean because there isn't much room for them to regress — they're already near the population mean. So, if you have a sample, even a nonrandom one, that is a pretty good subsample of the population, regression to the mean will be inconsequential (although it will be present). But if your sample is very extreme relative to the population (e.g., the lowest or highest x%), their mean is further from the population's and has more room to regress.

- The less correlated the two variables, the greater the regression to the mean. The other major factor that affects the amount of regression to the mean is the correlation between the two variables. If the two variables are *perfectly* correlated — the highest scorer on one is the highest on the other, next highest on one is next highest on the other, and so on — there will no be regression to the mean. But this is unlikely to ever occur in practice. We know from measurement theory that there is no such thing as "perfect" measurement — all measurement is assumed (under the true score model) to have some random error in measurement. It is only when the measure has no random error — is perfectly reliable — that we can expect it will be able to correlate perfectly. Since that just doesn't happen in the real world, we have to assume that measures have some degree of unreliability, and that relationships between measures will not be perfect, and that there will appear to be regression to the mean between these two measures, given asymmetrically sampled subgroups.

The Formula for the Percent of Regression to the Mean

You can estimate exactly the percent of regression to the mean in any given situation. The formula is:

P_{rm} = 100(1-r)

where:

P_{rm} = the percent of regression to the mean

r = the correlation between the two measures

Consider the following four cases:

- if r = 1, there is no (i.e., 0%) regression to the mean
- if r =.5, there is 50% regression to the mean
- if r =.2, there is 80% regression to the mean
- if r = 0, there is 100% regression to the mean.

In the first case, the two variables are perfectly correlated and there is no regression to the mean. With a correlation of.5, the sampled group moves *fifty percent* of the distance from the no-regression point to the mean of the population. If the correlation is a small.20, the sample will regress 80% of the distance. And, if there is no correlation between the measures, the sample will "regress" all the way back to the population mean! It's worth thinking about what this last case means. With zero correlation, knowing a score on one measure gives you absolutely no information about the likely score for that person on the other measure. In that case, your best guess for how any person would perform on the second measure will be the mean of that second measure.

Estimating and Correcting Regression to the Mean

Given our percentage formula, for any given situation we can estimate the regression to the mean. All we need to know is the mean of the sample on the first measure the population mean on both measures, and the correlation between measures. Consider a simple example. Here, we'll assume that the pretest population mean is 50 and that we select a low-pretest scoring sample that has a mean of 30. To begin with, let's assume that we do not give any program or treatment (i.e., the null case) and that the population is not changing over time on the characteristic being measured (i.e., steady-state). Given this, we would predict that the population mean would be 50 and that the sample would get a posttest score of 30 *if there was no regression to the mean*. Now, assume that the correlation is.50 between the pretest and posttest for the population. Given our formula, we would expect that the sampled group would regress 50% of the distance from the no-regression point to the population mean, or 50% of the way from 30 to 50. In this case, we would observe a score of 40 for the sampled group, which would constitute a 10-point pseudo-effect or regression artifact.

Now, let's relax some of the initial assumptions. For instance, let's assume that between the pretest and posttest the population gained 15 points on average (and that this gain was uniform across the entire distribution, that is, the variance of the population stays the same across the two measurement occasions). In this case, a sample that had a pretest mean of 30 would be expected to get a posttest mean of 45 (i.e., 30+15) if there is no regression to the mean (i.e., r=1). But here, the correlation between pretest and posttest is.5 so we expect to see regression to the mean that covers 50% of the distance from the mean of 45 to the population posttest mean of 65. That is, we would observe a posttest average of 55 for our sample, again a pseudo-effect of 10 points.

Regression to the mean is one of the trickiest threats to validity. It is subtle in its effects, and even excellent researchers sometimes fail to catch a potential regression artifact. You might want to learn more about the regression to the mean phenomenon. One good way to do that would be to simulate the phenomenon. If you're not familiar with simulation, you can get a good introduction in the The Simulation Book. If you already understand the basic idea of simulation, you can do a manual (dice rolling) simulation of regression artifacts or a computerized simulation of regression artifacts.

INTRODUCTION TO DESIGN

Research design can be thought of as the *structure* of research — it is the "glue" that holds all of the elements in a research project together. We often describe a design using a concise notation that enables us to summarize a complex design structure efficiently. What are the "elements" that a design includes? They are:

- Observations or Measures: These are symbolized by an 'O' in design notation. An O can refer to a single measure (e.g., a measure of body weight), a single instrument with multiple items (e.g., a 10-item self-esteem scale), a complex multi-part instrument (e.g., a survey), or a whole battery of tests or measures given out on one occasion. If you need to distinguish among specific measures, you can use subscripts with the O, as in O_1, O_2, and so on.
- Treatments or Programs: These are symbolized with an 'X' in design notations. The X can refer to a simple intervention (e.g., a one-time surgical technique) or to a complex hodgepodge program (e.g., an employment training program). Usually, a no-treatment control or

comparison group has no symbol for the treatment (some researchers use X+ and X-to indicate the treatment and control respectively). As with observations, you can use subscripts to distinguish different programs or program variations.

- Groups: Each group in a design is given its own line in the design structure. If the design notation has three lines, there are three groups in the design.
- Assignment to Group: Assignment to group is designated by a letter at the beginning of each line (i.e., group) that describes how the group was assigned. The major types of assignment are:
- R = random assignment
- N = nonequivalent groups
- C = assignment by cutoff
- Time

Time moves from left to right. Elements that are listed on the left occur before elements that are listed on the right.

Design Notation Examples

It's always easier to explain design notation through examples than it is to describe it in words. Let's go through each of the parts of the design. There are two lines in the notation, so you should realize that the study has two groups. There are four Os in the notation, two on each line and two for each group. When the Os are stacked vertically on top of each other it means they are collected at the same time. In the notation you can see that we have two Os that are taken before (i.e., to the left of) any treatment is given — the pretest — and two Os taken after the treatment is given — the posttest. The R at the beginning of each line signifies that the two groups are randomly assigned (making it an experimental design). The design is a treatment versus comparison group one because the top line (treatment group) has an X while the bottom line (control group) does not. You should be able to see why many of my students have called this type of notation the "tic-tac-toe" method of design notation — there are lots of Xs and Os!

With this simple set of rules for describing a research design in notational form, you can concisely explain even complex design structures. And, using a notation helps to show common design sub-structures across different designs that we might not recognize as easily without the notation.

TYPES OF DESIGNS

What are the different major types of research designs? We can classify designs into a simple threefold classification by asking some key questions. First, does the design use random assignment to groups? [Don't forget that random *assignment* is not the same thing as random *selection* of a sample from a population!] If random assignment is used, we call the design a randomized experiment or true experiment. If random assignment is not used, then we have to ask a second question: Does the design use *either* multiple groups or multiple waves of measurement? If the answer is yes, we would label it a quasi-experimental design. If no, we would call it a non-experimental design. This threefold classification is especially useful for describing the design with respect to internal validity. A randomized experiment generally is the strongest of the three designs when your interest is in establishing a cause-effect relationship. A non-experiment is generally the weakest in this respect. I have to hasten to add here, that I don't mean that a non-experiment is the weakest of the three designs *overall*, but only with respect to internal validity or causal assessment. In fact, the simplest form of non-experiment is a one-shot survey design that consists of nothing but a single observation O. This is probably one of the most common forms of research and, for some research questions — especially descriptive ones — is clearly a strong design. When I say that the non-experiment is the weakest with respect to internal validity, all I mean is that it isn't a particularly good method for assessing the cause-effect relationship that you think might exist between a program and its outcomes.

To illustrate the different types of designs, consider one of each in design notation. The first design is a posttest-only randomized experiment. You can tell it's a randomized experiment because it has an R at the beginning of each line, indicating random assignment. The second design is a pre-post nonequivalent groups quasi-experiment. We know it's not a randomized experiment because random assignment wasn't used. And we know it's not a non-experiment because there are both multiple groups and multiple waves of measurement. That means it must be a quasi-experiment. We add the label "nonequivalent" because in this design we do not explicitly control the assignment and the groups may be nonequivalent or not similar to each other.

Finally, we show a posttest-only nonexperimental design. You might use this design if you want to study the effects of a natural disaster like a flood or tornado and you want to do so by interviewing survivors. Notice that in this design, you don't have a comparison group (e.g., interview in a town down the road the road that didn't have the tornado to see what differences the tornado caused) and you don't have multiple waves of measurement (e.g., a pre-tornado level of how people in the ravaged town were doing before the disaster). Does it make sense to do the non-experimental study? Of course! You could gain lots of valuable information by well-conducted post-disaster interviews. But you may have a hard time establishing which of the things you observed are due to the disaster rather than to other factors like the peculiarities of the town or pre-disaster characteristics.

EXPERIMENTAL DESIGN

Experimental designs are often touted as the most "rigorous" of all research designs or, as the "gold standard" against which all other designs are judged. In one sense, they probably are. If you can implement an experimental design well (and that is a big "if" indeed), then the experiment is probably the strongest design with respect to internal validity. Why? Recall that internal validity is at the center of all causal or cause-effect inferences. When you want to determine whether some program or treatment *causes* some outcome or outcomes to occur, then you are interested in having strong internal validity. Essentially, you want to assess the proposition:

If X, then Y

or, in more colloquial terms:

If the program is given, then the outcome occurs.

Unfortunately, it's not enough just to show that when the program or treatment occurs the expected outcome also happens. That's because there may be lots of reasons, other than the program, for why you observed the outcome. To really show that there is a causal relationship, you have to simultaneously address the two propositions:

If X, then Y

and

If *not* X, then *not* Y

Or, once again more colloquially:

If the program is given, then the outcome occurs

and

If the program is *not* given, then the outcome does *not* occur

If you are able to provide evidence for both of these propositions, then you've in effect isolated the program from all of the other potential causes of the outcome. You've shown that when the program is present the outcome occurs and when it's not present, the outcome doesn't occur. That points to the causal effectiveness of the program.

Think of all this like a fork in the road. Down one path, you implement the program and observe the outcome. Down the other path, you don't implement the program and the outcome doesn't occur. But, how do we take *both* paths in the road in the same study? How can we be in two places at once? Ideally, what we want is to have the same conditions — the same people, context, time, and so on — and see whether when the program is given we get the outcome and when the program is not given we don't. Obviously, we can never achieve this hypothetical situation. If we give the program to a group of people, we can't simultaneously not give it! So, how do we get out of this apparent dilemma?

Perhaps we just need to think about the problem a little differently. What if we could create two groups or contexts that are as similar as we can possibly make them? If we could be confident that the two situations are comparable, then we could administer our program in one and not give the program in the other. And, if the two contexts are comparable, then this is like taking both forks in the road simultaneously! We can have our cake and eat it too, so to speak.

That's exactly what an experimental design tries to achieve. In the simplest type of experiment, we create two groups that are "equivalent" to each other. One group (the program or treatment group) gets the program and the other group (the comparison or control group) does not. In all other respects, the groups are treated the same. They have similar people, live in similar contexts, have similar backgrounds, and so on. Now, if we observe differences in outcomes between these two groups, then the differences must be due to the only thing that differs between them — that one got the program and the other didn't.

OK, so how do we create two groups that are "equivalent"? The approach used in experimental design is to assign people randomly from a common pool of people into the two groups. The experiment relies on this idea of random assignment to groups as the basis for obtaining two groups that are similar. Then, we give one the program or treatment and we don't give it to the other. We observe the same outcomes in both groups.

The key to the success of the experiment is in the random assignment. In fact, even with random assignment we never expect that the groups we create will be exactly the same. How could they be, when they are made up of different people? We rely on the idea of probability and assume that the two groups are "probabilistically equivalent" or equivalent within known probabilistic ranges.

So, if we randomly assign people to two groups, and we have enough people in our study to achieve the desired probabilistic equivalence, then we may consider the experiment to be strong in internal validity and we probably have a good shot at assessing whether the program causes the outcome(s).

But there are lots of things that can go wrong. We may not have a large enough sample. Or, we may have people who refuse to participate in our study or who drop out part way through. Or, we may be challenged successfully on ethical grounds (after all, in order to use this approach we have to deny the program to some people who might be equally deserving of it as others). Or, we may get resistance from the staff in our study who would like some of their "favourite" people to get the program. Or, they mayor might insist that her daughter be put into the new program in an educational study because it may mean she'll get better grades.

The bottom line here is that experimental design is intrusive and difficult to carry out in most real world contexts. And, because an experiment is often an intrusion, you are to some extent setting up an artificial situation so that you can assess your causal relationship with high internal validity. If so, then you are limiting the degree to which you can generalize your results to real contexts where you haven't set up an experiment. That is, you have reduced your external validity in order to achieve greater internal validity.

In the end, there is just no simple answer (no matter what anyone tells you!). If the situation is right, an experiment can be a very strong design to use. But it isn't automatically so. My own personal guess is that randomized experiments are probably appropriate in no more than 10% of the social research studies that attempt to assess causal relationships.

Experimental design is a fairly complex subject in its own right. I've been discussing the simplest of experimental designs — a two-group program versus comparison group design. But there are lots of experimental design variations that attempt to accomplish different things or solve different problems. In this section you'll explore the basic design and then learn some of the principles behind the major variations.

TWO-GROUP EXPERIMENTAL DESIGNS

The simplest of all experimental designs is the two-group posttest-only randomized experiment. In design notation, it has two lines — one for each group — with an R at the beginning of each line to indicate that the groups were randomly assigned. One group gets the treatment or program (the X) and the other group is the comparison group and doesn't get the program (note that this you could alternatively have the comparison group receive the standard or typical treatment, in which case this study would be a relative comparison).

Notice that a pretest is not required for this design. Usually we include a pretest in order to determine whether groups are comparable prior to the program, but because we are using random assignment we can assume that the two groups are probabilistically equivalent to begin with and the pretest is not required (although you'll see with covariance designs that a pretest may still be desirable in this context).

In this design, we are most interested in determining whether the two groups are different after the program. Typically we measure the groups on one or more measures (the Os in notation) and we compare them by testing for the differences between the means using a t-test or one way Analysis of Variance (ANOVA).

The posttest-only randomized experiment is strong against the single-group threats to internal validity because it's not a single group design! (Tricky, huh?) It's strong against the all of the multiple-group threats except for selection-mortality. For instance, it's strong against selection-testing and selection-instrumentation because it doesn't use repeated measurement. The selection-mortality threat is especially salient if there are differential rates of dropouts in the two groups. This could result if the treatment or program is a noxious or negative one (e.g., a painful medical procedure like chemotherapy) or if the control group condition is painful or intolerable. This design is susceptible to all of the social interaction threats to internal validity. Because the design requires random assignment, in some institutional settings (e.g., schools) it is more likely to utilize persons who would be aware of each other and of the conditions they've been assigned to.

The posttest-only randomized experimental design is, despite its simple structure, one of the best research designs for assessing cause-effect relationships. It is easy to execute and, because it uses only a posttest, is relatively inexpensive. But there are many variations on this simple experimental design. You can begin to explore these by looking at how we classify the various experimental designs.

PROBABILISTIC EQUIVALENCE

What do I mean by the term probabilistic equivalence? Well, to begin with, I certainly *don't* mean that two groups are equal to each other. When we deal with human beings it is impossible to ever say that any two individuals or groups are equal or equivalent. Clearly the important term in the phrase is "probabilistic". This means that the type of equivalence we have is based on the notion of probabilities. In more concrete terms, probabilistic equivalence means that we know *perfectly* the odds that we will find a difference between two groups. Notice, it doesn't mean that the means of the two groups will be equal. It just means that we know the odds that they won't be equal.

We achieve probabilistic equivalence through the mechanism of random assignment to groups. When we randomly assign to groups, we can calculate the chance that the two groups will differ just because of the random assignment (i.e., by chance alone). Let's say we are assigning a group of first grade students to two groups. Further, let's assume that the average test scores for these children for a standardized test with a population mean of 50 were 49 and 51 respectively. We might conduct a t-test to see if the means of our two randomly assigned groups are statistically different. We know — through random assignment and the law of large numbers — that the chance that they will be different is 5 out of 100 when we set our significance level to.05 (i.e., *alpha* =.05). In other words, 5 times out of every 100, when we randomly assign two groups, we can expect to get a significant difference at the.05 level of significance.

When we assign randomly, the only reason the groups can differ is because of chance assignment because their assignment is entirely based on the randomness of assignment. If, by chance, the groups differ on one variable, we have no reason to believe that they will automatically be different on any other. Even if we find that the groups differ on a pretest, we have no reason to suspect that they will differ on a posttest. Why? Because their pretest difference had to be a chance one. So, when we randomly assign, we are able to assume that the groups do have a form of equivalence. We don't expect them to be equal. But we do expect that they are "probabilistically" equal.

RANDOM SELECTION & ASSIGNMENT

Random *selection* is how you draw the sample of people for your study from a population. Random *assignment* is how you assign the sample that you draw to different groups or treatments in your study.

It is possible to have *both* random selection and assignment in a study. Let's say you drew a random sample of 100 clients from a population list of 1000 current clients of your organization. That is random sampling. Now, let's say you randomly assign 50 of these clients to get some new additional treatment and the other 50 to be controls. That's random assignment.

It is also possible to have *only one of these* (random selection or random assignment) but not the other in a study. For instance, if you do not randomly draw the 100 cases from your list of 1000 but instead just take the first 100 on the list, you do not have random selection. But you could still randomly assign this nonrandom sample to treatment versus control. Or, you could randomly select 100 from your list of 1000 and then nonrandomly (haphazardly) assign them to treatment or control.

And, it's possible to have *neither* random selection nor random assignment. In a typical nonequivalent groups design in education you might nonrandomly choose two 5th grade classes to be in your study. This is nonrandom selection. Then, you could arbitrarily assign one to get the new educational program and the other to be the control. This is nonrandom (or nonequivalent) assignment.

Random selection is related to sampling. Therefore it is most related to the external validity (or generalizability) of your results. After all, we would randomly sample so that our research participants better represent the larger group from which they're drawn. Random assignment is most related to design. In fact, when we randomly assign participants to treatments we have, by definition, an experimental design. Therefore, random assignment is most related to internal validity. After all, we randomly assign in order to help assure that our treatment groups are similar to each other (i.e., equivalent) prior to the treatment.

CLASSIFYING EXPERIMENTAL DESIGNS

Although there are a great variety of experimental design variations, we can classify and organize them using a simple signal-to-noise ratio metaphor. In this metaphor, we assume that what we observe or see can be divided into two components, the signal and the noise (by the way, this is directly analogous to the true score theory of measurement).

In most research, the signal is related to the key variable of interest — the construct you're trying to measure, the program or treatment that's being implemented. The noise consists of all of the random factors in the situation that make it harder to see the signal — the lighting in the room, local distractions, how people felt that day, etc. We can construct a ratio of these two by dividing the signal by the noise. In research, we want the signal to be high relative to the noise. For instance, if you have a very powerful treatment or program (i.e., strong signal) and very good measurement (i.e., low noise) you will have a better chance of seeing the effect of the program than if you have either a strong program and weak measurement or a weak program and strong measurement.

With this in mind, we can now classify the experimental designs into two categories: signal enhancers or noise reducers. Notice that doing either of these things — enhancing signal or reducing noise — improves the quality of the research. The *signal-enhancing experimental designs* are called the factorial designs. In these designs, the focus is almost entirely on the setup of the program or treatment, its components and its major dimensions. In a typical factorial design we would examine a number of different variations of a treatment. There are two major types of *noise-reducing experimental designs*: covariance designs and blocking designs. In these designs we typically use information about the makeup of the sample or about pre-program variables to remove some of the noise in our study.

FACTORIAL DESIGNS

Probably the easiest way to begin understanding factorial designs is by looking at an example. Let's imagine a design where we have an educational program where we would like to look at a variety of program variations to see which works best. For instance, we would like to vary the amount of time the children receive instruction with one group getting 1 hour of instruction per week and another getting 4 hours per week. And, we'd like to vary the setting with one group getting the instruction in-class (probably pulled off into a corner of the classroom) and the other group being pulled-out of the classroom for instruction in another room. We could think about having four separate groups to do this, but when we are varying the amount of time in instruction, what setting would we use: in-class or pull-out? And, when we were studying setting, what amount of instruction time would we use: 1 hour, 4 hours, or something else?

With factorial designs, we don't have to compromise when answering these questions. We can have it both ways if we cross each of our two time in instruction conditions with each of our two settings. Let's begin by doing some defining of terms. In factorial designs, a factor is a major independent variable. In this example we have two factors: time in instruction and setting. A level is a subdivision of a factor. In this example, time in instruction has two levels and setting has two levels. Sometimes we depict a factorial design with a numbering notation. In this example, we can say that we have a 2 x 2 (spoken "two-by-two) factorial design. In this notation, the *number of numbers* tells you how many factors there are and the *number values* tell you how many levels. If I said I had a 3 x 4 factorial design, you would know that I had 2 factors and that one factor had 3 levels while the other had 4. Order of the numbers makes no difference and we could just as easily term this a 4 x 3 factorial design. The number of different treatment groups that we have in any factorial design can easily be determined by multiplying through the number notation. For instance, in our example we have 2 x 2 = 4 groups. In our notational example, we would need 3 x 4 = 12 groups.

We can also depict a factorial design in design notation. Because of the treatment level combinations, it is useful to use subscripts on the treatment (X) symbol.

Now, let's look at a variety of different results we might get from this simple 2 x 2 factorial design. And each outcome is shown in table form (the 2 x 2 table with the row and column averages) and in graphic form (with each factor taking a turn on the horizontal axis). You should convince yourself that the information in the tables agrees with the information in both of the graphs. The lines that are shown in the graphs are technically not necessary — they are used as a visual aid to enable you to easily track where the averages for a single level go across levels of another factor. Keep in mind that the values shown in the tables and graphs are group averages on the outcome variable of interest. In this example, the outcome might be a test of achievement in the subject being taught. We will assume that scores on this test range from 1 to 10 with higher values indicating greater achievement. You should study carefully the outcomes in each figure in order to understand the differences between these cases.

The Null Outcome

Let's begin by looking at the "null" case. The null case is a situation where the treatments have no effect. This figure assumes that even if we didn't give the training we could expect that students would score a 5 on average on the outcome test. You can see in this hypothetical case that all four groups score an average of 5 and therefore the row and column averages must be 5. You can't see the lines for both levels in the graphs because one line falls right on top of the other.

The Main Effects

A main effect is an outcome that is a consistent difference between levels of a factor. For instance, we would say there's a main effect for setting if we find a statistical difference between the averages for the in-class and pull-out groups, *at all levels* of time in instruction. The first figure depicts a main effect of time. For all settings, the 4 hour/week condition worked better than the 1 hour/week one. It is also possible to have a main effect for setting (and none for time).

In the second main effect graph we see that in-class training was better than pull-out training for all amounts of time.

Finally, it is possible to have a main effect on both variables simultaneously as depicted in the third main effect figure. In this instance 4 hours/week always works better than 1 hour/ week and in-class setting always works better than pull-out.

Interaction Effects

If we could only look at main effects, factorial designs would be useful. But, because of the way we combine levels in factorial designs, they also enable us to examine the interaction effects that exist between factors. An *interaction effect* exists when differences on one factor depend on the level you are on another factor. It's important to recognize that an interaction is between factors, not levels. We wouldn't say there's an interaction between 4 hours/week and in-class treatment. Instead, we would say that there's an interaction between time and setting, and then we would go on to describe the specific levels involved.

How do you know if there is an interaction in a factorial design? There are three ways you can determine there's an interaction. First, when you run the statistical analysis, the statistical table will report on all main effects and interactions. Second, you know there's an interaction when can't talk about effect on one factor without mentioning the other factor. if you can say at the end of our study that time in instruction makes a difference, then you know that you have a main effect and not an interaction (because you did not have to mention the setting factor when describing the results for time). On the other hand, when you have an interaction it is impossible to describe your results accurately without mentioning both factors. Finally, you can always spot an interaction in the graphs of group means — whenever there are lines that are not parallel there is an interaction present! If you check out the main effect graphs above, you will notice that all of the lines within a graph are parallel. In contrast, for all of the interaction graphs, you will see that the lines are not parallel.

In the first interaction effect graph, we see that one combination of levels — 4 hours/week and in-class setting — does better than the other three. In the second interaction we have a more complex "cross-over" interaction. Here, at 1 hour/week the pull-out group does better than the in-class group while at 4 hours/week the reverse is true. Furthermore, the both of these combinations of levels do equally well.

RANDOMIZED BLOCK DESIGNS

The Randomized Block Design is research design's equivalent to stratified random sampling. Like stratified sampling, randomized block designs are constructed to reduce noise or variance in the data. How do they do it? They require that the researcher divide the sample into relatively homogeneous subgroups or blocks (analogous to "strata" in stratified sampling). Then, the experimental design you want to implement is implemented within each block or homogeneous subgroup. The key idea is that the variability within each block is less than the variability of the entire sample. Thus each estimate of the treatment effect within a block is more efficient than estimates across the entire sample. And, when we pool these more efficient estimates across blocks, we should get an overall more efficient estimate than we would without blocking.

Here, we can see a simple example. Let's assume that we originally intended to conduct a simple posttest-only randomized experimental design. But, we recognize that our sample has several intact or homogeneous subgroups. For instance, in a study of college students, we might expect that students are relatively homogeneous with respect to class or year. So, we decide to block the sample into four groups: freshman, sophomore, junior, and senior. If our hunch is correct, that the variability within class is less than the variability for the entire sample, we will probably get more powerful estimates of the treatment effect within each block. Within each of our four blocks, we would implement the simple post-only randomized experiment.

Notice a couple of things about this strategy. First, to an external observer, it may not be apparent that you are blocking. You would be implementing the same design in each block. And, there is no reason that the people in different blocks need to be segregated or separated from each other. In other words, blocking doesn't necessarily affect anything that you do with the research participants. Instead, blocking is a strategy for grouping people in your data analysis in order to reduce noise — it is an analysis strategy. Second, you will only benefit from a blocking design if you are correct in your hunch that the blocks are more homogeneous than the entire sample is. If you are wrong — if different college-level classes aren't relatively homogeneous with respect to your measures — you will actually be hurt by blocking (you'll get a less powerful estimate of the treatment effect). How do you know if blocking is a good idea? You need to consider carefully whether the groups are relatively homogeneous. If you are measuring political attitudes, for instance, is it reasonable to believe that freshmen are more like each other than they are like sophomores or juniors? Would they be more homogeneous with respect to measures related to drug abuse? Ultimately the decision to block involves judgment on the part of the researcher.

How Blocking Reduces Noise

So how does blocking work to reduce noise in the data? To see how it works, you have to begin by thinking about the non-blocked study. We use the 'X' symbol to indicate a program group case and the 'O' symbol for a comparison group member. You can see that for any specific pretest value, the program group tends to outscore the comparison group by about 10 points on the posttest. That is, there is about a 10-point posttest mean difference.

Now, let's consider an example where we divide the sample into three relatively homogeneous blocks. To see what happens graphically, we'll use the pretest measure to block. This will assure that the groups are very homogeneous. Let's look at what is happening within the third block. Notice that the mean difference is still the same as it was for the entire sample — about 10 points within each block. But also notice that the variability of the posttest is much less than it was for the entire sample. Remember that the treatment effect estimate is a signal-to-noise ratio. The signal in this case is the mean difference. The noise is the variability. But, we have changed the noise — the variability on the posttest is much smaller within each block that it is for the entire sample. So, the treatment effect will have less noise for the same signal.

It should be clear from the graphs that the blocking design in this case will yield the stronger treatment effect. But this is true only because we did a good job assuring that the blocks were homogeneous. If the blocks weren't homogeneous — their variability was as large as the entire sample's — we would actually get worse estimates than in the simple randomized experimental case. We'll see how to analyse data from a randomized block design in the Statistical Analysis of the Randomized Block Design.

COVARIANCE DESIGNS

The basic Analysis of Covariance Design (ANCOVA or ANACOVA) is a just pretest-posttest randomized experimental design. The notation shown here suggests that the pre-program measure is the same one as the post-program measure (otherwise we would use subscripts to distinguish the two), and so we would call this a pretest. But you should note that the pre-program measure doesn't have to be a pretest — it can be any variable measured prior to the program intervention. It is also possible for a study to have more than one covariate.

The pre-program measure or pretest is sometimes also called a "covariate" because of the way it's used in the data analysis — we "covary" it with the outcome variable or posttest in order to remove variability or noise. Thus, the ANCOVA design falls in the class of a "noise reduction" experimental design.

In social research we frequently hear about statistical "adjustments" that attempt to control for important factors in our study. For instance, we might read that an analysis "examined posttest performance after adjusting for the income and educational level of the participants." In this case, "income" and "education level" are covariates. Covariates are the variables you "adjust for" in your study. Sometimes the language that will be used is that of "removing the effects" of one variable from another. For instance, we might read that an analysis "examined posttest performance after removing the effect of income and educational level of the participants."

How Does A Covariate Reduce Noise?

One of the most important ideas in social research is how we make a statistical adjustment — adjust one variable based on its covariance with another variable. If you understand this idea, you'll be well on your way to mastering social research. What I want to do here is to show you a series of graphs that illustrate pictorially what we mean by adjusting for a covariate.

Now, let's fit some straight lines to the data. The lines on the graph are regression lines that describe the pre-post relationship for each of the groups. The regression line shows the expected posttest score for any pretest score. The treatment effect is even clearer with the regression lines. You should see that the line for the treated group is about 10 points higher than the line for the comparison group at any pretest value.

What we want to do is remove some of the variability in the posttest while preserving the difference between the groups. Or, in other terms, we want to "adjust" the posttest scores for pretest variability. In effect, we want to "subtract out" the pretest. You might think of this as subtracting the line from each group from the data for each group. How do we do that? Well, why don't we actually subtract?!? Find the posttest difference between the line for a group and each actual value. We call each of these differences a residual — it's what's left over when you subtract a line from the data.

Now, here comes the tricky part. What does the data look like when we subtract out a line? You might think of it almost like turning the above graph clockwise until the regression lines are horizontal.

HYBRID EXPERIMENTAL DESIGNS

Hybrid experimental designs are just what the name implies — new strains that are formed by combining features of more established designs. There are lots of variations that could be constructed from standard design features. Here, I'm going to introduce two hybrid designs. I'm featuring these because they illustrate especially well how a design can be constructed to address specific threats to internal validity.

The Solomon Four-Group Design

The Solomon Four-Group Design is designed to deal with a potential testing threat. Recall that a testing threat occurs when the act of taking a test affects how people score on a retest or posttest. It's probably not a big surprise that this design has four groups. Note that two of the groups receive the treatment and two do not. Further, two of the groups receive a pretest and two do not. One way to view this is as a 2x2 (Treatment Group X Measurement Group) factorial design. Within each treatment condition we have a group that is pretested and one that is not. By explicitly including testing as a factor in the design, we are able to assess experimentally whether a testing threat is operating.

Possible Outcomes. Let's look at a couple of possible outcomes from this design. The first outcome graph shows what the data might look like if there is a treatment or program effect and there is no testing threat. You need to be careful in interpreting this graph to note that there are six dots — one to represent the average for each O in the design notation. To help you visually see the connection between the pretest and posttest average for the same group, a line is used to connect the dots. The two dots that are not connected by a line represent the two post-only groups. Look first at the two pretest means. They are close to each because the groups were randomly assigned. On the posttest, both treatment groups outscored both controls. Now, look at the posttest values. There appears to be no difference between the treatment groups, even though one got a pretest and the other did not. Similarly, the two control groups scored about the same on the posttest. Thus, the pretest did not appear to affect the outcome. But both treatment groups clearly outscored both controls. There is a main effect for the treatment.

Now, look at a result where there is evidence of a testing threat. In this outcome, the pretests are again equivalent (because the groups were randomly assigned). Each treatment group outscored it's comparable control group. The pre-post treatment outscored the pre-post control. And, the post-only treatment outscored the post-only control. These results indicate that there is a treatment effect. But here, both groups that had the pretest outscored their comparable non-pretest group. That's evidence for a testing threat.

SWITCHING REPLICATIONS DESIGN

The Switching Replications design is one of the strongest of the experimental designs. And, when the circumstances are right for this design, it addresses one of the major problems in experimental designs — the need to deny the program to some participants through random assignment. The design notation indicates that this is a two group design with three waves of measurement. You might think of this as two pre-post treatment-control designs grafted together. That is, the implementation of the treatment is repeated or *replicated*. And in the repetition of the treatment, the two groups *switch* roles — the original control group becomes the treatment group in phase 2 while the original treatment acts as the control. By the end of the study all participants have received the treatment.

The switching replications design is most feasible in organizational contexts where programs are repeated at regular intervals. For instance, it works especially well in schools that are on a semester system. All students are pretested at the beginning of the school year. During the first semester, Group 1 receives the treatment and during the second semester Group 2 gets it. The design also enhances organizational efficiency in resource allocation. Schools only need to allocate enough resources to give the program to half of the students at a time.

Possible Outcomes. Let's look at two possible outcomes. In the first example, we see that when the program is given to the first group, the recipients do better than the controls. In the second phase, when the program is given to the original controls, they "catch up" to the original program group. Thus, we have a converge, diverge, reconverge outcome pattern. We might expect a result like this when the program covers specific content that the students master in the short term and where we don't expect that they will continue getting better as a result.

Now, look at the other example result. During the first phase we see the same result as before — the program group improves while the control does not. And, as before, during the second phase we see the original control group, now the program group, improve as much as did the first program group. But now, during phase two, the original program group continues to increase even though the program is no longer being given them. Why would this happen? It could happen in circumstances where the program has continuing and longer term effects. For instance, if the program focused on learning skills, students might continue to improve even after the formal program period because they continue to apply the skills and improve in them.

4

Hypotheses, Concepts and Measurement

Concepts, as abstract units of meaning, play a key role in the development and testing of hypotheses. Concepts are the basic components of hypotheses. Most formal hypotheses connect concepts by specifying the expected relationships between concepts. For example, a simple relational hypothesis such as "education increases income" specifies a positive relationship between the concepts "education" and "income." This abstract or conceptual hypothesis cannot be tested. First, it must be operationalized or situated in the real world by rules of interpretation. Consider again the simple hypothesis "Education increases Income." To test the hypothesis the abstract meaning of education and income must be derived or operationalized. The concepts should be measured. Education could be measured by "years of school completed" or "highest degree completed" etc. Income could be measured by "hourly rate of pay" or "yearly salary" etc.

When a set of hypotheses are grouped together they become a type of conceptual framework. When a conceptual framework is complex and incorporates causality or explanation it is generally referred to as a theory. According to noted philosopher of science Carl Gustav Hempel "An adequate empirical interpretation turns a theoretical system into a testable theory: The hypothesis whose constituent terms have been interpreted become capable of test by reference to observable phenomena.

Frequently the interpreted hypothesis will be derivative hypotheses of the theory; but their confirmation or disconfirmation by empirical data will then immediately strengthen or weaken also the primitive hypotheses from which they were derived."

Hempel provides a useful metaphor that describes the relationship between a conceptual framework and the framework as it is observed and perhaps tested (interpreted framework). "The whole system floats, as it were, above the plane of observation and is anchored to it by rules of interpretation. These might be viewed as strings which are not part of the network but link certain points of the latter with specific places in the plane of observation. By virtue of those interpretative connections, the network can function as a scientific theory" Hypotheses with concepts anchored in the plane of observation are ready to be tested. In "actual scientific practice the process of framing a theoretical structure and of interpreting it are not always sharply separated, since the intended interpretation usually guides the construction of the theoretician." It is, however, "possible and indeed desirable, for the purposes of logical clarification, to separate the two steps conceptually."

Statistical Hypothesis Testing

When a possible correlation or similar relation between phenomena is investigated, such as, for example, whether a proposed remedy is effective in treating a disease, that is, at least to some extent and for some patients, the hypothesis that a relation exists cannot be examined the same way one might examine a proposed new law of nature: in such an investigation a few cases in which the tested remedy shows no effect do not falsify the hypothesis. Instead, statistical tests are used to determine how likely it is that the overall effect would be observed if no real relation as hypothesized exists. If that likelihood is sufficiently small (e.g., less than 1%), the existence of a relation may be assumed. Otherwise, any observed effect may as well be due to pure chance. In statistical hypothesis testing two hypotheses are compared, which are called the null hypothesis and the alternative hypothesis. The null hypothesis is the hypothesis that states that there is no relation between the phenomena whose relation is under investigation, or at least not of the form given by the alternative hypothesis. The alternative hypothesis, as the name suggests, is the alternative to the null hypothesis: it states that there *is* some kind of relation. The alternative hypothesis may take several forms, depending on the nature of the hypothesized relation; in particular, it can be two-sided (for example: there is *some* effect, in a yet unknown direction) or one-sided (the direction of the hypothesized relation, positive or negative, is fixed in advance).

Conventional significance levels for testing the hypotheses are.10,.05, and.01. Whether the null hypothesis is rejected and the alternative hypothesis is accepted, all must be determined in advance, before the observations are collected or inspected. If these criteria are determined later, when the data to be tested is already known, the test is invalid.

It is important to mention that the above procedure is actually dependent on the number of the participants (units or sample size) that is included in the study. For instance, the sample size may be too small to reject a null hypothesis and, therefore, is recommended to specify the sample size from the beginning. It is advisible to define a small, medium and large effect size for each of a number of the important statistical tests which are used to test the hypotheses.

THEORY AND HYPOTHESIS

A theory is a well-established principle that has been developed to explain some aspect of the natural world. A theory arises from repeated observation and testing and incorporates facts, laws, predictions, and tested hypotheses that are widely accepted.

A hypothesis is a specific, testable prediction about what you expect to happen in your study. For example, a study designed to look at the relationship between study habits and test anxiety might have a hypothesis that states, "This study is designed to assess the hypothesis that students with better study habits will suffer less test anxiety." Unless your study is exploratory in nature, your hypothesis should always explain what you expect to happen during the course of your experiment or research.

While the terms are sometimes used interchangeably in general practice, the difference between a theory and a hypothesis is important when studying experimental design. Some important distinctions to note include:

- A theory predicts events in general terms, while a hypothesis makes a specific prediction about a specified set of circumstances.
- A theory is has been extensively tested and is generally accepted, while a hypothesis is a speculative guess that has yet to be tested.

HYPOTHESIS TESTING

Social science research, and by extension business research, uses a number of different approaches to study a variety of issues. This research may be a very informal, simple process or it may be a formal, somewhat sophisticated process. Regardless of the type of process, all research begins with a generalized idea in the form of a research question or a hypothesis. A research question usually is posed in the beginning of a research effort or in a specific area of study that has had little formal research. A research question may take the form of a basic question about some issue or phenomena or a question about the relationship between two or more variables. For example, a research question might be: Do flexible work hours improve employee productivity?" Another question might be: "How do flexible hours influence employees' work?"

A hypothesis differs from a research question; it is more specific and makes a prediction. It is a tentative statement about the relationship between two or more variables. The major difference between a research question and a hypothesis is that a hypothesis predicts an experimental outcome. For example, a hypothesis might state: "There is a positive relationship between the availability of flexible work hours and employee productivity."

Hypotheses provide the following benefits:

1. They determine the focus and direction for a research effort.
2. Their development forces the researcher to clearly state the purpose of the research activity.
3. They determine what variables will not be considered in a study, as well as those that will be considered.
4. They require the researcher to have an operational definition of the variables of interest.

The worth of a hypothesis often depends on the researcher's skills. Since the hypothesis is the basis of a research study, it is necessary for the hypothesis be developed with a great deal of thought and contemplation. There are basic criteria to consider when developing a hypothesis, in order to ensure that it meets the needs of the study and the researcher. A good hypothesis should:

1. Have logical consistency. Based on the current research literature and knowledge base, does this hypothesis make sense?
2. Be in step with the current literature and/or provide a good basis for any differences. Though it does not have to support the current body of literature, it is necessary to provide a good rationale for stepping away from the mainstream.
3. Be testable. If one cannot design the means to conduct the research the hypothesis means nothing.
4. Be stated in clear and simple terms in order to reduce confusion.

HYPOTHESIS TESTING PROCESS

Hypothesis testing is a systematic method used to evaluate data and aid the decision-making process. Following is a typical series of steps involved in hypothesis testing:

1. State the hypotheses of interest
2. Determine the appropriate test statistic
3. Specify the level of statistical significance

4. Determine the decision rule for rejecting or not rejecting the null hypothesis
5. Collect the data and perform the needed calculations
6. Decide to reject or not reject the null hypothesis.

Each step in the process will be discussed in detail, and an example will follow the discussion of the steps.

Stating the Hypotheses

A research study includes at least two hypotheses—the null hypothesis and the alternative hypothesis. The hypothesis being tested is referred to as the null hypothesis and it is designated as H It also is referred to as the hypothesis of no difference and should include a statement of equality (=, e”, or £). The alternative hypothesis presents the alternative to the null and includes a statement of inequality (“‘). The null hypothesis and the alternative hypothesis are complementary.

The null hypothesis is the statement that is believed to be correct throughout the analysis, and it is the null hypothesis upon which the analysis is based. For example, the null hypothesis might state that the average age of entering college freshmen is 21 years.

H_0 The average age of entering college freshman = 21 years

If the data one collects and analyses indicates that the average age of entering college freshmen is greater than or less than 21 years, the null hypothesis is rejected. In this case the alternative hypothesis could be stated in the following three ways: (1) the average age of entering college freshman is not 21 years (the average age of entering college freshmen “‘ 21); (2) the average age of entering college freshman is less than 21 years (the average age of entering college freshmen < 21); or (3) the average age of entering college freshman is greater than 21 years (the average age of entering college freshmen > 21 years).

The choice of which alternative hypothesis to use is generally determined by the study's objective. The preceding second and third examples of alternative hypotheses involve the use of a "one-tailed" statistical test. This is referred to as "one-tailed" because a direction (greater than [>] or less than [<]) is implied in the statement. The first example represents a “two-tailed” test. There is inequality expressed (age 21 years), but the inequality does not imply direction. One-tailed tests are used more often in management and marketing research because there usually is a need to imply a specific direction in the outcome. For example, it is more likely that a researcher would want to know if Product A performed better than Product B (Product A performance > Product B performance), or vice versa (Product A performance < Product B performance), rather than whether Product A performed differently than Product B (Product A performance `” Product B performance). Additionally, more useful information is gained by knowing that employees who work from 7:00 a.m. to 4:00 p.m. are more productive than those who work from 3:00 p.m. to 12:00 a.m. (early shift employee production > late shift employee production), rather than simply knowing that these employees have different levels of productivity (early shift employee production `” late shift employee production).

Both the alternative and the null hypotheses must be determined and stated prior to the collection of data. Before the alternative and null hypotheses can be formulated it is necessary to decide on the desired or expected conclusion of the research. Generally, the desired conclusion of the study is stated in the alternative hypothesis. This is true as long as the null hypothesis can include a statement of equality. For example, suppose that a researcher is interested in exploring the effects of amount of study time on tests scores. The researcher believes that students who study longer perform better on tests. Specifically, the research suggests that students who spend four hours studying for an exam will get a better score than those who study two hours. In this case the hypotheses might be:

H_0 The average test scores of students who study 4 hours for the test = the average test scores of those who study 2 hours.

H_1 The average test score of students who study 4 hours for the test < the average test scores of those who study 2 hours.

As a result of the statistical analysis, the null hypothesis can be *rejected* or *not rejected.* As a principle of rigorous scientific method, this subtle but important point means that the null hypothesis cannot be *accepted.* If the null is rejected, the alternative hypothesis can be accepted; however, if the null is not rejected, we can't conclude that the null hypothesis is true. The rationale is that evidence that supports a hypothesis is not conclusive, but evidence that negates a hypothesis is ample to discredit a hypothesis. The analysis of study time and test scores provides an example. If the results of one study indicate that the test scores of students who study 4 hours are significantly better than the test scores of students who study two hours, the null hypothesis can be rejected because the researcher has found one case when the null is not true. However, if the results of the study indicate that the test scores of those who study 4 hours are not significantly better than those who study 2 hours, the null hypothesis cannot be rejected. One also cannot conclude that the null hypothesis is accepted because these results are only one set of score comparisons. Just because the null hypothesis is true in one situation does not mean it is always true.

Determining the Appropriate test Statistic

The appropriate test statistic (the statistic to be used in statistical hypothesis testing) is based on various characteristics of the sample population of interest, including sample size and distribution. The test statistic can assume many numerical values. Since the value of the test statistic has a significant effect on the decision, one must use the appropriate statistic in order to obtain meaningful results.

Specifying the Statistical Significance Level

As previously noted, one can reject a null hypothesis or fail to reject a null hypothesis. A null hypothesis that is rejected may, in reality, be true or false. Additionally, a null hypothesis that fails to be rejected may, in reality, be true or false. The outcome that a researcher desires is to reject a false null hypothesis or to fail to reject a true null hypothesis. However, there always is the possibility of rejecting a true hypothesis or failing to reject a false hypothesis. Rejecting a null hypothesis that is true is called a Type I error and failing to reject a false null hypothesis is called a Type II error. The probability of committing a Type I error is termed á and the probability of committing a Type II error is termed â.

As the value of á increases, the probability of committing a Type I error increases. As the value of â increases, the probability of committing a Type II error increases. While one would like to decrease the probability of committing of both types of errors, the reduction of á results in the increase of â and vice versa. The best way to reduce the probability of decreasing both types of error is to increase sample size.

The probability of committing a Type I error, á, is called the level of significance.

Before data is collected one must specify a level of significance, or the probability of committing a Type I error (rejecting a true null hypothesis). There is an inverse relationship between a researcher's desire to avoid making a Type I error and the selected value of á; if not making the error is particularly important, a low probability of making the error is sought.

The greater the desire is to not reject a true null hypothesis, the lower the selected value of á. In theory, the value of á can be any value between 0 and 1. However, the most common values used in social science research are.05,.01, and.001, which respectively correspond to the levels of 95 percent, 99 percent, and 99.9 percent likelihood that a Type I error is not being made. The tradeoff for choosing a higher level of certainty (significance) is that it will take much stronger statistical evidence to ever reject the null hypothesis.

Determining the Decision Rule

Before data are collected and analysed it is necessary to determine under what circumstances the null hypothesis will be rejected or fail to be rejected. The decision rule can be stated in terms of the computed test statistic, or in probabilistic terms. The same decision will be reached regardless of which method is chosen.

Collecting the Data and Performing the Calculations

The method of data collection is determined early in the research process. Once a research question is determined, one must make decisions regarding what type of data is needed and how the data will be collected. This decision establishes the bases for how the data will be analysed. One should use only approved research methods for collecting and analyzing data.

WHAT IS A HYPOTHESIS?

Definition: A hypothesis is a tentative statement about the relationship between two or more variables. A hypothesis is a specific, testable prediction about what you expect to happen in your study. For example, a study designed to look at the relationship between sleep deprivation and test performance might have a hypothesis that states, "This study is designed to assess the hypothesis that sleep deprived people will perform worse on a test than individuals who are not sleep deprived."

Unless you are creating a study that is exploratory in nature, your hypothesis should always explain what you *expect* to happen during the course of your experiment or research.

SOCIAL WORKERS' STRATEGIES FOR TREATMENT HYPOTHESIS TESTING

Social workers, like other clinicians, face a complex and uncertain task in trying to understand the dynamics of and the factors responsible for the problems that their clients present. The process assessment for the purpose of formulating the client's presenting problems in professionally meaningful concepts "is a basis for formulating treatment hypotheses". Problem formulation is an inferential product and involves the clinician in generating and then testing hypotheses about the origins, dynamics, and possible consequences of a client's problems. Testing of treatment hypotheses is viewed as a process in which practitioners actively seek, gather, and integrate information to compare with their initial hypotheses, as well as seek additional information to test new hunches. In testing treatment hypotheses, practitioners make decisions about what information to collect, how to gather the information, and when to stop. These decisions constitute the hypothesis-testing strategy used to determine the correctness of an hypothesis. However, it has been shown repeatedly that the processes involved in clinical hypothesis testing, in clinical inferences, and in judgment are vulnerable to problems and biases that encroach on the validity of the product. Because judgment and inference are critical and inseparable elements in formulation of and decisions about clinical hypotheses, investigation of the factors that influence these activities are important areas of research.

We addressed hypothesis testing in terms of two interrelated components—process and strategy. The process involves workers' search for the information viewed as necessary to test the treatment hypotheses and also involves the intended use of that information. In that manner, similarly with Gambrill (1990) and Haverkamp (1993), we viewed the process of hypothesis testing as involving more than the mere search of information.

The other component of hypothesis testing is the strategy the worker uses as part of the process. We distinguish two types of strategies—information search strategies that can be confirmatory or disconfirmatory of the hypothesis; the other type of strategy inolves the manner in which the information is intended to be used—biased or unbiased. Our conception of these strategies is informed by work done in clinical and nonclinical domains, which is reviewed briefly in the following section.

* A clear preference for a confirmatory strategy of information gathering was found in social psychological studies. In these studies, confirmatory information strategies were considered as biased and distinguished from disconfirmatory and from "equal opportunity" strategies, as follows:
* A confirmatory strategy was defined as a search for or gathering only of information that is consistent with the hypothesis, coupled by inattention to information that is inconsistent with or could discredit the hypothesis.

* A disconfirmatory strategy is the search for or gathering of information that would support an alternative hypothesis that is contradictory to the original hypothesis.
* The equal opportunity strategy involves search for both confirmatory and disconfirmatory information. Researchers working in the clinical domain called such strategies unbiased strategies.

Snyder and colleagues' studies (1978, 1980, 1988) of hypothesis testing strategies influenced research in the clinical domain. Haverkamp (1993) found confirmatory bias in practice situations, and Strohmer and colleagues found that counsellors recalled more information that confirmed their clinical hypotheses about clients even when the reports they received contained more information to disconfirm their hypotheses. But other studies found that practitioners preferred both confirmatory and disconfirmatory hypothesis-testing strategies.

THE WORKING HYPOTHESIS IN SOCIAL REFORM

There are some consequences that follow from the attempt to establish the theory of social reform among the inductive sciences that need emphasis. That to which I wish to refer is the implication of the hypothesis.

Socialism, in one form or another, lies back of the thought directing and inspiring reform. While socialistic utopias have been recognized as impotent to lead to better conditions, and opportunists have succeeded to the programists, the assumption that it will be possible to effect by constructive legislation radical changes that will lead to greater social equality is still very widely present. The success of municipal ownership, in means of transportation and various common necessities within cities, has aroused the expectation that this success can be achieved in other industries as fast as they are so organized as to become so-called natural monopolies. I think that a great deal of this confidence is inspired by the socialistic schemes of an essentially a priori character, rather than by a study of the conditions which these municipal concerns represent. We fail often to notice that government as an institution has essentially changed its character in so far as it has assumed these new functions. The government has become a business concern, which enters into the business world on a basis that is determined by the latter. It has assumed a certain amount of invested capital, where business risk has ceased, in the interests of its members, and has undertaken to carry on an enterprise that has already been worked out as regards its methods and technique. In a word, the municipality has become a business body operating for the benefit of those that make it up, and is therefore not different in principle from any stock company. The number of enterprises, that such a body could undertake as a commercial body are, so far, necessarily small, and we have no reason to assume that in the end anything but business conditions will determine what the municipality may successfully manage. There is no reason why the German government, as a social individual, should not buy up and manage such a business as the railroad; only so far as the business itself is concerned it must conduct it upon the principles which control the industrial world as a whole. It may introduce such reforms into it as are demanded by the public sentiment that finds expression in legislation, sooner than they will be introduced into other concerns. But it becomes at once in tendency as conservative as other great concerns, and must adapt itself to the demands of the business world of which it is a part. The government has then separate functions. On the one side, it formulates and brings to a focus public sentiment in so-called legislation, and conducts a police activity, national and international, over against classes of society and human impulses which are as yet not so socially organized as are the bulk of its members with their dominant impulses. On the other side, being an institution which is as definitely independent as other corporations within the community, it may undertake a very limited number of industrial and commercial concerns, which business evolution has carried to such a point of perfection that they lie safely within its domain.

While we recognize this possibility, we must, on the other side, recognize with equal distinctness that the functions of government, as an institution, are merging with equal rapidity into the industrial world which it is supposed to control. The whole work of legislation is not only dependent upon public sentiment, at least in democratic countries, but it is finding constantly fuller expression in other channels of publicity. The newspaper, in its various forms of journal and magazine, is effecting changes that are assumed to be those which follow governmental action. If only it becomes possible to focus public sentiment upon an issue in the delicate organism of the modern civilized community, it is as effective as if the mandate came from legislative halls, and frequently more so. This is true, not simply in the public reaction upon the justice of movements like those of great strikes and lockouts, but even in the interpretation of the methods of industrial and commercial activity. What the court does in reinterpreting laws is being done in increasing extent by simply closer organization of the business world-an organization that depends most immediately upon growing publicity. The study of the criminal and defective classes, as an expression of the conditions of the social body in which they are found, and their treatment from this new standpoint, as well as the movement toward arbitration for the solution of international differences, all point to the passing of functions which are supposed to inhere in the government into activities that belong to the community simply through its organization apart from government as a separate institution. On the other hand, certainly one of the most important so-called governmental functions, that is characteristic of the time, is the committee work, which is but a part of the general process of gaining publicity as regards what is going on in the country and the world. This is often done, not by a legislative commission, but by the university as well as the newspaper. In attempting to forecast what is to be the result of the movement of municipal ownership, we have to consider, therefore, not only the development of the municipal corporation and the industry that it conducts, but also that of a government that is changing fully as rapidly as the industrial and commercial world.

CONFIDENCE ABOUT THE HYPOTHESIS

Preliminary research suggests that the extent of clinicians' confidence in their hypothesis is related to the information search strategy, and that such relationship may be harmful to a good clinical process. When feeling confident in their hypotheses, clinicians' use of confirmatory strategies may reduce their vigilance and thus bias their information search, resulting in misdiagnosing. Empirically, extent of confidence was found to be positively associated with the use of confirmatory search strategies. However, they did not study the extent to which information search strategies were biased or unbiased.

The literature emphasizes that a search for alternative explanations is one of the main strategies that can be used to avoid premature acceptance of an explanation. Earlier studies suggest that the adoption of alternative hypotheses reduces the likelihood of a bias in hypothesis testing. Alternative hypotheses may be complementary or contradictory to the primary hypothesis stated. Whether the alternative hypotheses are complementary or contradictory also may be associated with whether a confirmatory or disconfirmatory information search strategy is adopted. For example, when the alternative hypotheses are contradictory, a process using a confirmatory strategy is likely to be less biased compared with testing alternative hypotheses that are complementary.

Participants

Participants were 104 direct practice social workers employed by four central social services agencies of Jerusalem, Israel, and by their satellite neighbourhood units. The social workers were all professionally trained and certified with at least a BA degree in social work. This degree is comparable in training to the MSW degree in the United States. The research instruments were administrated by the investigators at a monthly staff meeting to the 104 social workers who were present, out of a total of 124 direct practice line social workers at these agencies. Twenty of the 124 eligible workers did not attend the staff meeting when the data were collected for various reasons. Eighty-two percent of the 104 participants were women; the mean age was 34.2 (SD = 7.60), with an average of 6.87 years of practice experience (SD = 5.36). Four participants did not complete the research instrument and were dropped from the study, yielding data on 100 participants.

Research Instrument

The research instrument was adapted from Haverkamp's (1993) method for studying clinicians' self-generated hypotheses about client's problems and what information they used to check them. This method is open-ended and relatively unstructured, which we preferred over closed-ended responses. We wanted to avoid influencing the content and form of workers' responses, except in presenting the stimulus case and the tasks to be performed on the basis of it. We believe that this open-ended method approximates real-life hypothesis testing better than closed-ended responding used in some studies. One advantage of our method is that it creates a common structure for responding for all participants, which is necessary to elicit data that are comparable. As mentioned earlier, the extent to which workers, in fact, approach their hypothesis testing in such an explicit and organized manner as our structuring demanded is a question yet to be addressed. In any event, our method's compromise on ecological validity was necessary given the present state of knowledge regarding the process of hypothesis testing.

We randomly distributed to each participant one of two replicate intake summaries of actual cases. We used replicate cases to assess the possible influence of case characteristics on workers' hypothesis testing process. Workers were given either case 1 (a husband's drinking problem) or case 2 (an unemployed divorced man), which were judged by eight senior social workers as the most typical for the agency service out of an initial group of four case summaries. Participants were told that the study concerned the process of problem formulation and information gathering. Using their case summary they were asked to do the following tasks in sequential order:

* List all the client's problems.
* Select one problem that they believed was primary and required immediate focus.
* In relation to that problem, list in order (on provided sheets of paper) all their explanations (hypotheses) regarding factors responsible for the problem.

* For each explanation (hypothesis) indicate on a 1 to 10 Likert-type scale the extent of their confidence in the correctness of the hypothesis.
* For each hypothesis, list additional information needed to check the correctness of the hypothesis; specifically, "In order to check the correctness of your initial hypothesis, what additional information would you seek? And what is the source(s) of that information?"
* For each item of information that they sought, write down the reasons for viewing the information as useful for testing their hypotheses.

The final research instrument and the procedures were based on a pretest with a panel of 10 experienced social workers. In particular, comments of the pretest panel influenced revision of the fifth item by adding a request for the source of information. This was done to distinguish source of information from the content of the information, so that workers would not give the source instead of the substantive information they would look for. Our queries of the pretest panel indicated also that asking workers to check the correctness of the hypotheses was perceived as open-ended—thus allowing search for information that would either confirm or disconfirm the hypothesis.

Measures

Information Search Strategies. Operationally, we assessed information search strategies from the content of the information that social workers sought. This content was classified as reflecting a confirmatory strategy, disconfirmatory strategy, or irrelevant content strategy according to our conceptualization, which follows Swann & Giuliano's (1987) categorization. The different items of information sought by the workers for each of the hypotheses were considered as separate responses.

When the information in the response was consistent with the stated hypothesis, the response was considered confirmatory. For example, if the hypothesis stated that the client drinks because he is an uncontrolled alcoholic (this example will be used throughout), then seeking information on the duration or intensity of drinking was classified as confirmatory. A disconfirmatory response sought information that was contradictory to the hypothesis (that is, inconsistent with it). For example, seeking information on factors responsible for client ability to control his drinking was classified as disconfirmatory (that is, ability to control drinking being inconsistent with alcoholism). Responses were classified as irrelevant if the information sought could neither confirm nor disconfirm the hypothesis. For example, asking the client if he likes his job.

For every worker, a ratio score of responses in each of the categories of confirmatory, disconfirmatory and irrelevant to the total responses was computed.

Intended Use of Information. In accordance with Haverkamp (1993) and Skov and Sherman (1986), social workers' intended use of the information, biased or unbiased, was assessed from the reasons they gave for why the information was needed. We believe that it is preferable methodologically to learn the intended use of the information directly from the social workers rather than infer the use from the sought information. Therefore, we queried the social workers on the reasons for seeking the information.

The reasons social workers gave for the intended use of the information were classified as unbiased, biased, and other strategies, based on the concepts of Trope and colleagues (Trope et al., 1984). Intended use strategies were defined as follows:

Unbiased Responses. The reasons for information use were classified as unbiased if they explicitly indicated or implied the use of that information for comparing the likelihood of the primary hypothesis with an alternative hypothesis (whether the social worker stated an alternative hypothesis or not); for example, "I wanted to know about client's drinking at work because I wanted to know whether or not he drinks in all situations." Such a response was classified as unbiased because it kept open the possibility of nondrinking, although it seems to be confirmatory of the hypothesis that the client had an uncontrolled drinking problem. In another example, "The reason I asked the client about his periods of sobreity was to try and rule out alcoholism," the worker provides an unbiased response by explicitly mentioning an alternative hypothesis to the uncontrolled drinking hypothesis.

Biased Responses. The worker gives reasons for how the information gathered will be used to test the hypothesis without allowing for a possibility of an alternative hypothesis; for example: "To make sure he was an alcoholic I asked him whether he was dependent on hard liqueur, wine, or beer."

Reasons given by workers that could not be classified as unbiased or biased were classified as "other."

Coding

The information that the worker indicated was necessary to test each of the hypotheses and the reasons worker gave for the intended use of the information were coded according to the concepts and their definitions. After being trained in and using procedures developed by the investigators two judges, a social work doctoral student and a psychology student, coded the data independently. Coding began when there was an average three-way interrater agreement of 85 percent between the two coders and the first author in coding the pretest questionnaires. Reliability checks between the two coders were conducted in study's data. Agreement for the information search strategies ranged from 81 percent (kappa =.75) to 88 percent (kappa =.82), and, agreement for the reasons for information use ranged from 79 percent (kappa =.72) to 91 percent (kappa =.86).

Independent Variables

Number of Hypotheses. This variable was measured by the number of separate explanatory hypotheses about the client's problem that a participant listed.

Relationship between Hypotheses. This variable was measured when more than one hypothesis was stated by a worker. The additional hypotheses were designated as complementary, contradictory, or unrelated to the primary hypothesis. Two hypotheses were considered contradictory when they could not coexist with one another; that is, both hypotheses could not logically be correct with respect to the same client.

Complementary hypotheses were those for which one of the hypotheses added to the explanatory power of the other hypothesis, and they could both coexist logically. Two hypotheses were deemed unrelated when each of the hypotheses provided an explanation for a different problem. Three scores were obtained: (1) the ratio of complementary hypotheses to the total number of hypotheses, (2) the ratio of contradictory hypotheses to the total number of hypotheses, and (3) the ratio of unrelated hypotheses to the total number of hypotheses. Workers that only stated one hypothesis had no such scores. There was 84.7 percent agreement (kappa =.79) between the two independent coders in coding this variable

Confidence in the Hypothesis. This variable was measured by the degree of certainty (on a scale of 1 to 10 ranging from uncertain to certain) indicated by the respondent that the hypothesis was true. For each hypothesis, the confidence score was the scale number indicated by the worker.

Results

For the two dependent variables, information search strategies and intended use of information, analyses of variance found no significant differences ($p > .05$) in responding between workers presented with case 1 (marital problems and heavy drinking) and workers presented with case 2 (unemployed and divorced person) [$F(1, 99) = .124$; $F(1, 99) = .291$; $F(1, 99) = .039$, for confirmation, disconfirmation, and irrelevant, respectively; and $F(1, 99) = .196$, $F(1, 99) = .262$, $F(1, 99) = .026$, for unbiased, biased, and other, respectively]. Therefore, the data from the two conditions were collapsed in subsequent analyses.

When the respondents' formulation of hypotheses were coded, we noticed that some workers departed from the instructions. Rather than provide an explanatory hypothesis for the primary problem of the client, 33 of the workers either rephrased the problem or described a plan of treatment. Because the focus of the study was on strategies for testing the explanatory hypotheses, we decided to eliminate from the sample the workers who responded with pseudo-hypotheses (hypotheses that did not contain explanations for the problem). The 33 workers who departed from the instructions and provided pseudo-hypotheses did not differ from the others in age or years of experience [mean age: 33.77, 34.41, respectively, t(1, 98) =-.350, p =.728; mean of years of experience: 6.58, 7.02, respectively, t(1, 98) =-.390, p =.698].

For the remaining 67 workers, the average number of hypotheses was 1.66, with 54 percent of participants formulating more than one hypothesis. Of the multiple hypotheses, 45 percent were contradictory, 11 percent were complementary, and 44 percent were unrelated hypotheses. Hypothesis confidence ratings averaged about 7 on a 1 to 10 Likert-type scale, with slight, not statistically significant (p <.05) variations by whether the hypothesis was the primary or not. Of the 523 units of information sought by the total sample for testing the hypotheses, 53 percent were confirmatory; 11 percent were disconfirmatory and 36 percent were irrelevant units. Analyses of the 230 reasons given for the information sought indicated that 36 percent of the reasons were unbiased, 24 percent biased, and 40 percent were other. The third research question aimed to identify likely sources of variability in the dependent variables. We examined the extent that the information search strategies (percentage of confirmatory and percentage of disconfirmatory units) and the reasons for the information used (percentage of unbiased and percentage of biased reasons) were affected by the extent of confidence in the hypotheses, the number of hypotheses stated, and whether the relationship between the hypotheses was complementary or contradictory.

Separate step-wise multiple regression analyses were performed for each of the two dependent variables as the criteria and the three independent variables as predictors. These analyses indicated that none of the independent variables significantly accounted for the information search strategies—either for percentage of confirmatory or for percentage of disconfirmatory units. The regression analyses for the second dependent variable, reasons given for information use (unbiased or biased), were statistically significant (p <.05).

The proportion of contradictory hypotheses was positively related to the proportion of unbiased reasons; and the extent of confidence in hypothesis 2 was negatively related to the proportion of biased reasons. This latter finding, however, is based on an appreciably reduced n and therefore the relationship is more likely to be spurious.

CONTACT HYPOTHESIS

In criminology and sociology, the contact hypothesis is a way of improving relations among groups that are experiencing conflict. Gordon W. Allport (1954) is credited with the development of the Contact Hypothesis, also known as Intergroup Contact Theory. The premise of Allport's theory states that under appropriate conditions interpersonal contact is one of the most effective ways to reduce prejudice between majority and minority group members. Issues of stereotyping, prejudice, and discrimination are commonly occurring issues between rival groups. Allport's proposal was that properly managed contact between the groups should reduce these problems and lead to better interactions.

In order for this to occur, the following must be present:

- Equal Status, both groups taken into an equal status relationship,
- Common Goals, both groups work on a problem/task and share this as a common goal, sometimes called a *superordinate goal*,
- Intergroup Cooperation, the task must be structured so that individual members of both groups are interdependent on each other to achieve this common goal,
- Support of authorities, law or customs, some authority that both groups acknowledge and define social norms that support the contact and interactions between the groups and members.

The reduction of prejudice through intergroup contact is best explained as the *reconceptualization of group categories*. Gordon Allport (1954) claims that prejudice is a direct result of generalizations and over-simplifications made about an entire group of people based on incomplete or mistaken information.

The basic rationale is that prejudice may be reduced as one learns more about a category of people. Rothbart and John (1985) describe belief change through contact as "an example of the general cognitive process by which attributes of category members modify category attributes". An individual's beliefs can be modified by that person coming into contact with a culturally distinct category member and subsequently modifying or elaborating the beliefs about the category as a whole.

A study conducted by Rothbart and John (1985) found that the Contact Hypothesis is an effective technique for reducing prejudice and stereotyping if three criterion are met.

1. The minority group members behavior is not consistent with their stereotype
2. Contact between group members occurs often and in a variety of social contexts
3. The minority members are perceived as typical of their cultural group.

Parasocial Contact Hypothesis

Schiappa, Gregg and Hewes proposed a communication analogue to Allport's (1954) Contact Hypothesis named the Parasocial Contact Hypothesis. Two years after the release of Gordon Allport's novel, *The Nature of Prejudice*, Horton and Wohl (1956) pushed for studying what they referred to as "para-social" interaction: "One of the most striking characteristics of the new mass media including radio, television and the movies is that they give the illusion of face-to-face relationships with the performer". The illusion of a face to face interaction via the mass media is under consideration for scholars due to its implication to change, shape and/or reinforce stereotypes and prejudices. The theory works under the assumption that people cognitively process mass mediated interactions in a matter similar to interpersonal interactions. Therefore, these individuals should benefit from these mediated intercultural interactions (Parasocial contact) in a similar fashion to face to face interactions. Research studies have concluded that parasocial contact is associated with lower levels of prejudice and changes in beliefs about the attributes of minority group categories. A complementary approach to the parasocial contact hypothesis is provided by Ortiz & Harwood who suggest that observing intergroup interaction in the media (e.g., watching a gay and straight character interact on TV) can be particularly powerful in influencing attitudes. Members of groups can model effective intergroup interaction by observing such interaction in the media.

Contact via Other Media

In addition to work on the parasocial contact hypothesis, additional research has examined the effects of exposure to characters in children's literature, for instance, using Wright et al.'s extended contact idea. Other work has examined whether online interaction has similar effects as direct face-to-face interaction. Some attempts have been made to provide .ntegrated frameworks for examining intergroup contact across a wide variety of mediated contexts and discussing how the process might differ from direct face-to-face contact

CONTACT HYPOTHESIS AND HOMOSEXUALITY

The Contact Hypothesis has proven to be highly effective in alleviating prejudice directed toward homosexuals. Applying the Contact Hypothesis to heterosexuals and homosexuals, Herek (1987) found that college students who had pleasant interactions with a homosexual tend to generalize from that experience and accept homosexuals as a group. Herek and Glunt's (1993) national study of interpersonal contact and heterosexuals' attitudes toward gay men found that increased contact "predicted attitudes toward gay men better than did any other demographic or social psychological variable"; such variables included gender, race, age, education, geographic residence, marital status, number of children, religion and political ideology. Herek and Capitanio (1996) found that contact experiences with two or three homosexuals are associated with more favourable attitudes than are contact experiences with only one individual.

An Example

Competitions are the reasons behind rivalries and fights.

Many sports teams, sororities, fraternities, and businesses use the contact hypothesis technique. Having the two groups in competitions do something that requires the groups to work together helps break the rivalries and fights. The groups are given a project to complete, like raising money for a charity or hosting an event. The two groups must be given something that one group cannot complete by itself. This will allow the groups to share a common goal and have equal status and cooperation. The most commonly seen version of contact hypothesis is in the juvenile system. Petty criminals perform community service together to decrease the amount of fights and competition in the system. This also helps the community and the individuals that might have been hurt by the petty criminal.

Once this task is complete it is hypothesized that the groups will find cohesion. The Contact Hypothesis (Allport, 1954), has influenced a broad application of this concept, attributing to the racial desegregation of schools and research on reducing racial, homosexual, age and AIDS based prejudices.

5

Critical Action Research: A Model for Social Work

As a profession committed to the empowerment of oppressed groups, social work has struggled with the role of scientific inquiry and the "correct" epistemology for social work. However, during the past several decades, in the increasingly competitive human services climate, social workers have come to the realization that they must use research to examine the need for as well as to support the outcomes of practice. Although the role of research has been defined as an essential professional survival activity, the debate over what inquiry models best serve social workers and their mission continues. On one end of the epistemology debate is the view that quantitative and positivist approaches to inquiry are the most efficacious way to support practice need and outcome. These approaches view research as a professional activity that is conceptualized, conducted, and used by professionals. However, in addition and sometimes contrary to that perspective is the notion that social workers need to consider qualitative, naturalistic inquiry to capture the uniqueness, diversity, and complexity of the issues and client populations from their own perspective. Moreover, the notion of knowledge as power adds another important dimension to the debate over epistemology by raising questions about who should generate, have access to, and determine the use of knowledge in the social work field.

In response to the important philosophical and methodological questions being asked in social work, this article presents a model for social work knowing founded on the tenets of critical theory synthesized with principles and practices from action research. We suggest that this model not only provides the essential empirical support for social work interventions and outcomes but also is consistent with the social work code of ethics and commitment to elimination of oppression.

THEORETICAL AND PHILOSOPHICAL BACKGROUND

As stated by Finn (1994), a major challenge facing social work is the "call for change-oriented, value-based models of knowledge development that address people, power and praxis". Thus, the qualitative-quantitative debate deservedly becomes obfuscated by the critical need to develop purposive models of knowing to serve oppressed populations by moving beyond the perpetuation of dominance and privilege by and for resource-rich groups.. Critical theory and action research provide sound philosophical and methodological grounding for the development of a model to meet the need identified by Finn.

Critical Theory

As implied by the name, critical theory is not a research method but a worldview that suggests both an epistemology and a purpose for conducting research. Whether critical theory is a philosophical, political, or sociological school of thought has been debated in the contemporary literature. In essence, critical theory is a response to post-Enlightenment philosophies, positivism in particular, which "deconstructs" the notion of a unitary truth that can be known by one way or method. That is to say, critical theory is a movement that lives in the world of philosophy. Because critical theory is inspired by so many diverse schools of thought, including those informed by Marx, Hegel, Kant, Foucault, Derrida, and Kristeva, it is not a unitary approach but rather a complex set of strategies that are united by the commonality of sociopolitical purpose.

Critical theorists seek to understand human experience as a means of changing the world. The common purpose of researchers who approach investigation through critical theory therefore is to come to know about human experience to promote social change. Critical theory originated at the Social Institute of the Frankfurt School in the 1920s. As the Nazis gained power in Germany, critical theorists moved to Columbia University in New York City and further developed their notions of power and justice, particularly in response to the hegemony of positivism in the United States. With their focus on social change, critical theorists came to view knowledge as power and the production of knowledge as "socially and historically determined". Derived from this view is an epistemology that upholds pluralism or in which coming to know about phenomena occurs in multiple ways. Furthermore, knowing is dynamic, changing, and influenced by the sociopolitical context of the times.

Action Research

Action research has evolved during the past 30 years into its current use. When this strategy originated in the 1960s, it consisted of the application of anthropological research methods to investigation and resolution of social problems. Scholars such as Lewin and Goodenough were associated with this radical form of social action through inquiry. However, current models, although aimed at providing data on which to take action, have a broader purpose than radical social action, although this purpose is still visible in some action research inquiry.

The action approach to research most frequently is used as a prerequisite to planning and enacting solutions to community problems or service dilemmas and thus shares its purposive elements with critical theory, albeit less politically radical than critical inquiry in its contemporary form. Many models and descriptions of action research have been advanced in the literature. Moreover, there are similar and overlapping terms such as participatory research, participatory action research, and collaborative research that describe similar philosophical and process approaches to the generation and use of knowledge. Although there are differences among authors and specific types of action research, there are several basic tenets common to all. First, action research is founded on the principle that those who experience a phenomenon are the most qualified to investigate it. To capture knowledge of human experience, individuals who typically have been in the role of participants in positivist research become full participants in designing, conducting, and reporting research.

Second, as implied in the name, the purpose of "action" research is to generate knowledge to inform action. Third, action research is based on four principle values: (1) democracy, (2) equity, (3) liberation, and (4) life enhancement. By democracy, it is meant that action research is participatory. That is, all individuals who are stakeholders in a problem or issue and its resolution are included in the research process. The principle of equity ensures that all are equally valued in the research process, regardless of previous experience in research. Liberation suggests that action research is a design aimed at decreasing oppression. Finally, the principle of life enhancement positions action research as a systematic inquiry strategy to promote the expression of full human potential.

Action research can use action processes from both experimental and naturalistic traditions or an integration of the two. However, consistent with its principles, all research occurs within its natural context, and most action re search relies on strategies that characteristically are interpretive in nature.

Sequentially, action research is cyclical, beginning with the identification of a problem or dilemma that calls for action, moving to systematic inquiry, and culminating in planning, using the findings of the inquiry. However, these elements are not necessarily mutually exclusive.

SYNTHESIZING CRITICAL THEORY AND ACTION RESEARCH

Action research and critical theory are not mutually exclusive and thus, their philosophical foundations are complimentary. Both value a grassroots approach to identifying and resolving social problems, a democratic perspective, and a social change outcome. Moreover, critical theory and, to a lesser extent, action research attend to the power imbalance of positivism and the elitist use of knowledge generated by traditional and professionally dominated methods of inquiry. Of particular use to social workers is the capacity of action research to inform social change at multiple systemic levels because of the participation of all stakeholders in the research process.

The literature on use of participatory inquiry is increasing, thereby illustrating the potential depth and breadth of these egalitarian strategies. For example, Rains and Ray (1995) illustrated the value of community participation in the development of health promotion programs in a rural community, whereas Ervin (1996) discussed similar approaches to urban planning. In the educational arena, participatory research and planning have been used to develop many interventions and system changes, such as those described by Billingsley and Houck (1988), in which the needs of students with learning disabilities in a secondary school were ascertained and addressed through a participatory action effort. For the most part, the use of participatory strategies has been applied to problem resolution for marginalized and oppressed populations (Finn, 1994), and therefore these approaches provide an excellent vehicle for social change that emerges from and is controlled by those affected by the systems that are in need of revision. However, the use of participatory strategies need not be restricted to the concerns of disempowered groups. Action research, however, must involve disenfranchised stakeholders democratically in change oriented inquiry. A key element in participatory strategies is to ensure that the resources for the conduct of an inquiry and for the application of the knowledge to social change are available. Thus, egalitarian collaboration among professional and lay investigators is essential. Methodologically, although qualitative strategies have dominated participatory and critical inquiry, no methods are dismissed. Choice of method is purposive and collaborative and thus may include qualitative as well as quantitative techniques.

Review of the literature on participatory action research across disciplines, such as public administration, business, medicine, education, anthropology, and sociology (Cole, 1993) reveals that although full participation is supported theoretically, it remains sparsely used in social work and in these other fields. Moreover, when participatory strategies were used, they typically were directed by researchers with consumer input elicited through interviews. Although participatory strategies were supported as most desirable, only one study (Sarri, 1992) involved consumers in research design and data analysis. More characteristic are studies such as that discussed by Simonson and Bushaw (1993), who conducted a community needs assessment in which participation of lay researchers was limited and thus seriously hampered by methodological dominance by the researchers.

How to operationalize the egalitarian, inclusive principles of action research needs continued development and modeling. As articulated by Argyris (1989), "the challenge is to define and meet standards of appropriate rigor with out sacrificing relevance". Therefore, the model presented in this article and its illustration provide guidelines on how to meet this challenge.

The Model

On the basis of the literature briefly overviewed earlier, we advance a model of social work research. This model is distinguished from other participatory approaches by its inclusive governance and composition and active involvement of all stakeholder groups throughout the entire planning, research, and dissemination processes.

RECOGNITION AND ARTICULATION OF A SOCIAL PROBLEM

The first step of the model is the identification of a social problem. Although professionals and researchers usually have been in the position of formally identifying a problem that lends itself to inquiry, in this model, the recognition may emerge from any group. The critical element of this step is for experienced researchers to collaborate with those affected by the problem to clearly articulate it, its scope and all stakeholders. Once the problem is formally stated and stakeholders are identified, the next step occurs. Convention of a Steering Committee Composed of All Stakeholder Groups. The composition of the steering committee is crucial to the social work model of action research. All stakeholders need to be represented. How the steering committee accomplishes that task is driven by resources and purpose and is unique to each project. At minimum, the steering committee should be appointed or selected by a collaborative process among the professional and lay communities.

Identification of the Research Scope and Social Change Purpose by the Steering Committee. Once the steering committee is convened, it is the task of that group to delimit the research scope and to articulate clearly the object of change that the research is designed to accomplish. In this early stage of the action research process, the steering committee takes on the governance functions of oversee and guide to ensure that the research effort is inclusive, participatory, and purposive.

Selection of a Collaborative Research Team. Selection of the collaborative research team can be done in many ways. It is possible to seek nominations or volunteers or to recruit those who are already committed to the social problem being studied. The steering committee ultimately approves of the research team, using the evaluative criteria of skill adequacy, inclusive representation from stakeholders, and potential for the team to collaborate. The research team must have lay and professional researchers on it, each of whom identifies his or her strengths, skills, values, and roles on the team. As indicated in the literature, recruitment and continued engagement of lay researchers may be time-consuming and difficult. Methods for obtaining and maintaining a viable and consistent team include but certainly are not limited to the payment of stipends, distance communication strategies, participation in dissemination activities following the research, collaborative publications, and the recruitment of those who are passionate about the goals of the project.

Training of Lay Researchers in Designing, Conducting, and Using Inquiry. Before the project is designed and conducted, the lay researchers must have the language and skill to be full participants in the inquiry. Training in relevant research "thinking and action" skills should be done in a manner that is meaningful to all participants in the research team, so that all understand and are capable of upholding empirical rigor. It may be possible for training to be conducted by the professional researchers, or it may be that the lay researchers seek training elsewhere. The nature, timing, and structure of the training is a collaborative and purposive decision to ensure that all team members have the knowledge and skills to be valuable contributors to the project.

Design of the Inquiry: Specify Research Questions, Design, and Analytic Strategy. As is the case with all research efforts, designing the inquiry is a detailed thinking process. In this model, the design is collaborative and consensual. Issues of validity, reliability, trustworthiness, and credibility are negotiated and decided on at this stage with particular guidance from the team members who are well versed in research method. The scope of the inquiry and its potential applicability to other populations needs to be discussed and decided on in the design phase, such that the research process maintains its rigor.

Conduct Inquiry and Analysis. As agreed on in the previous step, the research team conducts the inquiry as planned. In this phase, it is critical that the team meet regularly to evaluate the process and to make changes as needed. Criteria for ensuring rigor need to be upheld throughout the research process.

Report Findings in Accessible Formats to All Stakeholder Groups. Unlike traditional research reports, which follow a prescribed format, the reporting phase in this model is flexible and purposive. The team meets to decide the content and structure of research reporting. It is not only possible but also likely that several reports, developed fur diverse audiences, may be produced and disseminated. Because the research is used for social change, accessible, credible, useful, and understandable reporting is essential.

Submit Findings to Social Change Planning and Action. Unlike many other research endeavours, this step of the model is its purposive culmination. In this step, the research team, the steering committee, and other stakeholder groups use the research findings to inform social planning and change, as stipulated early in the process. Accessible reporting enhances this step. Evaluation of the usefulness of the research findings must take into account the extent to which the new knowledge contributed to desirable social change.

Identification by Steering Committee of Further Areas for Inquiry. Because social change is ongoing, it follows that social inquiry is continuous as well. Consistent with Stringer's (1996) notion of action research as cyclical, the end of the initial research inquiry leads to the beginning of the next effort. To illustrate the model, the following case example is offered.

The Maine Adolescent Transition Project

The Maine Adolescent Transition (MAT) project began with an initial identification by providers and parents of a social problem throughout the state. Essentially, it became clear that although some services were in place for adolescents with special health care needs during the high school years, transition to adulthood was problematic. (Adolescents were defined as youths between the ages of 12 and 25, who required services and supports for medical or disabling conditions.) Moreover, for adolescents who were not attending school, transition was even less supported, because so many of the support services for this population were delivered through the school system. A statewide steering committee consisting of adolescents with special health care needs, parents, health and social services providers, educators, policymakers, and potential employers was convened to address the social problem. The committee decided to seek extramural funding and initiated a grant proposal process. The University of Maine and a contracted grantsperson provided the grant proposal preparation expertise. Each draft that was written was submitted to the steering committee for input and revision. When the proposal was final, it was submitted to the Maine Bureau of Maternal and Child Health, and funding was obtained.

The proposal outlined a collaborative and critical action research project designed to obtain a comprehensive understanding of the transition needs of adolescents with special health care needs as a basis for future systems change and services revision. With use of the critical action research model, a statewide needs assessment study was conducted. At this stage of the process, problems were encountered when two universities competed to facilitate the research. The two universities were unable to collaborate because of political and organizational conflict, and the steering committee agreed on an application and interview process in which criteria for the selection of one university were explicated. Both universities prepared an application addressing the criteria. The steering committee selected the university that previously had demonstrated a commitment to inclusive research and planning. To retain the expertise of the university that was not chosen, the project directors, with approval from the steering committee, added a representative to the steering committee from that university.

A design integrating qualitative and quantitative strategies was developed to answer the following six research questions:

1. What do adolescents with special health care needs, their families, providers, and policymakers articulate as positive transition outcomes?
2. How do adolescents with special health care needs, their families, providers, potential employers, and policymakers define independence for this population?
3. What barriers to successful transition are articulated by adolescents with special health care needs, their families, providers, potential employers, and policymakers?
4. What current and missing supports and services are needed by adolescents with special health care needs as articulated by adolescents with special health care needs, their families, providers, potential employers, and policymakers?
5. What geographic, ethnic, and socioeconomic differences exist in articulated positive transition outcomes, definitions of independence, perceived barriers, and current and needed services?
6. What differences in desired transition outcomes, definition of independence, and perceived service needs exist among adolescents with special health care needs,

their families, providers, potential employers, and policymakers?

Consistent with the model, the steering committee developed the research questions and provided input on the design. The steering committee appointed a participatory action team (PAT) to design a triangulated research project relying on focus group, survey, and life history methodology and to conduct all data collection activity and data analysis. The team, composed of adolescent, parent, health and human services provider, educator, employer, and policymaker representatives, was trained in focus group and interview methodology and in thematic and taxonomic data analysis techniques. The survey was selected by the university investigators but agreed on as a viable tool by the steering committee.

Nine focus groups, each with six to 10 participants, were conducted. To ensure that each interest group was heard, the following homogenous focus groups were convened: two adolescent groups, one parent group, three health and human services provider groups, one educator group, one employer group, and one policy maker group. Recruitment of focus group members occurred by nomination from PAT and the steering committee. The aim of this purposive recruitment was to obtain a range of conditions and disciplinary groups and a spectrum of the state's political, geographic, socioeconomic, and ethnic perspectives from each interest group. Once the group was scheduled, a two member team, consisting of a PAT representative of that interest group and a university investigator met with the group, obtained consent, and facilitated the group. Semi-structured questions to ensure adequacy of data to answer the research questions were posed to group members. All discourse was audiotaped and transcribed, with names and identifiers deleted to maintain confidentiality.

Thematic data analysis was conducted independently by the investigator and PAT member facilitating the group, and any differences in meaning were negotiated between the two analyzers. Quantitative analysis was conducted by one of the investigators and shared with PAT and steering committee.

Member checks with focus group participants were conducted to verify impressions and analysis.

Analysis of survey data was conducted by the university researcher, and findings were submitted to PAT and steering committee for review. Life history interviews were conducted by a two-member team of a university researcher and parent member of PAT. These data were analysed for "turnings," specific life events that have a significant influence in the future direction of one's life, by a two-member team, and all identifying information was deleted to maintain confidentiality prior to submission of the findings and analysis to the full PAT and steering committee.

Dissemination occurred in multiple formats, including presentations, online postings, and newsletter reviews for adolescents, parents, teachers, providers, employers, and policymakers, as well as oral and written papers to scholarly groups. In an effort that was consistent with the model, the steering committee worked with the university investigators to seek additional funding for systems change. A collaborative grant proposal to implement systems change for adolescents with special health care needs, based on the findings of the study, was written, and funding was obtained.

Next Step in the Model

The next step of the critical action research model currently is being implemented. To plan carefully for systems change, the steering committee agreed on the statewide conduct of force field analysis groups, in which the stakeholder groups examine the research findings and use them in this collaborative planning activity. In this step of the model, the conflicts and areas of dissent that surfaced in the research can be addressed. Each stakeholder group will be asked to consider all perspectives in developing plans for systems change. The steering committee is primarily responsible for the evaluation of the process and for ensuring that all stakeholder groups are represented and heard. Along with the university investigators, PAT members (after having been trained) conducted the force field analysis, in addition, specific goals for ongoing inquiry, with research questions identified by the steering committee, were written into the grant proposal and will be accomplished over the project timeline and beyond.

Some problems in the implementation of the model that surfaced in this project are worth noting. First, the steering committee members did not agree initially on the direction for the needs assessment. Significant negotiation to clarify the research focus and participants was necessary. To produce consensus, the entire steering committee convened, each individual stated his or her position, and a tally for the preferred direction was taken. In the process, some steering committee members decided to withdraw because they were unable to support the majority vote. One member initiated his own inquiry. However, because all stakeholder groups ultimately were included, despite the withdrawal of some individuals, the steering committee was satisfied that all perspectives would be heard fairly. Second, who would provide primary direction and oversight for the research was unclear and influenced by political and organizational territorialism. The steering committee addressed these issues and developed methods, as discussed earlier, to include both institutions without compromising the project.

A third critical issue was scheduling meeting times for PAT. Illness and weather as well as school commitments for adolescents interfered. We were able to maintain contact and conduct much of the work via e-mail. Because the project was supported by a grant, we were able to provide access to on-line resources for those who did not previously have these options.

Related to the practical issues of scheduling was the problem with individuals dropping out of PAT. Three of the initial members were unable to continue through the entire project. Although nothing can be done about maintaining those who are unable or unwilling to remain, modifying future strategies can be informed by examining the reasons that these problems occur. We found that those who dropped out did so because they moved out of the area. This point highlighted the need to obtain participants who were committed to the project and who anticipated being able to complete the work. When new individuals were recruited, they were approached with these criteria in mind and were trained in the research process before participating.

The final and most challenging issue is how to use findings that are controversial and conflicting. In the MAT project, the needs articulated by adolescents and parents were contradictory to the needs discussed by providers and teachers. These dissonant findings were reported as such and are being addressed in the planning process. Although such findings are potentially problematic in that the "consumer" perspective significantly challenges the status quo of the services provider domination, they are an intended outcome of the critical action model, in that the process unearths the perspectives of those who traditionally are silenced or invisible in the knowledge-generation process.. Thus, conflict arising from critical action approaches is not only beneficial to service revision but is essential to avoiding presumptions that emerge from a system where "knowing power" is held only by an elite few. Without the potential for such a conflict, egalitarian services and structures cannot be established.

Implications for Social Work Practice

As urged by social work scholars and practitioners, the model advanced and illustrated in this article provides a framework for social work inquiry that is consistent with the mission, values, and aims of the profession. The philosophical foundation of the model is purposive, inclusive, empowering, and action oriented. Moreover, in concert with the contemporary trends for accountability and evidence-based practice, action orientation using this model is well informed by sound and participatory inquiry.

At a time in the development of the profession when hesitance to conduct research has given way to the recognition that research is essential for survival, this model provides a bridge between the university and the community and between research and practice. In essence, inquiry in this model not only is a knowledge-generating endeavour but also is a practice intervention. Previously devalued groups are empowered by developing and using their own knowledge and by sharing resources and skills in an egalitarian manner with those who have previously held too much knowing power. Although implementing such a model is a complex process, with the potential to give lip service to egalitarianism, the critical action model provides systematic guidance through which multiple groups can assume a critical approach to knowledge that informs the development and implementation of social and human services, in this model, interest groups that have been silenced can be empowered with resources such that traditional models of knowledge generation and thus of services delivery can be challenged, with systems change being an outcome. In the implementation, measures to ensure that farther political advantage is not gained by dominant groups are essential, however, or the model becomes rhetorical and subverts the ultimate social work commitment to elimination of oppression.

MINDFUL INQUIRY AND ACTION RESEARCH

Given this enormous challenge, how can scholar-practitioners make the best and most productive use of the available information? Bentz and Shapiro suggest that knowledge of social science inquiry methods and theories for interpreting results and data will help practitioners evaluate the quality of the information and make intelligent choices.

As we get into a discussion of the major cultures of inquiry that researchers immerse themselves in, an important distinction needs to be made between what constitutes a "culture/tradition" of inquiry and what can merely be thought of as a "method" of inquiry. Many of us use these terms interchangeably, and it was therefore important for this author to make sense of what appears to be a general controversy. As a matter of fact, Bentz and Shapiro, may have, either inadvertently, or possibly by design, introduced an element of confusion when they make the following suggestion in their book: "Mindful inquiry has elements of hermeneutics, phenomenology, and critical social science, which we will explain briefly in this chapter. Later in this book, we discuss these approaches in some detail as cultures of inquiry—that is, as three specific traditions among a number of others, such as quantitative and behavioral science, ethnography, and action research, within which research is currently carried out in the human and social sciences."

The "subjectivity" of the human experience is sometimes considered by them as a research contaminant. As we get more involved in this discussion, we will discover that the subjectivity of both, the researcher and the research participant is a critical factor in social science research and cannot be discounted as either non-existent or inconsequential. It often determines the quality of data we will be able to gather in our field work, if we work in the hermeneutic culture of inquiry, as do these authors.

The implementation of conceptual structure assessment in many thesis takes hermeneutical approach. Hermeneutics is especially important in this aspect of the project because of the complexity of the ideas, conceptions, and theories that are incorporated into the discussion of for example adult learning in distance education in new social movements. One main contribution is to "allow the movements of understanding to happen on their own time". Hermeneutics rejects both foundationalism and nihilism (noddings, 1998). All of these characteristics point to the value of this approach for a theoretical inquiry that wants to analyse, synthesize and evaluate threads of thought.

Bentz and Shapiro suggest that hermeneutics is the study of texts and related theories for their "interpretation." Everything that we experience is interpreted through our existing filters (culture, language, symbols, and concepts). Originally used by theologians as a means of understanding and interpreting religious texts such as the Bible, the field has been extended to make sense of just about any system, using several layers of interpretation. In a reciprocal interpretative process, hermeneutics studies present day texts in a historical context, and vice-versa.

They have done a nice job of drawing a parallel between the twists and turns of each culture of inquiry, and a mechanical spring. One can experience different things as one travels along the twists and turns of the spring. It is particularly this experience of new revelations and insights that make social science research particularly intriguing. In action research, it is taken as axiomatic that the inquirer is connected to, embedded in, the issues and field they are studying. This is particularly evident when the "personal is political", as in inquiry into race, gender or deprivation of some sort, and when our studies take us beyond dominant frameworks and assumptions. However, we suggest that all researchers can benefit from exploring the ways in which they are connected to their research – in terms of topic and methodological approach – and how these connections influence their theorizing and practice.

Research is always carried out by an individual with a life and a lifeworld... a personality, social context, and various personal and practical challenges and conflicts, all of which affect the research, from the choice of a research question or topic, through the method used, to the reporting of the project's outcome.

Recognising that research is an engaged human, social and political activity invites and requires us to seek to account for these aspects in our research and role.

Systemic change in the relationships and boundary dynamics of schools involves a call for more qualitative research within school communities. Action research influences system change via participation, self-determination, and knowledge generation.

As we have indicated, the term 'action research' can be interpreted quite broadly. Its history is of relevance: Bentz and Shapiro (1998) traced its origin to 'two independent sources – Kurt Lewin, a person of science, and John Collier, a person of practical affairs.' They emphasised different aspects of inquiry. Lewin (1946) argued that 'realistic fact finding and evaluation are prerequisites for any learning', whereas Collier (1945) stressed 'the requirement for cooperation among the administrator, the scientist and the layperson'. Bentz and Shapiro comment that 'early studies ... were more concerned with changing the behaviour of persons or organisations in a specific direction than in using action research as a means of participant problem solving.'

They held that it was Paolo Freire who later 'developed a form of inquiry he called "participatory" action research.' The authors provide examples of this sort of work where the researcher: *'...act[s] as a facilitator of a process of inquiry involving as many stakeholders in the situation as wish to be involved. Ideally, these stakeholders will be involved in the research design, data gathering, data analysis, and implementation of action steps resulting from the research..*

It is generally recognised that there is no one method that is 'right' for action research. Any method could be used. What makes a piece of research 'action research', as opposed to mere audit or evaluation, is the commitment to change. As Bentz and Shapiro (1998) state:

'Action research is less a separate culture of inquiry than it is a statement of intention and values. The intention is to change a system, and the values are those of participation, self-determination, empowerment through knowledge, and change.'.

Given this as the broad aim, the choice of method may be more to do with the nature of the problem that one is seeking to understand and explain. For example, if there is genuine uncertainty about two approaches to do research, it may be appropriate to set up an experiment where one group of participants is treated by one method and the other by another.

The guest lecturer, Dr. Sayyed Mohsen Fatemi, explained about quantitative and qualitative research. Every science has its own ontology, epistemology and consequently its own methodologies. Ontology defines the fundamental categories of reality. Domain ontology as distinct from formal ontology is related to focus of study. Each research field has its own ontology. A biologist, who studies plants, differentiates the plants' specific constituent parts, actions and contexts. Similarly a sociologist will have implicit and/or explicit presuppositions about categories of reality that are fundamental and related in the human and social systems he studies. Where formal ontology inquiry is to say something general about reality, domain ontology says something specific about different areas of reality. Epistemology defines how we can know and reason that reality. As for domain ontology, each research field has its own epistemology: The maps applied by the biologist studying plants, are traditionally different from the maps applied by the sociologist in his studies of interacting humans. The methodologies of each of these two scientists have followed as different systems of investigative techniques within their focus of study. The biologist and the sociologist traditionally apply different procedures for accomplishing and approaching the phenomena they focus on. They use different scientific methods studying different domains with different epistemology and ontology.

Dr. Fatemi also described the act of creativity. It is not searching for the sameness, is not in pursuit of congruence or compatibility, and is not moving towards convergence. Creativity is not bound to coherence, cohesiveness, conformity, correspondence or consistency in a sign oriented paradigm. Creativity may represent an act of revelation where things are revealed in light of creativity and unconsciousness as it can be an act of disclosure where things are cryptically and yet creatively presented. Creativity is not dutifully at the service of the recognized order as it is not respectful of the relationships and their establishment within the government of signs. Creativity may bring chaos and disorder but this chaotic situation is only as a result of a comparison between the act of creativity and the previously identified system of order within the plane of signs.

A SIMPLIFIED FRAMEWORK FOR USING MULTIPLE IMPUTATION

Missing data are ubiquitous in social research, and missingness or nonresponse can represent a threat to the validity of inferences because of undue effects on efficiency, power, and parameter bias. Social work researchers are now addressing missing data in a more rigorous manner. Recently, Saunders et al. (2006) and Choi, Golder, Gillmore, and Morrison (2005) described important data imputation methods and dispelled misunderstandings regarding popular imputation methods, such as mean substitution. Recent advances in analytic methods, such as multiple imputation (MI), are taking hold in social work research. With MI, missing values are replaced with values repeatedly drawn from simulated conditional probability distributions (Schafer, 1997), thus creating multiple versions of the data set. Each version of the data set is analysed according to the data analysis model, and the multiple results are combined into point estimates (Rubin, 1996).

A critical task in MI is to devise an imputation model (Allison, 2002) or missing data model, which involves specifying the measures that are putatively associated with the missing values. Although this process adds additional steps, the specification of an imputation model and the creation of multiple data sets can produce less-biased estimates in the presence of missing data across a wide variety of data analysis techniques (Schafer, 1997).

Besides MI, there are many other methods for addressing missing data. An equally rigorous method known as direct or full information maximum likelihood (FIML) estimation can produce unbiased estimates and correct standard errors in the presence of missing data. When the number of imputations is sufficiently large, identical missing data models will produce the same estimates under MI and FIML (Graham et al., 2007). Unlike MI, FIML is limited to maximum likelihood analytic techniques and the missing data model must be included in the analysis model. Although we focus on MI, the steps we describe for developing an imputation model are equally appropriate for use in the missing data model for FIML. On the basis of the MI literature, this article describes a framework for developing an imputation model for use with any free or commercial software package that performs MI.

BRIEF REVIEW OF MISSING DATA CONCEPTS

Generally, both MI and a broad range of missing data issues have received ample attention in the applied literature. We briefly discuss the three types of distributions that describe the randomness of nonresponse given that this property has consequences for the development of an imputation model. For a discussion of general missing data concepts that are not critical to understanding our discussion of imputation model development, we refer readers to Schafer and Graham (2002).

Distribution of Nonresponse

The probability distribution of nonresponse—more frequently referred to as the missing data or nonresponse mechanism (Rubin, 1976)—is both an important factor in the decision to impute with MI and a context for the development of an imputation model. Technical definitions are available in Rubin (1976) and Schafer (1997); for less technical definitions see Saunders et al. (2006), Allison (2002), and von Hippel (2004). Schafer and Graham's (2002) work provides helpful diagrams and promotes use of the term distribution over that of mechanism because of the latter's misleading implication of an underlying process. The distribution describes the randomness of missing data in the context of observed data (that is, the extent to which being missing is systematically related to observed or missing values).

Completely Random. As described by Rubin (1976), data may be missing completely at random (MCAR). In MCAR, the probability of nonresponse is independent of either observed or missing values. When nonresponse is MCAR, deletion—also known as complete case analysis—is a potential strategy given that the randomness of the missing values does not induce bias, although efficiency and power will be negatively affected. However, deletion is the easiest strategy to implement and is regarded as desirable if the assumption of MCAR is supported. MCAR can be tested with a likelihood ratio chi-square test of the null MCAR hypothesis that compares the means of the observed data for the pattern of nonresponse observed on each variable.

Systematic. Nonresponse may be systematic, that is, it may be conditioned on observed or missing values. In the worst case scenario, nonresponse may be associated with the missing values, which is known variously as missing not at random (MNAR), not missing at random (NMAR) (von Hippel, 2004) or nonignorable (Allison, 2002). This type of nonresponse can be a problem because there is no widely available theoretically grounded strategy for handling MNAK missing data. A more desirable distribution occurs when nonresponse is randomly distributed over the unobserved data but is associated with the observed data. This type of nonresponse is known as missing at random (MAR). This is also referred to as ignorable (Allison, 2002). When the data are MAR, techniques used to create the multiple imputations eliminate missing data bias (Schafer, 1999).

Multiple Imputation

With MI, missing values are replaced with values repeatedly drawn from conditional probability distributions by using a simulation method called Markov Chain Monte Carlo (MCMC). As noted previously, this process yields multiple versions of a data set, and the same analysis (for example, a linear regression) is conducted on each version, generating multiple estimates for each parameter. By using a set of rules that adjusts the standard errors for the uncertainty of the imputed values, the multiple estimates are combined to obtain a single parameter estimate (Rubin, 1987). This process adds an additional step to data analysis because it requires the analyst to specify an imputation model before data analysis.

MI can produce unbiased estimates when the fraction of missing information approaches 90% (Graham et al., 2007). This does not imply that 90% of the data points can be missing: The fraction of missing information depends on the proportion of missing data points as well as the covariance of the missing data points with observed data; the lower this relationship is, the higher is the proportion of missing information (Graham et al., 2007). For example, if 50% of the data points on income were missing, then the fraction of missing information is likely to be lower if education is in the imputation model (which has a high putative association with income) than if it is excluded. Therefore, the proportion of missing data points alone is a poor measure for determining whether MI is appropriate for a given situation.

Unfortunately, the MAR assumption underlying MI may not be plausible. This assumption cannot be tested because doing so would require having access to the values that are missing. If the data cannot be tested for MAR, then at best they can only be assumed to be MNAR, and MI does not eliminate missing data bias when data are MNAR. However, Schafer (1997) and Allison (2002) argued that by using an informed and well-constructed imputation model, performing MI on MNAR data could at least reduce bias, even to negligible levels. As Schafer (1997) noted, "The crucial assumption made by [multiple imputation] is not that the propensity to respond is completely unrelated to the missing data, but that this relationship can be explained by data that are observed". For example, if income is frequently missing in a data set—and higher income respondents were less likely to respond—then the missing data are MNAR. However, MI may yield less bias if an observed variable such as education (which covaries with income) is included in the imputation; even less bias is produced when both education and gender (also a variable that is predictive of income) are included. Thus, the focus should be on constructing the best possible imputation model and, arguably, not on assumptions about the nonresponse distribution. The process of setting up an imputation model is complicated, and there is a risk of increasing parameter bias if it is done poorly.

DEVELOPING AN IMPUTATION MODEL

The intended purpose of the imputation model is to capture the association among variables as related to the missing values. Treatments of MI dealing directly with the development of the imputation model from an applied perspective are rare. Instead, most tend to focus on specific issues (for example, variable format) rather than a general strategy. In this article, we combine these treatments into a framework for development of an imputation model. We first discuss considerations for creating the model.

Considerations for the Imputation Model

Several considerations guide the development of imputation models, including the covariation of the imputation and analysis models, the distributions of the variables, and the amount of information not used in the data analysis but available for imputation.

Model for Data Analysis. The covariance structure of the model for data analysis must be accounted for in the imputation model; otherwise, parameters estimated from the imputed data may be biased (Rubin, 1996). This means that all variables to be analysed and any interactions must appear in the imputation model.

Joint Multivariate Normality. In MI, the variables are assumed to have a joint multivariate normal distribution (Allison, 2002). However, imputing categorical data by using a normal model usually performs well. Clustered and panel data structures, which violate the assumptions of joint multivariate normality, must also be addressed (Allison, 2002).

Relationship between Model Size and Bias. On balance, the more information included in an imputation model, the better. In other words, any variables that are assumed to have modest association with the missing values should be included in the imputation model because they are likely to improve estimates and reduce bias. In this sense, developing the imputation model is more like forecasting than model fitting: Instead of parsimony for achieving best fit, the set of variables for imputing is allowed to be large to predict values as close as possible to the real, unobserved values. This assumption implies that as many variables as possible should be included in the model. However, exceptions must be made for the robustness of the data set, including the potential for collinearity. The robustness of the data, rather than strictly the percentage of missing data points (which factors into the overall robustness by constraining the amount of variability), helps determine whether imputation is appropriate for a given set of variables (Schafer, 1997).

Preparing an Imputation Model

On the basis of these considerations, we describe a three-step reduction strategy for developing an imputation model from a data set containing many variables, some of which may be used in the data analytic model whereas others may not. The framework assumes that a data analysis model has been established, that this model is included in the imputation model, and that the Little (1988) MCAR test (available in SPSS) confirms deletion would produce biased estimates—thus requiring a more rigorous strategy, such as imputation.

Identify Potential Imputation Variables. The first step is to select variables that should be candidates for the imputation model. The selected variables should have at least minimal association with the variables containing missing values. The absence of the observed values from which to estimate correlations requires an external basis for claiming a putative association. For example, research has established a high correlation between gender and physical aggression in childhood. Therefore, it is advisable for the analyst to include a variable for gender when imputing for a model of aggressive behavior, even if gender is not a focus of the analysis. Allison (2000) cautions that relying solely on the association of the nonanalytic variables with the pattern of nonresponse is not appropriate because this association may increase bias if not informative of the missing values. Although variables with missing values can be used in the imputation model, those with relatively fewer missing values will provide more information at a lower cost (in terms of model size) (Schafer, 1997). We recommend eliminating variables that can be assumed to have no association with the missing values and those with more than a relatively small number of missing data points as both of these types increase the size of the model but contribute little to bias reduction. Interactions can be implemented in one of two ways: by performing separate imputations for each category of one of the interacted variables or by calculating a product of the interacted variables before imputation and including this product variable in the imputation model (Allison, 2002).

Address the Distribution Assumptions. Categorical, skewed, and range-limited variables pose special problems for imputation. A special package for imputing only categorical variables (CAT) has been developed in S-Plus and R (Schafer, 1997). When variables are both multivariate normal and categorical, another package (MIXED) is available for S-Plus and R (Schafer, 1997). However, Schafer (1997) demonstrated that using MI under the assumption of normality works well even when variables are nonnormal, including binomial. Consequently, if the missing values are dispersed between categorical and continuous variables, then software for multivariate normal variables can be used. In this situation, continuous variables should be given priority. Similarly, polychotomous variables with k levels may be converted into k-1 dummy variables (Allison, 2002). Dummy variables can be then imputed under the assumption of multivariate normality, which can result in imputed values besides zero and one. Nevertheless, out-of-range values should not be rounded after imputation, as this may induce bias. Variables that have skewed or range-limited distributions should be considered for transformation (for example, logarithmic transformation for right-skewed or nonnegative data), requiring retransformation afterward.

Strategies for imputing clustered data continue to be developed, but few imputation packages account explicitly for clustering. PAN is a package developed for the S-Plus and P-statistical computing languages designed for use with panel data (which suffers from the same failure of independence assumptions as does clustered data) (Schafer, 1997). Although some researchers have suggested that including the clustering variable in the imputation model may circumvent the problem of nesting in MCMC, this method is ad hoc and does not preserve the associations between cases within the same cluster as effectively as does specialized software such as PAN. For repeated measures on individual cases (longitudinal or panel data), Allison (2002) suggested that multivariate normal imputation software can be used by first reformatting the data so there is one observation per case and then performing a normal imputation. Subsequently, the data should be converted to the period-by-case form required for repeated measures analysis.

Remove Collinearity. Collinearity is often a problem when reducing data to a working imputation model, particularly when starting with hundreds of variables. Collinearity (including linear dependence) can result in a failure of the MCAR test to provide a meaningful result and a failure of MCMC to run properly (Schafer, 1997). Linear dependence often arises when scales and their constituent items are included in a data set; therefore, either the scales or the items should be excluded (with a preference for normally distributed variables, we recommend retaining the scales, particularly when the items are binomial). Linear dependence also occurs when [kappa] dummy variables, representing [kappa] categories, are included in the model. In MI, the solution is the same as in regression analysis: Omit one of the categories.

If the previous steps have been followed, then linear dependence should not be a problem. However, high collinearity among the variables selected in the previous steps may still produce biased estimates. Therefore, we recommend testing for collinearity with a variance inflation factor (VIF) test before the MCAP, test and imputation. AVIF is calculated for a variable as [(1-[R.sup.2]).sup.-1] using the coefficient of determination [R.sup.2] from a model regressing this variable on every other variable in the model (Kennedy, 2003). AVIF approaching 10 usually indicates high collinearity. Note, however, that a VIF test is a multivariate complete case analysis in which cases with missing values are deleted. Therefore, higher VIFs may emerge—and collinearity can seemingly worsen—as deletion of the missing data in this step reduces the sample size and produces a more homogenous sample. Therefore, we recommend using the VIF test only as a guide before imputation. Data robustness diagnostics that are conducted during the imputation, available in some software packages, can be reviewed after imputation. These are better indicators of the robustness of the model (Schafer, 1997) and are discussed in more detail in the following section. Conventional strategies for dealing with collinearity can be used when collinearity is found to be high, such as deletion of highly collinear variables or the use of a transformation such as mean centering.

Imputation

The theory behind imputation and the specific procedures and algorithms used in MI are described in nontechnical language by Schafer and Graham (2002), Allison (2002), and Saunders et al. (2006). A more technical and advanced treatment is available in Schafer (1997). These treatments also discuss decisions involved in the imputation process that are beyond the scope of this chapter. These include deciding on the number of iterations of the algorithms used in the simulation process and selecting diagnostics such as autocorrelation plots. Software documentation should be consulted to determine how to specify these options and diagnostics.

After Imputation

After imputation, the imputation diagnostics are reviewed to assess the robustness of the imputation model and then the desired analyses are conducted. Many programs report diagnostics statistics such as the fraction of missing information and relative efficiency for each variable. If a large number of imputations are performed, the fraction of missing information will be lower and relative efficiency can exceed 99% (Graham et al., 2007). The relative efficiency will be lower if parameter estimates vary widely across the imputations, which can occur as a result of either a poorly constructed imputation model or imputations with few imputed data sets (Graham et al., 2007). In the latter case, these statistics are potentially misleading (Allison, 2002). After reviewing the diagnostics, the researcher should conduct the desired analysis on each copy of the data set that is generated during the simulation process. The estimates from each version of the analysis should then be combined into a single set of parameter estimates using Rubin's (1987) rules for inference, which inflate the standard errors to account for the uncertainty of the simulated values.

MAJOR TYPES OF RESEARCH DESIGN

Research design plans manage and systematize quantitative or qualitative data collection. Quantitative research finds the answer to an inquiry by compiling numerical evidence. It counts and classifies components and creates statistical models to explain what is observed. Qualitative research is subjective in approach, and attempts to understand human behavior and the rationales that govern it. It generates mainly verbal data that is analysed and interpreted. Under each of these two main categories fall a variety of research designs suitable to particular studies.

Descriptive research is a quantitative research design that describes phenomena as they exist, taking care not to influence subjects or events in any way. Descriptive and survey research designs are used by social scientists to describe human behaviours, by market analysts to look at the habits of customers, and by businesses seeking insight about company practices. Descriptive research can be used to indicate what variables might be worth testing quantitatively.

An experimental research design is considered the most accurate method of research. Usually applied to the physical sciences, it attempts to prove or disprove a hypothesis numerically, using statistical analysis. Because of the exacting structure of this design, results can be statistically analysed, replicated and validated by other researches, greatly diminishing arguments about the accuracy of the results.

Used frequently in the social sciences and psychology, quasi-experiments lack a control group, making firm statistical analysis difficult. However, these experiments can be useful in generating data to indicate general trends. They are effective in obtaining a general overview that can be followed up with a quantitative or case study to focus on the underlying reasons for the results generated.

A historical research design can be applied to all fields of study, because it includes factors such as origins, growth, theories and significant persons. It can collect both quantitative and qualitative historical data. Primary sources — i.e., first-hand accounts — are the most highly valued in historical research, and include oral history interviews and recordings, eyewitness accounts and personal diaries. In conducting historical research, consider any possible prejudices or biases your sources may have.

Observational research compares subjects in situations in which the researcher has little control over the experiment, mainly for ethical reasons. For instance, in comparing the life expectancy of smokers with that of non-smokers, it would be unethical to ask a group of otherwise healthy people to smoke for 20 years to compare them with the control group of non-smokers. The weakness of this design is that results can be skewed by factors such as pollution, second-hand smoke and environmental working conditions.

DESCRIPTIVE RESEARCH

Descriptive research does not fit neatly into the definition of either quantitative or qualitative research methodologies, but instead it can utilize elements of both, often within the same study. The term descriptive research refers to the type of research question, design, and data analysis that will be applied to a given topic. Descriptive statistics tell what is, while inferential statistics try to determine cause and effect.

The type of question asked by the researcher will ultimately determine the type of approach necessary to complete an accurate assessment of the topic at hand. Descriptive studies, primarily concerned with finding out "what is," might be applied to investigate the following questions: Do teachers hold favourable attitudes toward using computers in schools? What kinds of activities that involve technology occur in sixth-grade classrooms and how frequently do they occur? What have been the reactions of school administrators to technological innovations in teaching the social sciences? How have high school computing courses changed over the last 10 years? How do the new multimediated textbooks compare to the print-based textbooks? How are decisions being made about using Channel One in schools, and for those schools that choose to use it, how is Channel One being implemented? What is the best way to provide access to computer equipment in schools? How should instructional designers improve software design to make the software more appealing to students? To what degree are special-education teachers well versed concerning assistive technology? Is there a relationship between experience with multimedia computers and problem-solving skills? How successful is a certain satellite-delivered Spanish course in terms of motivational value and academic achievement? Do teachers actually implement technology in the way they perceive? How many people use the AECT gopher server, and what do they use if for?

Descriptive research can be either quantitative or qualitative. It can involve collections of quantitative information that can be tabulated along a continuum in numerical form, such as scores on a test or the number of times a person chooses to use a-certain feature of a multimedia program, or it can describe categories of information such as gender or patterns of interaction when using technology in a group situation. Descriptive research involves gathering data that describe events and then organizes, tabulates, depicts, and describes the data collection. It often uses visual aids such as graphs and charts to aid the reader in understanding the data distribution. Because the human mind cannot extract the full import of a large mass of raw data, descriptive statistics are very important in reducing the data to manageable form. When in-depth, narrative descriptions of small numbers of cases are involved, the research uses description as a tool to organize data into patterns that emerge during analysis. Those patterns aid the mind in comprehending a qualitative study and its implications.

Most quantitative research falls into two areas: studies that describe events and studies aimed at discovering inferences or causal relationships. Descriptive studies are aimed at finding out "what is," so observational and survey methods are frequently used to collect descriptive data. Studies of this type might describe the current state of multimedia usage in schools or patterns of activity resulting from group work at the computer. An example of this is Cochenour, Hakes, and Neal's (1994) study of trends in compressed video applications with education and the private sector.

Descriptive studies report summary data such as measures of central tendency including the mean, median, mode, deviance from the mean, variation, percentage, and correlation between variables. Survey research commonly includes that type of measurement, but often goes beyond the descriptive statistics in order to draw inferences. Thick, rich descriptions of phenomena can also emerge from qualitative studies, case studies, observational studies, interviews, and portfolio assessments. Robinson's (1994) case study of a televised news program in classrooms and Lee's (1994) case study about identifying values concerning school restructuring are excellent examples of case studies.

Descriptive research is unique in the number of variables employed. Like other types of research, descriptive research can include multiple variables for analysis, yet unlike other methods, it requires only one variable. For example, a descriptive study might employ methods of analyzing correlations between multiple variables by using tests such as Pearson's Product Moment correlation, regression, or multiple regression analysis. Good examples of this are the Knupfer and Hayes (1994) study about the effects of the Channel One broadcast on knowledge of current events, Manaev's (1991) study about mass media effectiveness, McKenna's (1993) study of the relationship between attributes of a radio program and it's appeal to listeners, Orey and Nelson's (1994) examination of learner interactions with hypermedia environments, and Shapiro's (1991) study of memory and decision processes.

On the other hand, descriptive research might simply report the percentage summary on a single variable. Examples of this are the tally of reference citations in selected instructional design and technology journals by Anglin and Towers (1992); Barry's (1994) investigation of the controversy surrounding advertising and Channel One; Lu, Morlan, Lerchlorlarn, Lee, and Dike's (1993) investigation of the international utilization of media in education (1993); and Pettersson, Metallinos, Muffoletto, Shaw, and Takakuwa's (1993) analysis of the use of verbo-visual information in teaching geography in various countries.

Descriptive statistics utilize data collection and analysis techniques that yield reports concerning the measures of central tendency, variation, and correlation. The combination of its characteristic summary and correlational statistics, along with its focus on specific types of research questions, methods, and outcomes is what distinguishes descriptive research from other research types.

Three main purposes of research are to describe, explain, and validate findings. Description emerges following creative exploration, and serves to organize the findings in order to fit them with explanations, and then test or validate those explanations (Krathwohl, 1993). Many research studies call for the description of natural or man-made phenomena such as their form, structure, activity, change over time, relation to other phenomena, and so on. The description often illuminates knowledge that we might not otherwise notice or even encounter. Several important scientific discoveries as well as anthropological information about events outside of our common experiences have resulted from making such descriptions. For example, astronomers use their telescopes to develop descriptions of different parts of the universe, anthropologists describe life events of socially atypical situations or cultures uniquely different from our own, and educational researchers describe activities within classrooms concerning the implementation of technology. This process sometimes results in the discovery of stars and stellar events, new knowledge about value systems or practices of other cultures, or even the reality of classroom life as new technologies are implemented within schools.

Educational researchers might use observational, survey, and interview techniques to collect data about group dynamics during computer-based activities. These data could then be used to recommend specific strategies for implementing computers or improving teaching strategies. Two excellent studies concerning the role of collaborative groups were conducted by Webb (1982), and Rysavy and Sales (1991). Noreen Webb's landmark study used descriptive research techniques to investigate collaborative groups as they worked within classrooms. Rysavy and Sales also apply a descriptive approach to study the role of group collaboration for working at computers. The Rysavy and Sales approach did not observe students in classrooms, but reported certain common findings that emerged through a literature search.

Descriptive studies have an important role in educational research. They have greatly increased our knowledge about what happens in schools. Some of the important books in education have reported studies of this type: Life in Classrooms, by Philip Jackson; The Good High School, by Sara Lawrence Lightfoot; Teachers and Machines: The Classroom Use of Technology Since 1920, by Larry Cuban; A Place Called School, by John Goodlad; Visual Literacy: A Spectrum of Learning, by D. M. Moore and Dwyer; Computers in Education: Social,

Political, and Historical Perspectives, by Muffoletto and Knupfer; and Contemporary Issues in American Distance Education, by M. G. Moore. Henry J. Becker's (1986) series of survey reports concerning the implementation of computers into schools across the United States as well as Nancy Nelson Knupfer's (1988) reports about teacher's opinions and patterns of computer usage also fit partially within the realm of descriptive research. Both studies describe categories of data and use statistical analysis to examine correlations between specific variables. Both also go beyond the bounds of descriptive research and conduct further statistical procedures appropriate to their research questions, thus enabling them to make further recommendations about implementing computing technology in ways to support grassroots change and equitable practices within the schools. Finally, Knupfer's study extended the analysis and conclusions in order to yield suggestions for instructional designers involved with educational computing.

The Nature of Descriptive Research

The descriptive function of research is heavily dependent on instrumentation for measurement and observation (Borg & Gall, 1989). Researchers may work for many years to perfect such instrumentation so that the resulting measurement will be accurate, reliable, and generalizable. Instruments such as the electron microscope, standardized tests for various purposes, the United States census, Michael Simonson's questionnaires about computer usage, and scores of thoroughly validated questionnaires are examples of some instruments that yield valuable descriptive data. Once the instruments are developed, they can be used to describe phenomena of interest to the researchers.

The intent of some descriptive research is to produce statistical information about aspects of education that interests policy makers and educators. The National Center for Education Statistics specializes in this kind of research. Many of its findings are published in an annual volume called Digest of Educational Statistics. The center also administers the National Assessment of Educational Progress (NAEP), which collects descriptive information about how well the nation's youth are doing in various subject areas. A typical NAEP publication is The Reading Report Card, which provides descriptive information about the reading achievement of junior high and high school students during the past 2 decades.

On a larger scale, the International Association for the Evaluation of Education Achievement (IEA) has done major descriptive studies comparing the academic achievement levels of students in many different nations, including the United States. Within the United States, huge amounts of information are being gathered continuously by the Office of Technology Assessment, which influences policy concerning technology in education. As a way of offering guidance about the potential of technologies for distance education, that office has published a book called Linking for Learning: A New Course for Education, which offers descriptions of distance education and its potential.

There has been an ongoing debate among researchers about the value of quantitative versus qualitative research, and certain remarks have targeted descriptive research as being less pure than traditional experimental, quantitative designs. Rumors abound that young researchers must conduct quantitative research in order to get published in Educational Technology Research and Development and other prestigious journals in the field. One camp argues the benefits of a scientific approach to educational research, thus preferring the experimental, quantitative approach, while the other camp posits the need to recognize the unique human side of educational research questions and thus prefers to use qualitative research methodology. Because descriptive research spans both quantitative and qualitative methodologies, it brings the ability to describe events in greater or less depth as needed, to focus on various elements of different research techniques, and to engage quantitative statistics to organize information in meaningful ways. The citations within this chapter provide ample evidence that descriptive research can indeed be published in prestigious journals. Descriptive studies can yield rich data that lead to important recommendations. For example, Galloway (1992) bases recommendations for teaching with computer analogies on descriptive data, and Wehrs (1992) draws reasonable conclusions about using expert systems to support academic advising. On the other hand, descriptive research can be misused by those who do not understand its purpose and limitations. For example, one cannot try to draw conclusions that show cause and effect, because that is beyond the bounds of the statistics employed.

Borg and Gall (1989) classify the outcomes of educational research into the four categories of description, prediction, improvement, and explanation. They say that descriptive research describes natural or man-made educational phenomena that is of interest to policy makers and educators. Predictions of educational phenomenon seek to determine whether certain students are at risk and if teachers should use different techniques to instruct them. Research about improvement asks whether a certain technique does something to help students learn better and whether certain interventions can improve student learning by applying causal-comparative, correlational, and experimental methods. The final category of explanation posits that research is able to explain a set of phenomena that leads to our ability to describe, predict, and control the phenomena with a high level of certainty and accuracy. This usually takes the form of theories. The methods of collecting data for descriptive research can be employed singly or in various combinations, depending on the research questions at hand. Descriptive research often calls upon quasi-experimental research design. Some of the common data collection methods applied to questions within the realm of descriptive research include surveys, interviews, observations, and portfolios.

PARTICIPATORY ACTION RESEARCH

Action research or participatory action research is a recognized form of experimental research that focuses on the effects of the researcher's direct actions of practice within a participatory community with the goal of improving the performance quality of the community or an area of concern.

Action research involves utilizing a systematic cyclical method of planning, taking action, observing, evaluating (including self-evaluation) and critical reflecting prior to planning the next cycle. The actions have a set goal of addressing an identified problem in the workplace, for example, reducing the illiteracy of students through use of new strategies (Quigley, 2000) or improving communication and efficiency in a hospital emergency room. It is a collaborative method to test new ideas and implement action for change. It involves direct participation in a dynamic research process, while monitoring and evaluating the effects of the researcher's actions with the aim of improving practice. At its core, action research is a way to increase understanding of how change in one's actions or practices can mutually benefit a community of practitioners. Understanding action research.

"Essentially Participatory Action Research (PAR) is research which involves all relevant parties in actively examining together current action (which they experience as problematic) in order to change and improve it. They do this by critically reflecting on the historical, political, cultural, economic, geographic and other contexts which make sense of it. ... Participatory action research is not just research which is hoped that will be followed by action. It is action which is researched, changed and re-researched, within the research process by participants. Nor is it simply an exotic variant of consultation. Instead, it aims to be active co-research, by and for those to be helped. Nor can it be used by one group of people to get another group of people to do what is thought best for them-whether that is to implement a central policy or an organisational or service change. Instead it tries to be a genuinely democratic or non-coercive process whereby those to be helped, determine the purposes and outcomes of their own inquiry."-Wadsworth, Y. (1998) What is Participatory Action Research?

The "research" aspects of PAR attempt to avoid the traditional "extractive" research carried out by universities and governments where "experts" go to a community, study their subjects, and take away their data to write their papers, reports and theses. Research in PAR is ideally BY the local people and FOR the local people. Research is designed to address specific issues identified by local people, and the results are directly applied to the problems at hand.

PAR proceeds through repeated cycles, in which researchers and the community start with the identification of major issues, concerns and problems, initiate research, originate action, learn about this action and proceed to a new research and action cycle. This process is a continuous one. Participants in Action Research projects continuously reflect on their learning from the actions and proceed to initiate new actions on the spot. Outcomes are very difficult to predict from the outset, challenges are sizeable and achievements depend to a very large extent on researcher's commitment, creativity and imagination.

Examples of action research projects dissertations and masters thesis can be easily found by searching the internet. Some universities host sites where the best example of this form of research in corporate and university organizations, and school communities.

PAR should not be confused with PRA-Participatory rural appraisal. PRA is an assessment technique that could form part of a PAR process, but does not encompass the full action-reflection cycle.

Origins

PAR has many of its roots in social psychology. It builds on the Action research and Group Dynamics models developed by psychologist Kurt Lewin in the early-to-mid 1900s, as well as on the study of oral culture by such scholars as Milman Parry and Walter J. Ong. At its core, PAR revolves around three sets of relationships: relations between individuals within communities and groups, relations between those groups and communities, and relations between people and their physical environment. Management of group dynamics in its many aspects thus plays a central role in PAR processes, and PAR practitioners/facilitators must have a strong foundation in this field.

PAR builds on the critical pedagogy put forward by Paulo Freire as a response to the traditional formal models of education where the "teacher" stands at the front and "imparts" information to the "students" that are passive recipients. This was further developed in "adult education" models throughout

Latin America. Friere (1990) wrote, "The silenced are not just incidental to the curiosity of the researcher but are the masters of inquiry into the underlying causes of the events in their world. In this context research becomes a means of moving them beyond silence into a quest to proclaim the world."

Based on the work of Freire, it was Colombian sociologist Orlando Fals-Borda who gave PAR its worldwide recognition by organizing the first PAR conferences in Cartagena, Colombia. Based on his research with peasant groups in rural Boyaca and with other underserved groups, Fals-Borda was able to effectively incorporate the "Community Action" component into the research plans of many traditionally trained researchers. It was not until then that communities started to fully appreciate the benefits of this approach which had initially seemed too abstract for many.

Antonio Gramsci is less known for, yet very important in contrtibuting to PAR. Gramsci, writing in early 20th century Italy, argued that all people are intellectuals and philosophers. "Organic intellectuals" is how he terms people who take their local knowledge from life experiences, and use that knowledge to address changes and problems in society. The idea that PAR researchers are really co-learners and researchers with the people they meet in the research process promotes the validity that all people are intellectuals who develop intricate philosophies through lived experience. PAR also has its roots in phenomenology and postmodernism. These movements validated experience as a valid way of knowing, very much the foundation of the "action-reflection" model of Experiential learning and the PAR process. PAR is part of an important shift in paradigm from the traditional, positivist, science paradigm which arose to bring certainty and verifiability to research questions, to postpositivism which recognizes and tries to address complex human and social problems.

Finally, PAR has origins within the development discourse.

Recent developments

PAR has evolved through the 1990s and into the 21st century as it has been applied to various fields within international development. For example, participatory plant breeding (PPB) and participatory technology development (PTD) are two techniques that utilize PAR approaches. Other research approaches that often fall under the label of PAR include participatory research, critical action research, classroom action research, action learning, action science, soft systems approaches, and industrial action research. Additionally, more methods have been developed to add nuance and solidify key processes of "how" to do PAR, such as participatory development communication (PDC) and participatory video(PV). Practitioners have also recently tried to move away from the word "research" because of its extractive connotations and abstract meaning to many community and group members. Thus new names (with some new elements) are being used, such as "participatory action learning", "participatory learning-action", and "participatory action development".

PAR is a popular method used in teaching adult learners in low-income communities, and others how to explore, challenge, and react to their own needs. It is gaining popularity among community youth workers, as well as middle and senior high school teachers as a successful methodology for engaging youth voice in the classroom. According to Torre & Fine (2005), "Youth PAR projects are typically centered on issues of intimate, structural violence: educational justice, access to quality healthcare, the criminalization of youth, gang violence, police brutality, race/gender/sexuality oppression, gentrification and environmental issues." PAR is also increasingly used in service learning projects and provides the basis for a variety of secondary approaches such as Triple Task Method.

Critique

Many, such as Peter L. Berger and Robert Chambers, point out the intrinsically political nature of PAR. Participation is empowerment and empowerment is politics. Furthermore, it is very difficult for PAR to fully extricate itself from the researcher-community relationship that in itself affects local power dynamics. Community participation in such a context should be recognized for what it is-an externally motivated political act.

"However much the rhetoric changes to participation, participatory research, community involvement and the like, at the end of the day there is still an outsider seeking to change things... who the outsider is may change but the relation is the same. A stronger person wants to change things for a person who is weaker. From this paternal trap there is no complete escape."

However, in some cases, the participatory researcher may actually be a part of the community whose realities are being transformed. In Oakland, California, for example, Kitty Kelly Epstein is a longtime local resident, a grassroots activist and a participatory researcher. She has used the combination of these three roles successfully to help change policies and power dynamics.

Others would point to the irony of citing participatory evangelist Chambers, ally of the World Bank, in a section on critique. Arturo Escobar argues that concepts of participation and sustainability only help to foster a gentler image of development than usual. In some situations, as highlighted by Diane Rocheleau, participatory methods can also serve as Trojan horses to bring global and environmental restructuring processes directly to rural communities, bypassing national institutional buffers and pre-empting critical review. They can also be manipulated by various actors to deliberately affect power dynamics, often with a more centralizing effect than democratizing, as explored by Triulzi. This point of view was summarised in Bill Cooke and Uma Kothari's *Participation: The New Tyranny?* in 2001.

PAR has also been criticized for lacking the methodological rigor and technical validity that is the gold standard of much academic research. It is suggested that this weakness is a necessary tradeoff of a collaborative and adaptive research design. Supporters, however, counter that sacrificing some level of methodological and technical rigor is well worth the additional face validity and practical significance that is gained through a PAR approach. Additionally, many academic supporters would assert that there are ways to conduct PAR that is sound by academic standards.

6

Sampling Methods of Social Research

When a small group has taken as a representative of the whole, it's called as sampling. It's the small unit which make a good use in analysis of research finding.

TYPES OF SAMPLING

Random Sampling

It's called as the proportional sampling. It assures each individual or elements in the universe has equal chance of being selected or choosed research unit. It's a popular method in statistics to justify the method of research.

Lottery Sampling

Some time it's impossible to cover all the area, so the researcher may do the lottery system to select a particular area for her/his research designing.

Sequential Sampling

The scholar collects the sequential list to select her/his samples. In a sequence if a number is more samples are drawn from that sequence. Usually alphabetical order dominate in sequential sampling.

Grid Sampling

Grid sampling refers to election of a particular area from

the total Universe. In such a method of sampling the entire universe is divided into different greed and segments and the scholar prepares a map of the entire universe and places the greed in that map out of which he selects her/his samples for study & research.

Biased Sampling

Biased sampling means a researcher selects the samples according to her/his choice and is free to choose one & reject the other.

Stratified Sampling

It includes both perpessive and random sampling. Strata implies groups. The entire universe is divided into different groups or strata and samples are done from each group or strata.

Quota Sampling

Quota sampling is a type of perpessive sampling, the entire universe is divided into different groups, strata or physical regions and from each group, strata or region we draws specific samples according to our quota that means, selection must be according to the need of the area.

Multi-stage Sampling

The universe is always very large and there must be a proper parameter to select samples, which adequately represents the universe. For that purpose we divide the total universe into different stages and accordingly we select samples.

Convenience Sampling

Where the universe isn't very clear to understand for research, the researcher use this type off sampling.

Self-selected Sampling

Selection is done by the people. In such cases the researcher needn't go to the respondents, rather the respondent run after the researcher for selection.

SAMPLING

Sampling is that part of statistical practice concerned with the selection of a subset of individual observations within a population of individuals intended to yield some knowledge about the population of concern, especially for the purposes of making predictions based on statistical inference. Sampling is an important aspect of data collection. Researchers rarely survey the entire population for two reasons : the cost is too high, and the population is dynamic in that the individuals making up the population may change over time. The three main advantages of sampling are that the cost is lower, data collection is faster, and since the data set is smaller it is possible to ensure homogeneity and to improve the accuracy and quality of the data.

Each observation measures one or more properties (such as weight, location, color) of observable bodies distinguished as independent objects or individuals. In survey sampling, survey weights can be applied to the data to adjust for the sample design. Results from probability theory and statistical theory are employed to guide practice. In business and medical research, sampling is widely used for gathering information about a population.

Process

The sampling process comprises several stages:

- Defining the population of concern
- Specifying a sampling frame, a set of items or events possible to measure
- Specifying a sampling method for selecting items or events from the frame
- Determining the sample size
- Implementing the sampling plan
- Sampling and data collecting.

Population Definition

Successful statistical practice is based on focused problem definition. In sampling, this includes defining the population from which our sample is drawn. A population can be defined as including all people or items with the characteristic one wishes to understand. Because there is very rarely enough time or money to gather information from everyone or everything in a population, the goal becomes finding a representative sample (or subset) of that population. Sometimes that which defines a population is obvious. For example, a manufacturer needs to decide whether a batch of material from production is of high enough quality to be released to the customer, or should be sentenced for scrap or rework due to poor quality. In this case, the batch is the population.

Although the population of interest often consists of physical objects, sometimes we need to sample over time, space, or some combination of these dimensions. For instance, an investigation of supermarket staffing could examine checkout line length at various times, or a study on endangered penguins might aim to understand their usage of various hunting grounds over time. For the time dimension, the focus may be on periods or discrete occasions. In other cases, our 'population' may be even less tangible. For example, Joseph Jagger studied the behaviour of roulette wheels at a casino in Monte Carlo, and used this to identify a biased wheel. In this case, the 'population' Jagger wanted to investigate was the overall behaviour of the wheel (i.e. the probability distribution of its results over infinitely many trials), while his 'sample' was formed from observed results from that wheel. Similar considerations arise when taking repeated measurements of some physical characteristic such as the electrical conductivity of copper.

This situation often arises when we seek knowledge about the cause system of which the *observed* population is an outcome. In such cases, sampling theory may treat the observed population as a sample from a larger 'superpopulation'. For example, a researcher might study the success rate of a new 'quit smoking' program on a test group of 100 patients, in order to predict the effects of the program if it were made available nationwide. Here the superpopulation is "everybody in the country, given access to this treatment"-a group which does not yet exist, since the program isn't yet available to all.

Note also that the population from which the sample is drawn may not be the same as the population about which we actually want information. Often there is large but not complete overlap between these two groups due to frame issues etc. Sometimes they may be entirely separate-for instance, we might study rats in order to get a better understanding of human health, or we might study records from people born in 2008 in order to make predictions about people born in 2009.

Time spent in making the sampled population and population of concern precise is often well spent, because it raises many issues, ambiguities and questions that would otherwise have been overlooked at this stage.

Sampling Frame

In the most straightforward case, such as the sentencing of a batch of material from production (acceptance sampling by lots), it is possible to identify and measure every single item in the population and to include any one of them in our sample. However, in the more general case this is not possible. There is no way to identify all rats in the set of all rats. Where voting is not compulsory, there is no way to identify which people will actually vote at a forthcoming election (in advance of the election). These imprecise populations are not amenable to sampling in any of the ways below and to which we could apply statistical theory. As a remedy, we seek a sampling frame which has the property that we can identify every single element and include any in our sample. The most straightforward type of frame is a list of elements of the population (preferably the entire population) with appropriate contact information. For example, in an opinion poll, possible sampling frames include an electoral register and a telephone directory.

Probability and Nonprobability Sampling

A probability sampling scheme is one in which every unit in the population has a chance (greater than zero) of being selected in the sample, and this probability can be accurately determined. The combination of these traits makes it possible to produce unbiased estimates of population totals, by weighting sampled units according to their probability of selection.

Probability sampling includes: Simple Random Sampling, Systematic Sampling, Stratified Sampling, Probability Proportional to Size Sampling, and Cluster or Multistage Sampling. These various ways of probability sampling have two things in common:

1. Every element has a known nonzero probability of being sampled and
2. involves random selection at some point.

Nonprobability sampling is any sampling method where some elements of the population have *no* chance of selection (these are sometimes referred to as 'out of coverage'/ 'undercovered'), or where the probability of selection can't be accurately determined.

It involves the selection of elements based on assumptions regarding the population of interest, which forms the criteria for selection.

Hence, because the selection of elements is nonrandom, nonprobability sampling does not allow the estimation of sampling errors. These conditions give rise to exclusion bias, placing limits on how much information a sample can provide about the population. Information about the relationship between sample and population is limited, making it difficult to extrapolate from the sample to the population.

Sampling Methods

Within any of the types of frame identified above, a variety of sampling methods can be employed, individually or in combination. Factors commonly influencing the choice between these designs include:

- Nature and quality of the frame
- Availability of auxiliary information about units on the frame
- Accuracy requirements, and the need to measure accuracy
- Whether detailed analysis of the sample is expected
- Cost/operational concerns.

SIMPLE RANDOM SAMPLING

In a simple random sample ('SRS') of a given size, all such subsets of the frame are given an equal probability. Each element of the frame thus has an equal probability of selection: the frame is not subdivided or partitioned. Furthermore, any given *pair* of elements has the same chance of selection as any other such pair (and similarly for triples, and so on). This minimises bias and simplifies analysis of results. In particular, the variance between individual results within the sample is a good indicator of variance in the overall population, which makes it relatively easy to estimate the accuracy of results.

However, SRS can be vulnerable to sampling error because the randomness of the selection may result in a sample that doesn't reflect the makeup of the population. For instance, a simple random sample of ten people from a given country will *on average* produce five men and five women, but any given trial is likely to overrepresent one sex and underrepresent the other. Systematic and stratified techniques, discussed below, attempt to overcome this problem by using information about the population to choose a more representative sample.

SRS may also be cumbersome and tedious when sampling from an unusually large target population. In some cases, investigators are interested in research questions specific to subgroups of the population. For example, researchers might be interested in examining whether cognitive ability as a predictor of job performance is equally applicable across racial groups. SRS cannot accommodate the needs of researchers in this situation because it does not provide subsamples of the population. Stratified sampling, which is discussed below, addresses this weakness of SRS.

Simple random sampling is always an EPS design, but not all EPS designs are simple random sampling.

Systematic Sampling

Systematic sampling relies on arranging the target population according to some ordering scheme and then selecting elements at regular intervals through that ordered list. Systematic sampling involves a random start and then proceeds with the selection of every *k*th element from then onwards. In this case, *k*=(population size/sample size). It is important that the starting point is not automatically the first in the list, but is instead randomly chosen from within the first to the *k*th element in the list. A simple example would be to select every 10th name from the telephone directory (an 'every 10th' sample, also referred to as 'sampling with a skip of 10').

As long as the starting point is randomized, systematic sampling is a type of probability sampling. It is easy to implement and the stratification induced can make it efficient, *if* the variable by which the list is ordered is correlated with the variable of interest. 'Every 10th' sampling is especially useful for efficient sampling from databases.

Stratified Sampling

Where the population embraces a number of distinct categories, the frame can be organized by these categories into separate "strata." Each stratum is then sampled as an independent sub-population, out of which individual elements can be randomly selected. There are several potential benefits to stratified sampling.

First, dividing the population into distinct, independent strata can enable researchers to draw inferences about specific subgroups that may be lost in a more generalized random sample.

Second, utilizing a stratified sampling method can lead to more efficient statistical estimates (provided that strata are selected based upon relevance to the criterion in question, instead of availability of the samples). Even if a stratified sampling approach does not lead to increased statistical efficiency, such a tactic will not result in less efficiency than would simple random sampling, provided that each stratum is proportional to the group's size in the population.

Third, it is sometimes the case that data are more readily available for individual, pre-existing strata within a population than for the overall population; in such cases, using a stratified sampling approach may be more convenient than aggregating data across groups (though this may potentially be at odds with the previously noted importance of utilizing criterion-relevant strata).

Finally, since each stratum is treated as an independent population, different sampling approaches can be applied to different strata, potentially enabling researchers to use the approach best suited (or most cost-effective) for each identified subgroup within the population.

There are, however, some potential drawbacks to using stratified sampling. First, identifying strata and implementing such an approach can increase the cost and complexity of sample selection, as well as leading to increased complexity of population estimates. Second, when examining multiple criteria, stratifying variables may be related to some, but not to others, further complicating the design, and potentially reducing the utility of the strata. Finally, in some cases (such as designs with a large number of strata, or those with a specified minimum sample size per group), stratified sampling can potentially require a larger sample than would other methods (although in most cases, the required sample size would be no larger than would be required for simple random sampling.

A stratified sampling approach is most effective when three conditions are met

1. Variability within strata are minimized
2. Variability between strata are maximized
3. The variables upon which the population is stratified are strongly correlated with the desired dependent variable.

Advantages over other sampling methods

1. Focuses on important subpopulations and ignores irrelevant ones.
2. Allows use of different sampling techniques for different subpopulations.
3. Improves the accuracy/efficiency of estimation.
4. Permits greater balancing of statistical power of tests of differences between strata by sampling equal numbers from strata varying widely in size.

Disadvantages:

1. Requires selection of relevant stratification variables which can be difficult.
2. Is not useful when there are no homogeneous subgroups.
3. Can be expensive to implement.

Poststratification

Stratification is sometimes introduced after the sampling phase in a process called "poststratification". This approach is typically implemented due to a lack of prior knowledge of an appropriate stratifying variable or when the experimenter lacks the necessary information to create a stratifying variable during the sampling phase. Although the method is susceptible to the pitfalls of post hoc approaches, it can provide several benefits in the right situation. Implementation usually follows a simple random sample. In addition to allowing for stratification on an ancillary variable, poststratification can be used to implement weighting, which can improve the precision of a sample's estimates.

Oversampling

Choice-based sampling is one of the stratified sampling strategies. In choice-based sampling, the data are stratified on the target and a sample is taken from each stratum so that the rare target class will be more represented in the sample. The model is then built on this biased sample. The effects of the input variables on the target are often estimated with more precision with the choice-based sample even when a smaller overall sample size is taken, compared to a random sample. The results usually must be adjusted to correct for the oversampling.

PROBABILITY PROPORTIONAL TO SIZE SAMPLING

In some cases the sample designer has access to an "auxiliary variable" or "size measure", believed to be correlated to the variable of interest, for each element in the population. These data can be used to improve accuracy in sample design. One option is to use the auxiliary variable as a basis for stratification.

Another option is probability-proportional-to-size ('PPS') sampling, in which the selection probability for each element is set to be proportional to its size measure, up to a maximum of 1. In a simple PPS design, these selection probabilities can then be used as the basis for Poisson sampling. However, this has the drawback of variable sample size, and different portions of the population may still be over-or under-represented due to chance variation in selections. To address this problem, PPS may be combined with a systematic approach.

The PPS approach can improve accuracy for a given sample size by concentrating sample on large elements that have the greatest impact on population estimates. PPS sampling is commonly used for surveys of businesses, where element size varies greatly and auxiliary information is often available-for instance, a survey attempting to measure the number of guest-nights spent in hotels might use each hotel's number of rooms as an auxiliary variable. In some cases, an older measurement of the variable of interest can be used as an auxiliary variable when attempting to produce more current estimates.

Cluster Sampling

Sometimes it is cheaper to 'cluster' the sample in some way e.g. by selecting respondents from certain areas only, or certain time-periods only. (Nearly all samples are in some sense 'clustered' in time-although this is rarely taken into account in the analysis.) Cluster sampling is an example of 'two-stage sampling' or 'multistage sampling': in the first stage a sample of areas is chosen; in the second stage a sample of respondents *within* those areas is selected.

This can reduce travel and other administrative costs. It also means that one does not need a sampling frame listing all elements in the target population. Instead, clusters can be chosen from a cluster-level frame, with an element-level frame created only for the selected clusters. Cluster sampling generally increases the variability of sample estimates above that of simple random sampling, depending on how the clusters differ between themselves, as compared with the within-cluster variation. Nevertheless, some of the disadvantages of cluster sampling are the reliance of sample estimate precision on the actual clusters chosen. If clusters chosen are biased in a certain way, inferences drawn about population parameters from these sample estimates will be far off from being accurate.

Multistage sampling Multistage sampling is a complex form of cluster sampling in which two or more levels of units are embedded one in the other. The first stage consists of constructing the clusters that will be used to sample from. In the second stage, a sample of primary units is randomly selected from each cluster (rather than using all units contained in all selected clusters). In following stages, in each of those selected clusters, additional samples of units are selected, and so on. All ultimate units (individuals, for instance) selected at the last step of this procedure are then surveyed. This technique, thus, is essentially the process of taking random samples of preceding random samples. It is not as effective as true random sampling, but it probably solves more of the problems inherent to random sampling. Moreover, It is an effective strategy because it banks on multiple randomizations. As such, it is extremely useful.

Multistage sampling is used frequently when a complete list of all members of the population does not exist and is inappropriate. Moreover, by avoiding the use of all sample units in all selected clusters, multistage sampling avoids the large, and perhaps unnecessary, costs associated traditional cluster sampling.

Matched Random Sampling

A method of assigning participants to groups in which pairs of participants are first matched on some characteristic and then individually assigned randomly to groups. The procedure for matched random sampling can be briefed with the following contexts,

1. Two samples in which the members are clearly paired, or are matched explicitly by the researcher. For example, IQ measurements or pairs of identical twins.
2. Those samples in which the same attribute, or variable, is measured twice on each subject, under different circumstances. Commonly called repeated measures.

Examples include the times of a group of athletes for 1500m before and after a week of special training; the milk yields of cows before and after being fed a particular diet.

Quota Sampling

In quota sampling, the population is first segmented into mutually exclusive sub-groups, just as in stratified sampling. Then judgment is used to select the subjects or units from each segment based on a specified proportion. For example, an interviewer may be told to sample 200 females and 300 males between the age of 45 and 60. It is this second step which makes the technique one of non-probability sampling. In quota sampling the selection of the sample is non-random. For example interviewers might be tempted to interview those who look most helpful. The problem is that these samples may be biased because not everyone gets a chance of selection. This random element is its greatest weakness and quota versus probability has been a matter of controversy for many years.

Convenience Sampling or Accidental Sampling

Convenience sampling (sometimes known as grab or opportunity sampling) is a type of nonprobability sampling which involves the sample being drawn from that part of the population which is close to hand. That is, a sample population selected because it is readily available and convenient. It may be through meeting the person or including a person in the sample when one meets them or chosen by finding them through technological means such as the internet or through phone. The researcher using such a sample cannot scientifically make generalizations about the total population from this sample because it would not be representative enough. For example, if the interviewer was to conduct such a survey at a shopping center early in the morning on a given day, the people that he/she could interview would be limited to those given there at that given time, which would not represent the views of other members of society in such an area, if the survey was to be conducted at different times of day and several times per week. This type of sampling is most useful for pilot testing. Several important considerations for researchers using convenience samples include:

1. Are there controls within the research design or experiment which can serve to lessen the impact of a non-random convenience sample, thereby ensuring the results will be more representative of the population?
2. Is there good reason to believe that a particular convenience sample would or should respond or behave differently than a random sample from the same population?
3. Is the question being asked by the research one that can adequately be answered using a convenience sample?

In social science research, snowball sampling is a similar technique, where existing study subjects are used to recruit more subjects into the sample.

Line-intercept Sampling

Line-intercept sampling is a method of sampling elements in a region whereby an element is sampled if a chosen line segment, called a "transect", intersects the element.

Panel Sampling

Panel sampling is the method of first selecting a group of participants through a random sampling method and then asking that group for the same information again several times over a period of time. Therefore, each participant is given the same survey or interview at two or more time points; each period of data collection is called a "wave". This sampling methodology is often chosen for large scale or nation-wide studies in order to gauge changes in the population with regard to any number of variables from chronic illness to job stress to weekly food expenditures. Panel sampling can also be used to inform researchers about within-person health changes due to age or help explain changes in continuous dependent variables such as spousal interaction. There have been several proposed methods of analyzing panel sample data, including MANOVA, growth curves, and structural equation modeling with lagged effects.

Event Sampling Methodology

Event sampling methodology (ESM) is a new form of sampling method that allows researchers to study ongoing experiences and events that vary across and within days in its naturally-occurring environment. Because of the frequent sampling of events inherent in ESM, it enables researchers to measure the typology of activity and detect the temporal and dynamic fluctuations of work experiences. Popularity of ESM as a new form of research design increased over the recent years because it addresses the shortcomings of cross-sectional research, where once unable to, researchers can now detect intra-individual variances across time. In ESM, participants are asked to record their experiences and perceptions in a paper or electronic diary. There are three types of ESM:

1. Signal contingent – random beeping notifies participants to record data. The advantage of this type of ESM is minimization of recall bias.
2. Event contingent – records data when certain events occur
3. Interval contingent – records data according to the passing of a certain period of time.

ESM has several disadvantages. One of the disadvantages of ESM is it can sometimes be perceived as invasive and intrusive by participants. ESM also leads to possible self-selection bias. It may be that only certain types of individuals are willing to participate in this type of study creating a non-random sample. Another concern is related to participant cooperation. Participants may not be actually fill out their diaries at the specified times. Furthermore, ESM may substantively change the phenomenon being studied. Reactivity or priming effects may occur, such that repeated measurement may cause changes in the participants' experiences. This method of sampling data is also highly vulnerable to common method variance.

Further, it is important to think about whether or not an appropriate dependent variable is being used in an ESM design. For example, it might be logical to use ESM in order to answer research questions which involve dependent variables with a great deal of variation throughout the day. Thus, variables such as change in mood, change in stress level, or the immediate impact of particular events may be best studied using ESM methodology. However, it is not likely that utilizing ESM will yield meaningful predictions when measuring someone performing a repetitive task throughout the day or when dependent variables are long-term in nature (coronary heart problems).

Replacement of Selected Units

Sampling schemes may be *without replacement* or *with replacement*. For example, if we catch fish, measure them, and immediately return them to the water before continuing with the sample, this is a WR design, because we might end up catching and measuring the same fish more than once. However, if we do not return the fish to the water (e.g. if we eat the fish), this becomes a WOR design.

Sample Size

Formulas, tables, and power function charts are well known approaches to determine sample size.

Formulas

Where the frame and population are identical, statistical theory yields exact recommendations on sample size. However, where it is not straightforward to define a frame representative of the population, it is more important to understand the cause system of which the population are outcomes and to ensure that all sources of variation are embraced in the frame. Large number of observations are of no value if major sources of variation are neglected in the study. In other words, it is taking a sample group that matches the survey category and is easy to survey. Bartlett, Kotrlik, and Higgins (2001) published a paper titled *Organizational Research: Determining Appropriate Sample Size* in Survey Research Information Technology, Learning, and Performance Journal that provides an explanation of Cochran's (1977) formulas. A discussion and illustration of sample size formulas, including the formula for adjusting the sample size for smaller populations, is included.

A table is provided that can be used to select the sample size for a research problem based on three alpha levels and a set error rate.

Sampling and Data Collection

Good data collection involves:

- Following the defined sampling process
- Keeping the data in time order
- Noting comments and other contextual events
- Recording non-responses.

Most sampling books and papers written by non-statisticians focus only in the data collection aspect, which is just a small though important part of the sampling process.

Errors in Sample Surveys

Survey results are typically subject to some error. Total errors can be classified into sampling errors and non-sampling errors. The term "error" here includes systematic biases as well as random errors.

Sampling Errors and Biases

Sampling errors and biases are induced by the sample design. They include:

1. Selection bias: When the true selection probabilities differ from those assumed in calculating the results.
2. Random sampling error: Random variation in the results due to the elements in the sample being selected at random.

Non-sampling Error

Non-sampling errors are caused by other problems in data collection and processing. They include:

1. Overcoverage: Inclusion of data from outside of the population.
2. Undercoverage: Sampling frame does not include elements in the population.

3. Measurement error: E.g. when respondents misunderstand a question, or find it difficult to answer.
4. Processing error: Mistakes in data coding.
5. Non-response: Failure to obtain complete data from all selected individuals.

After sampling, a review should be held of the exact process followed in sampling, rather than that intended, in order to study any effects that any divergences might have on subsequent analysis. A particular problem is that of *non-response*.

Two major types of nonresponse exist: unit nonresponse and item nonresponse (submission or participation in survey but failing to complete one or more components/questions of the survey). In survey sampling, many of the individuals identified as part of the sample may be unwilling to participate, not have the time to participate (opportunity cost), or survey administrators may not have been able to contact them. In this case, there is a risk of differences, between respondents and nonrespondents, leading to biased estimates of population parameters. This is often addressed by improving survey design, offering incentives, and conducting follow-up studies which make a repeated attempt to contact the unresponsive and to characterize their similarities and differences with the rest of the frame. The effects can also be mitigated by weighting the data when population benchmarks are available or by imputing data based on answers to other questions.

Nonresponse is particularly a problem in internet sampling. Reasons for this problem include improperly designed surveys, over-surveying (or survey fatigue), and the fact that potential participants hold multiple e-mail addresses, which they don't use anymore or don't check regularly. Web-based surveys also tend to demonstrate nonresponse bias; for example, studies have shown that females and those from a white/Caucasian background are more likely to respond than their counterparts.

Survey Weights

In many situations the sample fraction may be varied by stratum and data will have to be weighted to correctly represent the population. Thus for example, a simple random sample of individuals in the United Kingdom might include some in remote Scottish islands who would be inordinately expensive to sample. A cheaper method would be to use a stratified sample with urban and rural strata. The rural sample could be under-represented in the sample, but weighted up appropriately in the analysis to compensate.

More generally, data should usually be weighted if the sample design does not give each individual an equal chance of being selected. For instance, when households have equal selection probabilities but one person is interviewed from within each household, this gives people from large households a smaller chance of being interviewed. This can be accounted for using survey weights. Similarly, households with more than one telephone line have a greater chance of being selected in a random digit dialing sample, and weights can adjust for this.

Weights can also serve other purposes, such as helping to correct for non-response.

History

Random sampling by using lots is an old idea, mentioned several times in the Bible. In 1786 Pierre Simon Laplace estimated the population of France by using a sample, along with ratio estimator. He also computed probabilistic estimates of the error. These were not expressed as modern confidence intervals but as the sample size that would be needed to achieve a particular upper bound on the sampling error with probability 1000/1001. His estimates used Bayes' theorem with a uniform prior probability and it assumed his sample was random. The theory of small-sample statistics developed by William Sealy Gossett put the subject on a more rigorous basis in the 20th century. However, the importance of random sampling was not universally appreciated and in the USA the 1936 *Literary Digest* prediction of a Republican win in the presidential election went badly awry, due to severe bias. More than two million people responded to the study with their names obtained through magazine subscription lists and telephone directories. It was not appreciated that these lists were heavily biased towards

Republicans and the resulting sample, though very large, was deeply flawed.

PREPARING FOR YOUR SOCIAL WORK INTERVIEW

Individual universities and colleges select and admit students for social work training programmes using their own criteria but they are also required to make a judgement on applicants' prospective suitability for professional registration with the General Social Care Council. The admissions tutor will assess your educational and employment details, your personal statement and reference from your UCAS application and will decide if you are to be short-listed and invited to attend for an interview.

It is likely that you will be asked to submit a short piece of written work beforehand based on your experience of social work or social care or on some current topical issue. Some universities may ask you to complete a questionnaire designed to assess qualities such as your ability to work with others, adaptability, resilience, commitment, organisational skills and communication skills. The interview is likely to explore your understanding of the knowledge and skills required for social work along with the reasons for your interest in social work, your personal qualities and ability to study at the required level. Interview panels are often made up of the course tutor and an experienced practising social worker. Users of social work services also contribute to the admissions process.

SOCIAL SURVEY

The Office for National Statistics carries out high quality social survey research for government departments and other public bodies on a range of social issues. This service began during the Second World War as the Wartime Social Survey and then the Government Social Survey. Since then we have been carrying out survey research for over 60 years, helping to develop government policies, inform public debate and monitor changes over time.

Survey Research

We currently carry out 8 continuous surveys throughout

the year every year, and over 30 ad-hoc surveys, which are commissioned to meet a particular information need. We collect information from more than half a million people each year through:

- personal interviews, mainly in people's own home
- telephone interviews, and
- postal surveys.

Methodological Work

We undertake methodological work to develop survey techniques building on our world-renowned expertise in quantitative survey methods.

Consultancy and advice: We provide consultancy and advice on all aspects of survey design to government departments and agencies and other public bodies.

Exploring the feasibility of developing an integrated approach to social surveys. There is a need for National Statistics to provide better information on key social and socio-economic variables between decennial censuses for a range of policy purposes. This project is looking to develop our ideas for the integration of the ONS-led continuous household surveys to meet this and related objectives

TAKING PART IN A SURVEY

Social surveys are a bridge between the people and the government. A good survey can provide accurate information about people's experiences and situation, which can help to make sure that government policies and services take account of everyone's needs. Good survey research depends on the co-operation of the people selected to take part.

We cannot include everyone in the country in every survey as this would be too expensive and take too much of everyone's time, so we select a sample of a few thousand people to represent the country as a whole. For example, for our household surveys, addresses are chosen at random from the Post Office's list of addresses throughout the country. All our surveys use random sampling to make sure that all groups of people are properly represented and everyone has an equal chance of being able to help with our surveys. Once a person or household has been chosen we cannot substitute other people because we could not be sure that we were talking to a representative cross-section of society.

Most of our surveys involve interviews, either face-to-face or by telephone. Most of our interviews take place in people's homes but we also interview in other places, such as schools and airports. Each survey is different and our interviewers will tell you more about the survey that you have been asked to take part in. Some of our surveys are quite quick, others are longer – but we are happy to make an appointment if necessary. Most of our surveys are straightforward and do not require any special knowledge on your part. Occasionally we may ask you to keep a note of an activity such as travel or household spending, but our interviewer will explain everything fully.

Yes, All information given is treated in confidence. The information is never used in any way that allows people to be identified. No identifiable information about anyone is passed to any outside bodies without their knowledge and agreement.

No, no-one has to take part if they do not want to, but we hope that, if people understand the importance of our work, people will choose to help us and make our surveys successful.

The information given by everyone who helps with the survey is combined and reports produced summarising the findings. These are then used by other government departments and other public bodies to develop policies and identify service needs. Some surveys provide information that is used for producing key economic indicators for the country.

GENERAL SOCIAL SURVEY

The General Social Survey (GSS) is a sociological survey used to collect data on demographic characteristics and attitudes of residents of the United States. The survey is conducted face-to-face with an in-person interview by the National Opinion Research Center at the University of Chicago, of a randomly-selected sample of adults (18+) who are not institutionalized. The survey was conducted every year from 1972 to 1994 (except in 1979, 1981, and 1992). Since 1994, it has been conducted every other year. The survey takes about 90 minutes to administer. As of 2008 27 national samples with 53,043 respondents and 5,364 variables had been collected. The data collected about this survey includes both demographic information and respondent's opinions on matters ranging from government spending to the state of race relations to the existence and nature of God. Because of the wide range of topics covered, and the comprehensive gathering of demographic information, survey results allow social scientists to correlate demographic factors like age, race, gender, and urban/rural upbringing with beliefs, and thereby determine whether, for example, an average middle-aged black male respondent would be more or less likely to move to a different U.S. state for economic reasons than a similarly situated white female respondent; or whether a highly educated person with a rural upbringing is more likely to believe in a transcendent God than a person with an urban upbringing and only a high-school education.

STATISTICAL SURVEY

Statistical survey is a method used to collect in a systematic way information from a sample of individuals. Although most people are familiar with public opinion surveys that are reported in the press, most surveys are not public opinion polls (such as political polling), but are used for scientific purposes. Surveys provide important information for all kinds of research fields, e.g., marketing research, psychology, health professionals and sociology..

A survey may focus on different topics such as preferences (e.g., for a presidential candidate), behavior (smoking and drinking behavior), or factual information(e.g., income), depending on its purpose. Since survey research is always based on a sample of the population, the success of the research is dependent on the representativeness of the population of concern.

Modes of Data Collection

There are several ways of administering a survey. The

choice between administration modes is influenced by several factors, including 1) costs, 2) coverage of the target population, 3) flexibility of asking questions, 4) respondents' willingness to participate and 5) response accuracy. The most common modes of administration are listed :

Telephone

- use of interviewers encourages sample persons to respond, leading to higher response rates.
- interviewers can increase comprehension of questions by answering respondents' questions.
- fairly cost efficient, depending on local call charge structure
- good for large national (or international) sampling frames
- some potential for interviewer bias (e.g. some people may be more willing to discuss a sensitive issue with a female interviewer than with a male one)
- cannot be used for non-audio information (graphics, demonstrations, taste/smell samples)
- unreliable for consumer surveys in rural areas where telephone density is low
- three types:
  - traditional telephone interviews
  - computer assisted telephone dialing
  - computer assisted telephone interviewing (CATI)

Mail

- the questionnaire may be handed to the respondents or mailed to them, but in all cases they are returned to the researcher via mail.
- An advantage is, is that cost is very low, since bulk postage is cheap in most countries
- long time delays, often several months, before the surveys are returned and statistical analysis can begin
- not suitable for issues that may require clarification

- respondents can answer at their own convenience (allowing them to break up long surveys; also useful if they need to check records to answer a question)
- no interviewer bias introduced
- large amount of information can be obtained: some mail surveys are as long as 50 pages
- response rates can be improved by using mail panels
    - o members of the panel have agreed to participate
    - o panels can be used in longitudinal designs where the same respondents are surveyed several times

Online Surveys

- can use web or e-mail. Web is preferred over e-mail because interactive HTML forms can be used
- often inexpensive to administer
- very fast results
- easy to modify
- response rates can be improved by using Online panels- members of the panel have agreed to participate
- honesty of responses can be an issue
- if not password-protected, easy to manipulate by completing multiple times to skew results
- data creation, manipulation and reporting can be automated and/or easily exported into a format that can be read by PSPP, DAP or other statistical analysis software
- data sets created in real time
- some are incentive based (such as Survey Vault or YouGov)
- may skew sample towards a younger demographic compared with CATI
- often difficult to determine/control selection probabilities, hindering quantitative analysis of data
- used in large scale industries.

Personal in-home Survey

- respondents are interviewed in person, in their homes (or at the front door)
- very high cost
- suitable when graphic representations, smells, or demonstrations are involved
- often suitable for long surveys (but some respondents object to allowing strangers into their home for extended periods)
- suitable for locations where telephone or mail are not developed
- skilled interviewers can persuade respondents to cooperate, improving response rates
- potential for interviewer bias

Personal Mall Intercept Survey

- shoppers at malls are intercepted-they are either interviewed on the spot, taken to a room and interviewed, or taken to a room and given a self-administered questionnaire
- socially acceptable-people feel that a mall is a more appropriate place to do research than their home
- potential for interviewer bias
- fast
- easy to manipulate by completing multiple times to skew results

How to Write good Survey Questions

Rules for writing good questions are given in classical survey books such as Dillman (1978)..A summary of these rules was made by Ten Brink (1992)..

- Rule 1. Use correct spelling, punctuation and grammar style.
- Rule 2. Use specific questions. For example, "did you read a newspaper yesterday?", instead of "did you read a newspaper?".

- Rule 3. Use a short introduction to question of behaviours. In this way you cannot only refresh the memory of the respondent, but also explain what you mean with the concept you are using. For example, with wines, you may not only mean red or white wine, but liqueurs, cordials, sherries, tables wines and sparkling wines.
- Rule 4. Avoid the use of technical terms and jargon. An exception to this rule are questions that are made for a specific group of respondents, who regularly use jargon, e.g., doctors, lawyers and researchers.
- Rule 5. Avoid questions that do not have a single answer. For example, "do you like to walk and to bike to school?". Somebody who likes to walk, but does not like to cycle, cannot answer this question in the right way.
- Rule 6. Avoid negative phrasing, e.g., "should the school not be improved?". This can lead to confusion and cost more effort to answer the question correctly.
- Rule 7. Avoid words and expressions with multiple-meanings, like any and just.
- Rule 8. Avoid stereotyping, offensive and emotionally loaded language.

Response Formats

Usually, a survey consists of a number of questions that the respondent has to answer in a set format. A distinction is made between open-ended and closed-ended questions. An open-ended question asks the respondent to formulate his own answer, whereas a closed-ended question has the respondent pick an answer from a given number of options.

The response options for a closed-ended question should be exhaustive and mutually exclusive. Four types of response scales for closed-ended questions are distinguished:

- Dichotomous, where the respondent has two options
- Nominal-polytomous, where the respondent has more than two unordered options

- Ordinal-polytomous, where the respondent has more than two ordered options
- (bounded) Continuous, where the respondent is presented with a continuous scale

A respondent's answer to an open-ended question is coded into a response scalc afterwards..

ADVANTAGES AND DISADVANTAGES OF SURVEYS

Advantages

- As in sample study few units are to be examined detailed study of the survey can be done.
- As few units are to be examined the survey work requires less time. Thus in this way sample survey saves time.
- As few units are to be examined the survey work requires less money. Thus in this way sample survey saves lots of money.
- In sample survey few persons are required for the survey work so experts can be appointed for the survey. This will increase the reliability of the survey results.
- When the test is of destructive nature, sampling is only the way out. In such cases the population survey is not possible.
- A large area can be covered under survey in the available time and money.
- If proper method is employed under the survey the results obtained will represent the population adequately. Surveys are relatively inexpensive (especially self-administered surveys).
- Surveys are useful in describing the characteristics of a large population. No other method of observation can provide this general capability.
- They can be administered from remote locations using mail, email or telephone.
- Consequently, very large samples are feasible, making the results statistically significant even when analyzing multiple variables.

- Many questions can be asked about a given topic giving considerable flexibility to the analysis.
- Sample survey make measurement more precise by enforcing uniform definitions upon the participants.
- Sample survey that similar data can be collected from groups then interpreted comparatively (between-group study).
- Sample survey is also used to check the accuracy of the census data (population survey).
- Surveys are an efficient way of collecting information from a large number of respondents. Very large samplings are possible. Statistical techniques can be used to determine validity, reliability, and statistical significance.
- Surveys are flexible in the sense that a wide range of information can be collected. They can be used to study attitudes, values, beliefs, and past behaviours.
- Because they are standardized, they are relatively free from several types of errors.
- They are relatively easy to administer.
- There is an economy in data collection due to the focus provided by standardized questions. Only questions of interest to the researcher are asked, recorded, codified, and analysed. Time and money is not spent on tangential questions.
- Sample surveys are usually cheaper to conduct than a full census.

Disadvantages

- They depend on subjects' motivation, honesty, memory, and ability to respond. Subjects may not be aware of their reasons for any given action. They may have forgotten their reasons. They may not be motivated to give accurate answers; in fact, they may be motivated to give answers that present themselves in a favourable light.

- Structured surveys, particularly those with closed ended questions, may have low validity when researching affective variables.
- Although the individuals chosen to participate in surveys are often randomly sampled, errors due to nonresponse may exist for more information on how to deal with nonresponsonders and biased data). That is, people who choose to respond on the survey may be different from those who do not respond, thus biasing the estimates. For example, polls or surveys that are conducted by calling a random sample of publicly available telephone numbers will not include the responses of people with unlisted telephone numbers, mobile (cell) phone numbers, people who are unable to answer the phone (e.g., because they normally sleep during the time of day the survey is conducted, because they are at work, etc.), people who do not answer calls from unknown or unfamiliar telephone numbers. Likewise, such a survey will include a disproportionate number of respondents who have traditional, land-line telephone service with listed phone numbers, and people who stay home much of the day and are much more likely to be available to participate in the survey (e.g., people who are unemployed, disabled, elderly, etc.).
- Survey question answer-choices could lead to vague data sets because at times they are relative only to a personal abstract notion concerning "strength of choice". For instance the choice "moderately agree" may mean different things to different subjects, and to anyone interpreting the data for correlation. Even yes or no answers are problematic because subjects may for instance put "no" if the choice "only once" is not available.

Nonresponse Reduction

Dilman (1978, chapter 7) gives detailed recommendations on how to reduce nonresponse in telephone and face-to-face surveys :

- Advance letter. A short letter is send in advance to

inform the sampled respondents about the upcoming survey. The style of the letter should be personalized but not overdone. First it announces that a phone call will be made/or an interviewer wants to make an appointment to do the survey face-to-face. Second the research topic will be describe. Last, an expression of the surveyor's appreciation to cooperate and an opening to ask questions on the survey.

- Training. The interviewers are thoroughly trained in how to ask respondents questions, how to work with computers and making schedules for callbacks to respondents who were not reached.
- Short introduction. The interviewer should always start with a short instruction about him or herself. She/he should give her name, the institute she is working for, the length of the interview and goal of the interview. Also it can be useful to make clear that you are not selling anything (De Leeuw, (2001) showed that this led to a slightly higher responding rate).
- Respondent-friendly survey questionnaire. The question asked must be clear, non offensive and easy to respond to for the subjects under study.

7

Social Work Research and Statistical Method

STATISTICS

The word 'Statistics' refers to some numerical facts relating to any phenomena in social sciences or exact sciences. Facts and figures pertaining to population, production, national income, profits, sales, bank rates, family patterns, dowry system, animal kingdom, plant life, bacteria; will all constitute statistics. The word 'statistics' seems to have derived from either the Latin word 'status' or the Italian word 'Statitsta' both meaning 'a political state'.

The word 'statistics' is presently referred to in two distinct senses. In its first reference as a plural noun, it means an aggregate or collection of numerical or quantitative expressions of facts i.e. 'numerical data' or simply 'data'. In its second reference as a singular noun, it means a body of principles and methods used in the collection, presentation, analysis and interpretation of numerical data.

Bowley defines statistics as the science of counting in one context. The emphasis made here is only on the collection of data. At another place he says: statistics may rightly be called the science of averages. Boddington defines statistics as the science of estimates and probabilities. According to Lovitt, the science of statistics deals with the collection. Classification and tabulation of numerical facts as the basis for explanation, description and comparison of phenomena. Seligman defines statistics as the science which deals with the methods of collecting classifying, presenting, comparing and interpreting numerical data collected to throw some light on any sphere of enquiry. Croxton and Cowden define statistics as the collection, presentation analysis and interpretation of numerical data.

Characteristics of Statistics

1. Statistics should be numerically expressed. For example the statement Rajan is of height 6' 1" makes the fact clear and easily understandable.
2. Statistics are aggregates of facts. Statistics means the facts pertaining to a group of individuals or individual item.
3. Statistics are affected to a market extent by a multiplicity of causes. There are a variety of forces or factors operating on the facts and figures in an aggregate. The influence of any particular factor cannot be isolated.
4. Statistics must be collected in a systematic manner for a predetermined purpose. Determination of the main purpose or objectives of any scientific study is the first and the most important step which in turn paves way for other operations to follow.
5. Statistics are enumerated or estimated according to reasonable standards of accuracy.
6. Statistics should be placed in relation to each other.

APPLICATIONS OF STATISTICS

Statistics and Sociology

Sociology is one of the social sciences aiming to discover the basic structure of human society, to identify the main forces that hold groups together or weaken them and to learn the conditions that transform social life. It highlights and illuminates aspects of social life that otherwise might be only obscurely recognized and understood. The sociologist may be called upon for help with a special problem such as social conflict, urban plight or the war on poverty or crimes. His practical contribution lies in the ability to clarify the underlaying nature of social problems to estimate more exactly their dimensions and to identify aspects that seem most amenable to remedy with the knowledge and skills at hand. He naturally lands in sociological research which is the purposeful effort to learn more about society than one can in the ordinary course of living. Keeping in view of the problem he sets forth his objectives collects materials or data and uses statistical techniques and the knowledge and theory already established on similar topics to achieve his objectives. So statistical data and statistical methods are quite indispensable for sociological research studies. There is a growing emphasis recently on social survey methods or research methodology in all faculties of arts.

Sociologists seek the help of statistical tools to study cultural change in the society, family pattern, prostitution, crime, marriage system etc. They also study statistically the relation between prostitution and poverty, crime and poverty, drunkness and crime, illiteracy and crime etc. Thus statistics is of immense use in various sociological studies.

Statistics and Government

The functions of a government are more varied and complex. Various depts in the state are required to collect and record statistical data in a systematic manner for an effective administration. Data pertaining to various fields namely population, natural resources, production both agricultural and industrial, finance, trade, exports and imports, prices, labour, transport and communication, health, education, defence, crimes etc. are the most fundamental requirements of the state for its administration. It is only on this basis of such data; the government decides on the priority areas, gives more attention to them through target oriented programmes and studies the impact of the programmes for its future guidelines.

Statistics and Planning

Modern age is an age of planning and statistics are indispensable for planning. According to Tippett planning greater or lesser degree according to the government in power is the order of the day and without statistics, planning is inconceivable. Based only on a correct assessment of various resources both human and material of the country proper planning can be made. A study of data relating to population, agriculture, industry, prices, employment, health, education enables the planners to fix up time-bound targets on the social and economic fronts evaluation of such economic and social programmes at different stages by means of related data gathered continuously and systematically is also done to decide whether the programmes are on towards the goal or targets set.

Statistics and Economics

In the fields of economics it is almost impossible to think of a problem which does not require an extensive use of statistical data. Most of the laws in economics are based on a study of a large number of units and their analysis is enabled by statistical data and the statistical methods.

The important economic aspects like production, consumption, exchange and distribution are described, compared and correlated with the aid of statistical tools. By a statistical study of time series on prices, sales, production one can study their trends, fluctuations and the underlaying causes. Thus statistics is indispensable in economic analysis.

THE RANGE OF A DISTRIBUTION

Most students are familiar with the grading scale in which "C" is assigned to average scores, "B" to above-average scores, and so forth. When grading exams "on a curve," instructors look to see how a particular score compares to the other scores. The letter grade given to an exam score is determined not by its relationship to just the high and low scores, but by its relative position among all the scores.

Percentile describes the relative location of points anywhere along the range of a distribution. A score that is at a certain percentile falls even with or above that percent of scores. The median score of a distribution is at the 50th percentile: It is the score at which 50% of other scores are below (or equal) and

50% are above. Commonly used percentile measures are named in terms of how they divide distributions. Quartiles divide scores into fourths, so that a score falling in the first quartile lies within the lowest 25% of scores, while a score in the fourth quartile is higher than at least 75% of the scores.

Quartile Finder

Find the quartile scores for the following distribution.

The divisions you have just performed illustrate quartile scores. Two other percentile scores commonly used to describe the dispersion in a distribution are decile and quintile scores which divide cases into equal sized subsets of tenths (10%) and fifths (20%), respectively. In theory, percentile scores divide a distribution into 100 equal sized groups. In practice this may not be possible because the number of cases may be under 100.

A box plot is an effective visual representation of both central tendency and dispersion. It simultaneously shows the 25th, 50th (median), and 75th percentile scores, along with the minimum and maximum scores. The "box" of the box plot shows the middle or "most typical" 50% of the values, while the "whiskers" of the box plot show the more extreme values. The length of the whiskers indicate visually how extreme the outliers are.

Below is the box plot for the distribution you just separated into quartiles. The boundaries of the box plot's "box" line up with the columns for the quartile scores on the histogram. The box plot displays the median score and shows the range of the distribution as well.

VARIANCE AND STANDARD DEVIATION

By far the most commonly used measures of dispersion in the social sciences are variance and standard deviation. Variance is the average squared difference of scores from the mean score of a distribution. Standard deviation is the square root of the variance.

In calculating the variance of data points, we square the difference between each point and the mean because if we summed the differences directly, the result would always be zero. For example, suppose three friends work on campus and earn \$5.50, \$7.50, and \$8 per hour, respectively. The mean of these values is \$(5.50 + 7.50 + 8)/3 = \$7 per hour. If we summed the differences of the mean from each wage, we would get (5.50-7) + (7.50-7) + (8-7) =-1.50 +.50 + 1 = 0. Instead, we square the terms to obtain a variance equal to 2.25 +.25 + 1 = 3.50. This figure is a measure of dispersion in the set of scores.

The variance is the minimum sum of squared differences of each score from *any* number. In other words, if we used any number other than the mean as the value from which each score is subtracted, the resulting sum of squared differences would be greater.

The standard deviation is simply the square root of the variance. In some sense, taking the square root of the variance "undoes" the squaring of the differences that we did when we calculated the variance.

Variance and standard deviation of a population are designated by and , respectively. Variance and standard deviation of a sample are designated by s^2 and s, respectively.

In these equations, is the population mean, is the sample mean, N is the total number of scores in the population, and n is the number of scores in the sample.

Computing Variance and Standard Deviation

This exercise shows you how to calculate variance and standard deviation for a data set. Click the button to calculate the variance and standard deviation, step by step, for the set of scores shown in the list. The mean of the scores has already been computed.

COMPARISONS OF MEASURES OF DISPERSION

When data are described by a measure of central tendency (mean, median, or mode), all the scores are summarized by a single value. Reports of central tendency are commonly supplemented and complemented by including a measure of dispersion. The measures of dispersion you have just seen differ in ways that will help determine which one is most useful in a particular situation.

Range. Of all the measures of dispersion, the range is the easiest to determine. It is commonly used as a preliminary indicator of dispersion. However, because it takes into account only the scores that lie at the two extremes, it is of limited use.

Quartile Scores are based on more information than the range and, unlike the range, are not affected by outliers. However, they are only infrequently used to describe dispersion because they are not as easy to calculate as the range and they do not have the mathematical properties that make them so useful as standard deviation and variance.

The standard deviation (or s) and variance (or s^2) are more complete measures of dispersion which take into account every score in a distribution.

The other measures of dispersion we have discussed are based on considerably less information. However, because variance relies on the squared differences of scores from the mean, a single outlier has greater impact on the size of the variance than does a single score near the mean. Some statisticians view this property as a shortcoming of variance as a measure of dispersion, especially when there is reason to doubt the reliability c some of the extreme scores.

For example, a researcher might believe that a person who reports watching television an average of 24 hours per day may have misunderstood the question. Just one such extreme score might result in an appreciably larger standard deviation, especially if the sample is small. Fortunately, since all scores are used in the calculation of variance, the many non-extreme scores (those closer to the mean) will tend to offset the misleading impact of any extreme scores.

The standard deviation and variance are the most commonly used measures of dispersion in the social sciences because:

- Both take into account the precise difference between each score and the mean. Consequently, these measures are based on a maximum amount of information.
- The standard deviation is the baseline for defining the concept of standardized score or "z-score".

- Variance in a set of scores on some dependent variable is a baseline for measuring the correlation between two or more variables (the degree to which they are related).

COMPARING MEASURES OF DISPERSION

Look at the distributions for the given variables. Compare the shapes of the distributions, their ranges and outliers, and answer the questions.

How Data Determines the Measures of Dispersion

Here is an activity that allows you to see how individual data points determine the different measures of dispersion. Click and drag to move points around, and notice when and how the measures change.

TESEARCHER AND PRACTITIONER PERSPECTIVES

In appointing the Task Force on Social Work Research in 1988, Lewis L. Judd, then director of the National Institute of Mental Health (NIMH), charged the group to analyse the state of research education, research resources, and research development in social work. Among its key findings, the Task Force on Social Work Research (1991) identified a significant lag in the contributions of practice-relevant research to the knowledge base of social work. The profession has since responded with an increased emphasis on building knowledge for services and policies. There is, for example, growing attention to developing models of social work practice that emphasize the importance of evidentiary knowledge bases and guidelines for applying knowledge in practice. Such models provide a framework for structuring the development and application of knowledge.

However, as Austin (1998) observed, the domain-specific nature of knowledge development and practice argues for a strategic approach to social work research that is based on fields of expertise, for example, child welfare, health, mental health, and gerontology. The author recommended that social work researchers critically assess the knowledge base, identify knowledge gaps, and establish research priorities to address those gaps in each of its substantive domains. Rosen and Proctor

(2003) echoed this call for a more systematic approach to knowledge development. They argued that to escape the profession's piecemeal approach, social work needed to formulate a clear, comprehensive, long-range agenda for intervention research.

Responding to the need for a methodical approach to developing social work knowledge, the John A. Hartford Foundation sponsored an effort to develop research priorities to help focus and organize social work research in the field of gerontology. Using a Delphi methodology, this project aimed to gain consensus from two national panels, one of academic researchers and one of expert practitioners, on research priorities for this field.

Delphi techniques provide a structured process to elicit and correlate expert panelists' informed opinions on a particular topic. Data are collected through the iterative administration of three or four questionnaires, interspersed with controlled feedback. The goal is to achieve consensus, typically on 10 to 15 top priority topics.

An earlier article detailed findings from the researcher panel. We summarize those findings and then present results from the practitioner panel with an eye to comparing the two panels.

ACADEMIC RESEARCHER PANEL

We began the two-phase Delphi project by identifying a panel of 46 gerontological social work academic researchers through the John A. Hartford Foundation's Geriatric SocialWork Faculty Scholars Program. We then designed and used a Web-based platform to collect three iterative waves of data via e-mail. The panel identified 49 research topics that reflect the range and diversity of gerontological social work and encompass core elements of the knowledge base for practice and policy in this field. Finally, we calculated priority and consensus scores for each of the 49 topics and then designated the 16 topics that achieved the highest priority and consensus ratings as topmost priorities. The researcher panel's highest-ranked priority, by a large margin, was developing and testing psychosocial interventions across specific populations and conditions. These 16 priority topics overlap and complement other national research agendas, including the National Institutes of Health Roadmap, the National Institute on Aging (NIA) Strategic Plan (2001-2005) (NIA, 2000), and the National Research Council (NRC) report on the NIH Committee on Future Directions for Behavioral and Social Science Research. Social work researchers are well positioned to make unique contributions to advancing these national agendas while addressing the profession's own knowledge needs.

For instance, social work expertise in individual, family, group, and community services to older adults and their families in a wide range of settings affords them a distinctive perspective on the knowledge needs and practice competencies required for grounded research. Likewise, social workers' expert knowledge about eligibility, availability, quality, and barriers to health and social services is key to intervention and services research. Social workers also bring a psychosocial perspective to interdisciplinary teams in medical, psychiatric, and long-term care settings, and they play an important role in formulation and analysis of public policy. Yet, the potential contributions of social workers to national and professional research agendas, including those focused on gerontology, are yet to be fully realized.

To incorporate this source of expertise, we conducted a second Delphi panel with expert practitioners. Earlier Delphi studies that aimed to establish priorities emphasized the need to represent the views of stakeholders, including researchers, practitioners, administrators, policymakers, grantmakers, educators, and consumers. Indeed, identifying topics that reflect common practitioner and academic priorities may help close the "bench to trench" gap that undermines the use of research by social work practitioners (NIMH, 1999).

METHOD

In concluding the researcher panel, we asked the panelists to nominate up to five expert gerontological social work practitioners who might participate in a replication of the process. To not unduly constrain or overly determine the range of expertise, we set limited nomination criteria. Participants could be either current or recent past practitioners and must have had at least five years of social work practice experience with older adults and demonstrated leadership in the field, for example, community involvement, conference presentations, elected positions, or various forms of publication. Researcher panelists nominated 93 practitioners: 72 agreed to participate and received the first questionnaire, and 52 completed round 1. Nonrespondents were contacted about three weeks after the survey was mailed, and most who declined participation reported lack of time as the reason.

Eighty-one percent of the 52 panelists were female. They were from 18 states (Mid-Atlantic = 14; Midwest = 25; Northwest = 3; Southeast = 3; West Coast = 7) and represented a range of social work settings and functions. Located in local and state public agencies and private profit and nonprofit organizations, they were practising in hospitals, health clinics, home health agencies, hospices, residential and nursing homes, senior centers, family services agencies, psychiatric services, Area Agencies on Aging, private counselling and case management services, Program of All Inclusive Care for the Elderly (PACE) work, and education and advocacy associations such as the Alzheimer's Association.

We collected three rounds of data, interspersed with controlled feedback. As several practitioners reported discomfort with Web-based questionnaires, we used postal mail. Strategies to maintain the panel included e-mail and phone reminders and second mailings at each round. Of the 72 practitioners who agreed to participate, 52 (72%) completed round 1. Of these 52 panelists, 42 (81%) completed round 2, and all 42 (100%) completed round 3.

Procedures

We used the same protocols and instruments developed and tested for the researcher panel with practitioners, with slight modifications for postal mailing. In round 1, panelists were asked to list up to five high-priority research topics; the

52 practitioners submitted a total of 253 topics. Next, two of the authors and two graduate social work students specializing in gerontology independently identified unique topics among the 253 submitted. The authors considered the four lists of topics developed by the independent coders, discussed and resolved inconsistencies, and distilled the list of 253 topics into 55 discrete topics. We erred in favor of more rather than fewer topics, and some overlap was inevitable. For example, to preserve the original topics submitted by panelists, two that are very similar but distinct—mental health: detection and treatment and depression assessment and treatment—are retained. In addition, to avoid altering topics put forth by practitioners, we attempted to retain the original level of abstraction. Thus, some topics are stated more broadly than others.

In round 2, we asked panelists to rate the importance of each of the 55 discrete topics, defined as "a topic's priority as an area in need of knowledge development for the field of aging." We also asked them to select and rank order the five topics they judged to be highest priority. We then calculated descriptive statistics on round 2 ratings. To further reduce the list of topics and move toward consensus, we eliminated 15 items with the lowest endorsement.

In round 3, panelists received the remaining list of 40 topics and descriptive statistics on the priority ratings derived from round 2. At this point, we also reorganized the presentation of topics to facilitate conceptual clarity by listing them under broader categories, such as mental health and social policy. We then asked panelists to again rate each topic and select and rank order five topics of highest priority. We also invited them to register and explain opinions that diverged from majority consensus at this final stage, although few did so.

This final round of data analysis aimed to derive priority and consensus scores for each topic. With respect to the one-to-five priority ratings, we used a procedure that treats nominal scale data as interval; that is, we grouped numeric priority ratings by dividing the sum of the scaled values by the number of ratings. We treated the value 2.5 as a neutral point, with boundaries distributed accordingly to avoid polarization of scores. As a result, mean priority ratings were grouped as highest (1.0-1.49), high (1.5-2.49), moderately high (2.5-3.49), moderately low (3.5-4.49), or low (4.5-5.0).

In the final analytic step, we calculated a consensus score for each topic using the quartile deviation. Consensus scores were calculated for each of the 40 topics in round 3 by determining the quartile range, subtracting the lower boundary of the range from the full value of the range, and then dividing the difference by 2 (Raskin, 1994). Consensus on a topic was deemed when all responses on the topic fell within the interquartile range, or between the 25th and 75th percentile estimates in the frequency distribution. Given the close clustering of scores with a deviation of less than one point on a five-point Likert scale, a quartile deviation less than 1.00 conventionally indicates group consensus. Examining the distribution of scores in this project, topics with a quartile deviation less than.60 were deemed high consensus, those equal to or more than.60 and less than 1.00, moderate consensus and those equal to or more than 1.00, low consensus. For example, the consensus score for "family interventions" was 0.5 (interquartile range 2.00-3.00), indicating that by the third and final round of data collection, panelists reached high consensus on their ratings of this topic.

Each topic was evaluated on two criteria to determine its priority: priority (highest, high, moderate, low, or lowest) and consensus (high, moderate, or low) ratings. These two criteria yielded a matrix of 15 possible combinations of endorsement levels for each topic.

FINDINGS

The 55 topics identified in round 1 and descriptive statistics for each topic generated from information collected in round 2. Mean priority ratings reflect the percentage of respondents endorsing the topic among their top five, and that this rating does not necessarily correspond with other assessments. For example, two of the highest rated topics, "determining best practices" and "gerontology education in social work," were also among respondents' top five priority topics. However, although the priority ranking for "living with disability and chronic conditions" was very high, only 11.9% of respondents selected this topic among their top five. Indeed, respondents could rate a topic important but not select it among the five most important. These two types of strategies for assessing the importance of research topics, both represented in the Delphi literature, yield valid but somewhat discordant findings.

Given our goal of producing a refined set of research priorities, we needed to further reduce the list of topics from round 3 of the practitioner panel, all of which attained a high or moderately high priority rating. Therefore, we chose only topics that achieved a high priority rating and then refined the list further by excluding topics that achieved only low consensus. This decision-making strategy yielded a final list of 16 topics.

To facilitate comparisons of the academic researcher and practitioner panels, we listed equivalent topics on the same line. The researcher panel's priority "developing and testing ethnic-sensitive assessment and interventions" is listed, for example, alongside the practitioner's topic on ethnic-sensitive interventions. In other instances, topics may not be identical but can be conceptualized under the same broad rubric. For example, although the practitioners' priority "outreach and service planning/delivery for underserved elders" lacks a precisely analogous priority on the researcher panel, it is subsumed under "Service Delivery" along with closely matched issues from the researcher panel. Finally, the practitioners identified several unique topics, categorized as social policy and capacity building.

There is considerable overlap in research priorities identified by the researcher and practitioner panels. Coincidentally, 16 topics from each panel achieved both highest or high priority and high or moderate consensus ratings. Nine topics (62%) were similar in content (or in the case of "outreach and service planning for underserved elders" classified in the same broad category). The researcher panel used broader conceptualizations that could easily accommodate the knowledge needs identified by practitioners. For example, researchers endorsed "developing and testing psychosocial and ecological interventions for cognitive and mental disorder," whereas practitioners endorsed "management of dementia." Likewise, we categorized "family interventions" on the practitioners' list with the researchers' topic "developing and testing psychosocial interventions across populations and conditions."

Others have described the pros and cons of Delphi techniques. Advantages include minimizing group pressure and equalizing opportunity for influence, two obvious pitfalls of group discussion. Also, panelists can be geographically distant from each other. Limitations, some of which are relevant to the present study, include the use of subjective judgments rather than objective data, lack of certainty about who qualifies as an expert, and less scientific rigor than other methods. Van Dijk (1990) argued that different techniques may yield different responses, and indeed, in the case of this study, a different group of practitioners could lead to different findings.

This study has several other limitations. First, the expert practitioners were referred to us by the academic researchers in our Delphi study on research priorities. It is difficult to know the extent to which the practitioners are representative, because they were not randomly selected. Furthermore, the practitioner and academic panels were not independent. The extent to which the participants from the two panels are colleagues and like-minded may render findings from the two panels more similar than if the panels had been independent. Finally, the expert practitioners from the Northeast and Midwest regions of the country were overrepresented, and the extent to which this uneven geographic dispersion affects the findings is not known.

Comparison of Panels

The overlapping topics represent consensus areas between gerontological social work researchers in academic settings and experts who are currently practising in the field. Consistent with the researcher panel, three practitioner topics relate to intervention research. Both groups endorse a need for more systematic development and testing of interventions. A recent review of social work research in gerontology published over the past five years revealed few effectiveness studies, further highlighting the gap between social work contributions in the practice arena and research contributions to practice. The panels' consensus on the need for intervention research also fits within a wider call by the NIMH (1999) and movement within the profession toward practice guidelines and evidence-based practice modalities.

The two panels also agreed about the need for research on workforce issues in an aging society. The researcher panel called for knowledge development in the recruitment and retention of professionals more generally; practitioners focused on social work. Indeed, practitioners identified gerontology social work education as the top research priority. This priority reflects a long-standing and increasingly urgent concern that the social work profession is not educating enough practitioners to meet the demands of rapidly changing demographics in our society. Practitioner panelists are also likely to experience the lack of trained colleagues more directly in their agencies and communities.

The practitioner panel suggests that this workforce crisis be addressed through research. Studies have explored related issues, including gerontological interest in professional organizations and student bodies, the social work labor market in aging-related jobs, and the number of schools that offer an aging specialization. Demonstration projects that assess training curriculums are also underway. These research efforts have heightened attention to gerontological social work education, and the profession is now benefiting from developmental efforts by several foundations.

However, demonstrable outcomes on the social work workforce are yet to be realized, and the practitioner panel suggests ongoing need to answer questions such as: What strategies are effective in recruiting and retaining social workers in gerontology? What course and fieldwork experiences and continuing education opportunities are most effective? What entry-level and advanced career opportunities exist? What reimbursement policies best support gerontological social work services? What practice boundaries between geriatric social work and other health care professions are firm and which are mutable ?

Both panels also ranked family caregiving as a top priority. Although most research published by gerontological social workers addresses family caregiving, neither panel suggested confidence that knowledge needs concerning caregiving are satisfied. This finding may reflect a gap between the production of knowledge on caregiving and its dissemination and use in the field; or it may signify a concern that research is not addressing practice-relevant questions. Both panels called for general intervention research on caregivers as well as studies targeted toward subgroups of caregivers, notably grandparent caregivers and caregivers for people with developmental disabilities.

In identifying mental health as a research priority, both panels echoed warnings of an impending crisis in geriatric mental health. Jeste and colleagues (1999) cautioned that the United States faces "an unprecedented explosion" of older adults with disabling mental disorders, with the number of elderly people with significant mental disorders expected to nearly quadruple between 1970 and 2030. The surgeon general has declared the health care needs of the elderly population a national priority, and an expert consensus group has recommended a 15-to 25-year plan for research on mental disorders of elderly people (Jeste et al., 1999).

Social workers practice with a disproportionate number of older adults with mental disorders in settings such as hospitals, home health agencies, day care centers,and nursing homes. They are also often the primary care providers for older adults whose living arrangements and family dynamics are strained by mental disorder. Social workers can certainly make important contributions to the development and implementation of knowledge on mental health and aging.

Both researchers and practitioners identified transitions in living arrangements as a high priority for knowledge development. This topic is particularly germane for the many social workers who practice at the intersections of community and residential care, acute and long-term care, and formal and informal care. Social workers play a key role in the admission and discharge of older adults from nursing homes, residential facilities, and day care centers and are responsible for discharge planning in hospitals and psychiatric facilities. They also help older people and their families obtain home care and initiate new routines. Indeed, social workers are proficient in managing the challenges of making the transition between and adjusting to different environments. Given that this transitional phase of care often shapes experience and outcomes in the service setting, research is needed to improve knowledge about this function.

There are also several notable differences between priorities identified by the two panels. The researchers endorsed the need for intervention research and for research on the service delivery system with greater specificity and breadth. Indeed, they identified four topics related to service delivery, whereas the practitioner panel identified only one related but distinct topic—"outreach and service planning/delivery for underserved populations." Perhaps academic researchers are more attuned to larger service delivery issues, such as access and integration, because of greater familiarity with a burgeoning multidisciplinary literature on these topics; whereas practitioners have a more immediate perspective geared toward identifying and meeting the service needs of older adults. Given that outreach, multidimensional assessment, and access and delivery of services to vulnerable elderly people is a hallmark of gerontological social work, social work researchers should lead efforts to formulate key research questions, design studies to address these questions, and disseminate practice-relevant findings to people in the service delivery system.

The practitioner panel endorsed seven unique topics. Two topics, income security and long-term care policy, are classified as social policy research. Gerontological social work researchers raise policy implications in their studies but have yet to assume a leadership role in documenting or analyzing the effects of policies. Perhaps social work researchers are not as well versed in policy research, or perhaps they view aging policy analysis as the responsibility of other disciplines. But, practitioners routinely experience the impact of policies on the daily lives of older adults and their families, and they more clearly express the need to advance policy research. Indeed, social workers should bring firsthand knowledge to the formulation and evaluation of social and health policy (Fahey, 1996). Researchers should respond to this challenge with rigorous investigations of all aspects of public policy and should bring this knowledge to public debates through timely and creative methods of dissemination.

The practitioner panel also identified three topics related to gerontological social work processes, which we categorized as capacity building: self-determination, decision making, and autonomy; empowerment strategies; and planning for later life with individuals and families. Academic researchers may not conceptualize these processes as standard research topics; yet, these topics are central to the daily work of practitioners and to the profession's code of ethics. The concept of capacity building in social work is under development. From this perspective, social workers enter into partnerships with individuals, families, and communities to increase their capacities to reach their goals. Capacity building principles include recognition of current and potential capabilities of clients; importance of articulating desired outcomes; development of client's knowledge, skills, and resources to pursue these outcomes; and creation of conditions that allow people to fulfill their capabilities. Clearly, the development of decision-making abilities and planning for future eventualities fit with these capacity-building principles.

The practitioner panel also endorsed quality of life in long-term care as a priority topic. It was surprising that the researchers did not endorse this topic as strongly: It was on their final list of high priority topics but did not achieve sufficient consensus. Practitioners identified normal and successful aging as a high-priority topic. Because a primary function of social work researchers is to formulate and investigate researchable questions on social problems, it is not surprising that they did not see normative processes of aging as a priority. Practitioners, on the other hand, may have more opportunities to interact with highly functioning older adults and, in community settings, to witness and participate in their decline over time. They also may sense that greater emphasis on productive aging would help dispel some of the myths, stereotypes, and stigma associated with the aging process.

Finally, we note a few general patterns in data from the two panels. First, the practitioners identified more topics than the researchers (235 original responses reduced to 55 topics compared with 181 reduced to 49 topics). The practitioners are likely to bring more diverse perspectives to a panel because they practice in a variety of settings, whereas all academic researchers were in university-based social work programs. Second, practitioners tended to assign higher, less variable ratings. In part, this may be because they regard their priorities as more urgent in their daily work. And researchers are also trained to be more sensitive to variation in measures.

CONCLUSION AND FUTURE DIRECTIONS

As in most stakeholder research, we conclude that researchers and practitioners express both convergent and divergent perspectives on knowledge needs for gerontological social work—and that both perspectives are valid. The next step in developing a unified research agenda is to combine both sets of priorities. We suggest that four broad substantive areas appear in both panels: housing and transitions in living arrangements; family caregiving; health and mental health; and workforce for an aging society. These are key areas for a social work research agenda and interdisciplinary agendas, such as those posed by the NIA and the NRC. Furthermore, there are four crosscutting themes that derive from the panels: intervention research, social policy, service delivery, and capacity building. Approaching the study of substantive areas with research questions that address these themes brings the unique perspective of social work to the forefront.

Many disciplines conduct research on housing and living arrangements, for example, but social workers bring unique expertise on interventions, policy, service delivery, and capacity building to this topic. They might implement psychosocial interventions to ease the transition to a new living arrangement or to enhance adjustment to a residential setting. Such interventions are not yet well developed, rigorously tested, or widely documented. However, social work researchers should lead efforts to develop knowledge on these aspects of housing and living arrangements. Social workers are also knowledgeable about how social policies shape access to different types of housing and living arrangements. They are familiar with the fragmentation that characterizes service delivery in housing complexes and naturally occurring retirement communities and with barriers to service use within a geographic area. Finally, social workers routinely engage older adults and families in capacity building as they seek to maximize autonomous decision-making and planning processes regarding living arrangements. Social workers bring specialized practice and policy experience and unique research perspectives to the substantive topic of housing and living arrangements.

A hypothetical grid that reflects the four core substantive topics and four crosscutting themes that capture the research priorities put forth by the two panels in this Delphi study could be used to further organize a research agenda for gerontological social work. A first step would be to review the current state of knowledge on topics in each of the 16 cells and summarize what is already known. Critical knowledge gaps could then be identified, and key research questions could be posed to guide our profession's research efforts. Such an endeavour would respond to Austin's (1998) call for a more systematic approach to social work research and his recommendation that each social work domain assess the state of its knowledge, identify critical knowledge gaps, and establish research needs and opportunities to fill those gaps. Identifying and addressing these gaps would, in turn, inform the development of a body of evidence-based knowledge and guidelines for gerontological social work practice.

8

Methods of Collecting Data

TECHNIQUES OF DATA COLLECTION

Social Survey

The basic procedure in survey is that people are asked a number of questions on that aspect of behavior which the sociologist is interested in. A number of people carefully selected so that their representation of their population being studied are asked to answer exactly the same question so that the replies to different categories of respondents may be examined for differences. One type of survey relies on contacting the respondents by letter and asking them to complete the questionnaire themselves before returning it. These are called Mail questionnaires. Sometimes questionnaires are not completed by individuals separately but by people in a group under the direct supervision of the research worker. A variation of the procedure can be that a trained interviewer asks the questions and records the responses on a schedule from each respondent.

These alternate procedures have different advantages and disadvantages. Mail questionnaires are relatively cheap and can be used to contact respondents who are scattered over a wide area. But at the same time the proportion of people who return questionnaires sent through post is usually rather small. The questions asked in main questionnaires have also to be very carefully worded in order to avoid ambiguity since the respondents cannot ask to have questions clarified for them.

Using groups to complete questionnaires means that the return rate is good and that information is assembled quickly and fairly. Administrating the interview schedules to the respondents individually is probably the most reliable method. Several trained interviewers may be employed to contact specific individuals. The questionnaires and schedules can consist of both close-ended and open-ended questions. Also a special attention needs to be paid to ensure that the questionnaires are filled in logical order.

Where aptitude questions are included great care must be exercised to ensure the proper words are used. In case of schedules emphasis and interactions may also be standardized between different individuals and from respondents to respondents. Finally proper sampling techniques must be used to ensure that the sample under study represents the universe of study. In order to enhance the reliability of data collected through questionnaires and schedules, these questionnaires and schedules must be pretested through pilot studies.

Interviewing

Social surveys may depend either on questionnaires that are self-administered or on schedules completed by trained research workers personally interviewing then is not a method of data collection distinct from social surveying but rather a technique which may vary from the brief formal contact as when the interviewer is working for the firms public opinion consultants or a market research organization and simply asks a housewife a few highly specific questions on limited range of topics to a long interview in which the research worker allows the respondents to develop points at leisure and take up others as he chooses.

The brief formal interview in which the working of the questions and the order in which they are asked is fixed is called structured interview while the freer discursive interview is called unstructured interview. The object of using structured interview is to standardize the interview as much as possible and thus to reduce the effect that the interviewer's personal approach or biases may have upon the result and even when structured interviews are used, proper training can do a lot to ensure further the reliability and validity of research. The personality of the interviewer and the social characteristics that the respondents attribute to him can be having influence on the result. The effort of interviewer's bias can be estimated by comparing one interviewer's result with other. The problem of interviewer's bias in an unstructured interview is much greater. Here the interviewer is left to his common devices as far as the way he approaches a respondent is concerned. There is no fixed list of questions to work through. Instead the interviewer may work from a guide that will remind him of the topics he wishes to cover.

The training of the interviewer is crucial here not simply training in the social skills of keeping the conversation going on a topic that the respondent may not be very interested in but also in acquiring sensitivity to those things his respondents tells him which are specially relevant to the theoretical topics he is pursuing. This means that unstructured interviews can be carried out by people trained in sociological theory. They are then able to size upon stray comments made by the respondents which can be developed and lead on to important theoretical insight.

Observation: Participant and non participant

The rationale behind the use of observation in sociological research is that the sociologist should become party to a set of social actions sufficiently able to be able to assess directly the social relationship involved. The degree of involvement may vary considerable from being merely a watcher on the sidelines to be deeply involved in and being a part of what is going on. The former type of observation techniques are called non-participant while the latter is called participant observation. Sometimes one way observations screen have been used to watch groups in actions that they are unaware that they are being watched and the observer cannot affect their actions by his presence. The sociologist is visibly present and is a part of the situation either as a sociologist or in another guise. Where the sociologist is merely an observer it is usually assumed that he knows enough about what the actors are doing to be able to understand their behaviour. Any sociological observer has then to some extent be a participant observer he must at least share sufficient cultural background with the actors to be able to construe their behavior meaningfully but the degree of participation and of sharing of meaning may vary considerably. Examples of such studies are Nel Anderson's study of Hobo-Indians and William White study of Street Corner Society.

Sampling

For practical and cost reasons, it is often impossible to collect information about the entire population of people or things in which social researchers are interested. In these cases, a sample of the total is selected for study. Most statistical studies are based on samples and not on complete enumerations of all the relevant data. The main criteria when sampling are to ensure that a sample provides a faithful representation of the totality from which it is selected, and to know as precisely as possible the probability that a sample is reliable in this way. Randomization meets these criteria, because it protects against bias in the selection process and also provides a basis on which to apply statistical distribution theory that allows an estimate to be made of the probability that conclusions drawn from the sample are correct. A statistical sample is a miniature picture or cross-section of the entire group or aggregate from which the sample is taken. The entire group from which a sample is chosen is known as the population, universe or supply.

SIMPLE RANDOM SAMPLING

The basic type of random sample is known as a simple random sample, one in which each person or item has an equal chance of being chosen. Often a population contains various distinct groups or strata that differ on the attribute that is being researched.

Stratified Random Sampling

Stratified random sampling involves sampling of each stratum separately. This increases precision, or reduces time, effort and cost of allowing smaller sample sizes for a given level of precision. For example, poverty is known to be most common among the elderly, the unemployed and single parent families, so research on the effect of poverty might will sample separately each of these three strata as part of a survey of poverty in the population as a whole which would permit the total sample size to be reduced because the investigator would know that the groups most affected by poverty were guaranteed inclusion.

Cluster Sampling

Cluster sampling is sometimes used when the population naturally congregates into clusters. For example, managers are clustered in organizations, so a sample of managers could be obtained by taking a random sample of organizations and investigating the managers in each of these. Interviewing or observing managers on this basis would be cheaper and easier than using a simple random sample of managers scattered across all organizations in the country. This is usually less precise than a simple random sample of the same size, but in practice the reduction in cost per element more than compensated for the decrease in precision.

Multi-stage Sampling

Sampling may be done as one process or in stages, known as multi-stage sampling. Multi-stage designs are common when populations are widely dispersed. Thus a survey of business managers might proceed by selecting a sample of corporations as first stage units, perhaps choosing these corporations with a probability proportionate to their size, and then selecting a sample of managers within these corporations at the second stage. Alternatively, a sample of individual factories or office buildings within each corporation could be chosen as the second stage units, followed by sample of managers in each of these as a third stage. Stratification can also be used in the design, if for example occupational sub-groups are known to differ from each other, by selecting state such as personnel, production, and finance management and sampling within each of these. For sampling to be representative, one needs a complete and accurate list of the first stage units that make up the relevant population, a basic requirement that is not always easily met. This forms the sampling frame. Selection from the frame is best done by numbering the items and using a table of random numbers to identify which items form the sample, though a quasi-random method of simply taking every item from the list is often appropriate. The reliability of a sample taken from a population can be assessed by the spread of the sampling distribution, measured by the standard deviation of this distribution, called the standard error. As a general rule, the larger is the size of the sample the smaller the standard error.

Area Sampling

In sampling of this kind small areas are designated as sampling units and the households interviewed include all or a specified fraction of those found in a canvass of these designated small areas. The basic sampling units or segments chosen may be relatively large or relatively small depending on such factors as the type of area being studied, population distribution, the availability of suitable maps and other information and the nature and desired accuracy of the data being collected.

ANALYZING COMPLEX SURVEY DATA

Increasingly, social work researchers are performing secondary analyses using data from large-scale surveys such as the National Health Interview Survey (NHIS) (National Center for Health Statistics, 1997), the National Education Longitudinal Study of 1988 (NELS:88), and the Longitudinal Study of Aging (LSOA). Generally, these surveys use complex probability sampling procedures such as stratification, multiple stages of selection, and oversampling to obtain a representative sample of the target population. Because of these sampling procedures, analyzing these data with traditional statistical software, such as SPSS or SAS, which use ordinary and generalized least squares estimation techniques, results in the underestimation of the standard error, inappropriate confidence intervals, and misleading tests of significance. Also, these statistical software packages assume a simple random sampling (Silbersiepe & Hardy) and do not control for features of the sampling design that affect observed outcomes (La Vange et al.). Given these aspects of traditional statistical software packages, they are considered inappropriate for analyzing complex survey data.

Analyzing complex survey data requires specialized software. SUDAAN and PC Carp are the most widely used packages Other software used are WesVarPC and Stata. Many social work researchers, however, are not using these specialized programs to analyse complex survey data. One reason may be that social work researchers may be unaware of the need to use such programs.

This article uses data from the 1994 AIDS Knowledge and Attitudes Supplement to the National Health Interview Survey (NHIS) to illustrate that biased point estimates, inappropriate standard errors, and misleading tests of significance can result from using traditional software packages for complex survey analysis. We also illustrate how results are affected by assuming a simple random sample (with and without the option of weighting), by using the sampling weights without controlling for complex survey design effect, by and controlling for complex survey design effects and using national estimate weights.

METHODOLOGICAL ISSUES

When analyzing data from complex surveys, researchers need to account for the sampling design use the sampling weights and the appropriate statistical software.

Accounting for the Sampling Design

Because the complex probability procedures used in large-scale surveys to obtain a representative sample of the target population do not result in a simple random sample, the consequences of these procedures on statistical inferences must be taken into account. To control for design effects, researchers need to alter the variance estimates by considering issues such as stratification, clustering, other proponents of nonindependence of observations, and oversampling or undersampling of subgroups of the population.

The simple definition of a design effect is the ratio of the estimated population variance taking the complex design features into account over the estimated population variance based on the same sample and assuming a simple random sample.

A design effect of one indicates that the variance estimate is the same regardless of the controls for the complex survey design. When the design effect is greater than one, the standard error (SE) calculated controlling for the complex survey design is larger than the SE calculated assuming a simple random sample. Therefore, the confidence interval around the point estimate is larger. This indicates that it is possible that P values based on the assumption of a simple random sample will indicate rejection of the null hypothesis erroneously (Type I error). When the design effect is less than one, the SE calculated controlling for the complex survey design is smaller than the SE calculated assuming a simple random sample. Therefore, the confidence interval around the point estimate is smaller. This indicates that it is possible that P values based on the assumption of a simple random sample will indicate acceptance of the null hypothesis erroneously (Type II error).

PRIMARY DATA AND INTEGRATIVE METHODS

HTA embraces a diverse group of methods that can be grouped into two broad categories. Primary data methods involve collection of original data, ranging from more scientifically rigorous approaches such as randomized controlled trials to less rigorous ones such as case studies. Integrative methods (also known as "secondary" or "synthesis" methods) involve combining data or information from existing sources, including from primary data studies. These can range from quantitative, structured approaches such as meta-analyses or systematic literature reviews to informal, unstructured literature reviews. Cost analysis methods, which can involve one or both of primary data methods and integrative methods, are discussed separately a following section.

Most HTA programs use integrative approaches, with particular attention to formulating findings that are based on distinguishing between stronger and weaker evidence drawn from available primary data studies. Some HTA programs do collect primary data, or are part of larger organizations that collect primary data. It is not always possible to conduct, or base an assessment on, the most rigorous types of studies. Indeed, policies often must be made in the absence, or before completion, of definitive studies. There is no standard methodological approach for conducting HTA. Given their varying assessment orientations, resource constraints and other factors, assessment programs tend to rely on different combinations of methods. Even so, the general trend in HTA is to call for and emphasize the more rigorous methods.

TYPES OF METHODOLOGICAL VALIDITY

Validity refers to whether what we are measuring is what we intend to measure. Methodological designs vary in their ability to produce valid findings. Understanding different aspects of validity helps in comparing alternative methodological designs and interpreting the results of studies using those designs. Although these concepts are usually addressed in reference to primary data methods, they apply as well to integrative methods.

Internal validity refers to the extent to which the findings of a study accurately represent the causal relationship between an intervention and an outcome in the particular circumstances of an investigation. This includes the extent to which a study minimizes any systematic or non-random error in the data.

External validity refers to the extent to which the findings obtained from an investigation conducted under particular circumstances can be generalized to other circumstances. To the extent that the circumstances of a particular investigation (e.g., patient characteristics or the manner of delivering a treatment) differ from the circumstances of interest, the external validity of the findings of that investigation may be questioned.

Face validity is the ability of a measure to represent reasonably a construct (i.e., a concept or domain of interest) as judged by someone with expertise in the health problem and interventions of interest. *Content validity* refers to the degree to which a measure covers that range of meanings or dimensions of a construct. As noted above, an outcome measure is often used as a marker or surrogate for a disease of interest. For example, how well do changes in prostate specific antigen (PSA) levels represent or predict the risk of prostate cancer? How well does performance on an exercise treadmill represent cardiovascular fitness?

Construct validity is the ability of a measure to correlate with other accepted measures of the construct of interest, and to discriminate between groups known to differ according to the variable. *Convergent validity* refers to the extent to which two different measures that are intended to measure the same construct do indeed yield similar results. *Discriminant validity,* opposite convergent validity, concerns whether different measures that are intended to measure different constructs do indeed fail to be positively associated with each other. *Concurrent validity* refers to the ability of a measure to accurately differentiate between different groups at the time the measure is applied, or the correlation of one measure with another at the same point in time. *Predictive validity* refers to the ability to use differences in a measure to predict future events or outcomes.

Primary Data Methods

The considerable and diverse array of primary data methods includes, e.g., true experiments such as randomized controlled trials (RCTs) and other controlled trials; other prospective but uncontrolled trials; observational studies such as case-control, cross-sectional studies, and surveillance studies; and simpler designs such as case series and single case reports or anecdotes. These methods can be described and categorized in terms of multiple attributes or dimensions, such as whether they are prospective or retrospective, interventional or observational, controlled or uncontrolled, and other attributes noted below. Some of these methods have alternative names, and many studies employ nearly limitless combinations of these attributes.

Some Fundamental Attributes

Prospective studies are planned and implemented by investigators using real-time data collection. These typically involve identification of one or more patient groups, collection of baseline data, delivering one or more interventions, collecting follow-up data, and comparing baseline to follow-up data for the patient groups. In retrospective studies, investigators collect samples of data from past events (interventions and outcomes) involving one or more patient groups. In an interventional study, investigators prospectively deliver, manipulate, or manage the intervention(s) of interest. In an observational study investigators only monitor or follow an intervention or exposure (e.g., of a risk factor) of interest, but do not themselves intervene in the delivery the intervention or exposure.

Many studies use separate control groups of patients as a basis of comparison to the one or more groups receiving an intervention of interest. Some studies do not use control groups; these uncontrolled studies rely on comparing patient measures before and after an intervention to determine whether the intervention had an effect. Control groups of patients are constituted in ways to ensure as much similarity as possible to patients in intervention groups. Except for the intervention of interest, the treatment and management of control groups and intervention groups are as similar as possible. By comparing changes in intervention groups to changes in control groups, investigators seek to isolate the effect of an intervention on patient outcomes from any effects on patient outcomes from extraneous factors. While most controlled studies used contemporaneous controls alongside (i.e., identified and followed at the same time as) intervention groups, investigators sometimes use historical control groups. In a crossover design study, patients start in one group (intervention or control) and then are switched to the other, thereby acting as their own controls.

Various means are used to ensure that intervention and control groups comprise patients with similar characteristics, so that "baseline" (initial) differences in these groups will not affect (confound) the relative changes in patient outcomes between the groups. Although such means as alternate assignment or using birthdays or identification numbers are used to assign patients to intervention and control groups, assignment based on randomization is preferred because it minimizes opportunities for bias to affect the composition of these groups at baseline. Knowledge of assignment of patients to one group or another, e.g., to a group receiving a new intervention or a group receiving standard care, can itself affect outcomes as experienced by patients and/or assessed by investigators. Therefore, some studies employ blinding of patients, and sometimes of investigators and data analysts, to knowledge of patient assignment to intervention and control groups in an effort to eliminate the confounding effects of such knowledge.

Alternative Methods Offer Tradeoffs in Validity

Although primary study investigators and assessors would prefer to have methods that are both internally and externally valid, they often find that study design attributes that increase one type of validity jeopardize the other. A well designed and conducted RCT is widely considered to be the best approach for ensuring internal validity, as it gives investigators the most control over factors that could confound the causal relationship between the a technology and health outcomes. However, for the reasons that a good RCT has high internal validity, its external validity may be limited.

Most RCTs are designed to investigate the effects of an intervention in specific types of patients so that the relationship between the intervention and outcomes is less likely to be confounded by patient variations. However, findings from an RCT involving a narrowly defined patient group may not be applicable for the same intervention given to other types of patients. Patients allowed to enroll in RCTs are often subject to strict inclusion and exclusion criteria pertaining, e.g., to age, risk factors, and previous and current treatments. This is done for various reasons, including to avoid confounding the treatment effect of the intervention in question by previous or current other treatments, and to limit the extent to which variations in patients' response to a treatment might dilute the treatment effect across the enrolled patient population. As a result, the patient population in an RCT may be less likely to be representative of the desired or potential target population in practice. As noted above, RCTs often involve special protocols of care and testing that may not be characteristic of general care, and are often conducted in university medical centers or other special settings that may not represent the general or routine settings in which most health care is provided.

Findings of some large observational studies (e.g., from large cross-sectional studies or registries) have external validity to the extent that they can provide insights into the types of outcomes that are experienced by different patient groups in different circumstances. However, these less rigorous designs are more subject to certain forms of bias that threaten internal validity, diminishing the certainty with which particular outcomes can be attributed to an intervention. Interesting or promising findings from weaker studies can raise hypotheses that can be tested using stronger studies. The use of "large, simple trials" (discussed below) is an attempt to combine the strengths of RCTs and observational studies.

RCTs Not Best Design for All Questions

While RCTs are the "gold standard" of internal validity for causal relationships, they are not necessarily the best method for answering all questions of relevance to an HTA. As noted by Eisenberg (1999):

"Those who conduct technology assessments should be as innovative in their evaluations as the technologies themselves.... The randomized trial is unlikely to be replaced, but it should be complemented by other designs that address questions about technology from different perspectives."

Other types of studies may be preferred to RCTs for different questions. For example, a good way to describe the prognosis for a given disease or condition may be a set of follow-up studies of patient cohorts at uniform points in the clinical course of a disease. Case control studies are often used to identify risk factors for diseases, disorders, and adverse events. The accuracy of a diagnostic test (as opposed to its ultimate effect on health outcomes) may be determined by a cross-sectional study of patients suspected of having a disease or disorder. Non-randomized trials or case series may be preferred for determining the effectiveness of interventions for otherwise fatal conditions, i.e., where little or nothing is to be gained by comparison to placebos or known ineffective treatments. Surveillance and registries are used to determine the incidence of rare, serious adverse events that may be associated with an interventions. For incrementally modified technologies posing no known additional risk, registries may be appropriate for determining safety and effectiveness.

Collecting New Primary Data

It is beyond the scope of this document to describe the planning, design, and conduct of clinical trials, observational studies, and other investigations for collecting new primary data. There is a considerable and evolving literature on these subjects. Also, there is a literature on priority setting and efficient resource allocation for clinical trials, and cost-effective design of clinical trials.

As noted above, compiling evidence for an assessment may entail collection of new primary data. An assessment program may determine that existing evidence is insufficient for meeting the desired policy needs, and that new studies are needed to generate data for particular aspects of the assessment. Once available, the new data can be interpreted and incorporated into the existing body of evidence.

In the US, major units of the NIH such as the National Cancer Institute and the National Heart, Lung and Blood Institute sponsor and conduct biomedical research, including clinical trials. Elsewhere at NIH, the Office of Medical Applications of Research coordinates the NIH Consensus Development Program, but does not collect primary clinical data, although it occasionally surveys physician specialists and other groups for which the NIH assessment reports are targeted. The Veterans Health Administration (VHA) Cooperative Studies Program is responsible for the planning and conduct of large multicenter clinical trials within the VHA, including approximately 60 cooperative studies at any one time. The FDA does not typically conduct primary studies related to the marketing of new drugs and devices; rather, the FDA reviews primary data from studies sponsored or conducted by the companies that make these technologies. The ability of most assessment programs to undertake new primary data collection, particularly clinical trials, is limited by such factors as programs' financial constraints, time constraints, responsibilities that do not include conducting or sponsoring clinical studies, and other aspects of the roles or missions of the programs. An HTA program may decide not to undertake and assessment if insufficient data are available. Whether or not an assessment involves collection of new primary data, the assessment reports should note what new primary studies should be undertaken to address gaps in the current body of evidence, or to meet anticipated assessment needs.

Health professional organizations and societies, e.g., the American College of Physicians and American College of Cardiology, work almost exclusively from existing data and do not do clinical research. Third-party payers generally do not sponsor clinical studies, but increasingly analyse claims data and other administrative data. Payers have supported trials of new technologies indirectly by paying for care associated with clinical studies of those technologies, or by paying unintentionally for uncovered new procedures that were coded as covered procedures. As noted above, some payers are providing conditional coverage for certain investigational technologies in selected settings in order to compile data that can be used to make more informed coverage decisions. One recent, controversial example, is the multicenter RCT of lung-volume reduction surgery, the National Emphysema Treatment Trial (NETT), funded by the NHLBI and the Centers for Medicare and Medicaid Services (CMS, which administers the US Medicare program).

PRIMARY DATA COLLECTION TRENDS RELEVANT TO HTA

Primary data collection methods have evolved in certain important ways that affect the body of evidence used in HTA. Among these, investigators have made progress in trying to combine some of the desirable attributes of RCTs and observational studies. For example, while retaining the methodological strengths of prospective, randomized design, "large, simple trials" use large numbers of patients, more flexible patient entry criteria and multiple study sites to improve external validity and gain effectiveness data. Also, fewer types of data may be collected for each patient, easing participation by patients and clinicians. Examples of these approaches include large, simple trials supported by NIH; certain large, multicenter RCTs coordinated by the VA Cooperative Studies Program, and "firm trials" involving random assignment of patients and providers to alternative teams to evaluate organizational and administrative interventions (Cebul 1991).

Clinical trials conducted for the purposes of advancing biomedical research or for achieving market clearance by regulatory bodies approval do not necessarily address clinical choices or policy decisions (e.g., coverage policies). The call for "pragmatic" or "practical" clinical trials (PCTs) is intended to meet these needs more directly. Among their main attributes, PCTs (1) select clinically relevant alternative interventions to compare, (2) include a diverse population of study participants, (3) recruit participants from heterogeneous practice settings, and (4) collect data on a broad range of health outcomes. PCTs will require that clinical and health policy decision makers become more involved in priority setting, research design, funding, and other aspects of clinical research (Tunis 2003).

Biomedical research organizations such as NIH and regulatory agencies such as FDA permit certain mid-trial changes in clinical trial protocols such as drug dosage modifications and patient cross-overs to alternative treatment groups to reflect the most recent scientific findings. Selected use of surrogate endpoints, especially biological markers, is employed where these are known to be highly correlated with "hard endpoints" such as morbidity and mortality that may not occur until months or years later. For example, a long-standing surrogate marker for stroke risk is hypertension, although understanding continues to evolve of the respective and joint roles of systolic and diastolic pressures in predicting stroke (Basile 2002). Trials of new drugs for HIV/AIDS use such biological markers as virological (e.g., plasma HIV RNA) and immunological (e.g., CD4+ cell counts) levels (Lalezari 2003).

Streamlining or combining clinical trial phases and "parallel track" availability of technologies to patients outside of ongoing formal RCTs are intended to speed regulatory approval and make technologies available to patients who are ineligible for RCT protocols but have exhausted other treatments. For example, the FDA provides several types of access to investigational treatments. "Emergency use" is allowed in situations where there is a need for an investigational technology in a manner that is not consistent with the approved investigational protocol or by a physician who is not part of the clinical trial, and may occur before FDA approval of the investigational plan (e.g., IND for drugs or IDE for devices). "Compassionate" use allows access for patients who do not meet the requirements for inclusion in an ongoing clinical trial but for whom the treating physician believes the technology may provide a benefit; this usually applies to patients with a serious disease or condition for whom there is no viable alternative treatment.

"Treatment use" refers to instances where data collected during a trial indicates that a technology is effective, so that during the trial or prior to full FDA review and approval for marketing, the technology may be provided to patients not in the trial, subject to the other requirements of the trial (e.g., under an IND for drugs or IDE for devices). "Continued access" allows continued enrollment of patients after the trial has been completed, in order to enable access to the investigational technology while the marketing application is being prepared by the sponsor or reviewed by the FDA. Although many of these adaptations were originally instituted for RCTs involving new drug treatments for HIV/AIDS, cancer, and other life-threatening conditions (Merigan 1990), their use in trials of treatments for other conditions is increasing.

Another important type of development in primary data collection is the incorporation of contemporaneous cost data collection in prospective clinical trials. Health care product companies increasingly are using such data in product promotion and to help secure favourable payment decisions. The generation of health and economic data are increasingly influenced by technical guidance for data submissions provided by national and regional HTA agencies, particularly in Canada, Europe, and Australia.

Integrative Methods

Having considered the merits of individual studies, an assessment group must begin to integrate, synthesize, or consolidate the available findings. For many topics in HTA, there is no single definitive primary study, e.g., that settles whether one technology is better than another for a particular clinical situation. Even where definitive primary studies exist, findings from different types of studies must be combined or considered in broader social and economic contexts in order to formulate policies.

Methods used to combine or integrate data include the following:

- Meta-analysis
- Modeling (e.g., decision trees, Markov models)
- Group judgment ("consensus development")
- Systematic literature review
- Unstructured literature review
- Expert opinion

The biases inherent in traditional means of consolidating literature (i.e., non-quantitative or unstructured literature reviews and editorials) are well recognized, and greater emphasis is given to more structured, quantified and better documented methods. The body of knowledge concerning how to strengthen and apply these integrative methods has grown substantially in recent years. Considerable work has been done to improve the validity of decision analysis and meta-analysis in particular. Experience with the NIH Consensus Development Program, the panels on appropriateness of selected medical and surgical procedures conducted by the RAND Corporation, the clinical practice guidelines activities sponsored until the mid-1990s by the former AHCPR (renamed as AHRQ), and others continues to add to the body of knowledge concerning group judgment processes.

Three major types of integrative methods—meta-analysis, decision analysis, and consensus development—are described below.

Meta-analysis

Meta-analysis refers to a group of statistical techniques for combining results of multiple studies to obtain a quantitative estimate of the overall effect of a particular technology (or variable) on a defined outcome. This combination may produce a stronger conclusion than can be provided by any individual study. The purposes of meta-analysis are to:

- Encourage systematic organization of evidence
- Increase statistical power for primary end points
- Increase general applicability (external validity) of findings
- Resolve uncertainty when reports disagree
- Assess the amount of variability among studies
- Provide quantitative estimates of effects (e.g., odds ratios or effect sizes)
- Identify study characteristics associated with particularly effective treatments
- Call attention to strengths and weaknesses of a body of research in a particular area
- Identify needs for new primary data collection.

Meta-analysis typically is used for topics that have no definitive studies, including topics for which non-definitive studies are in some disagreement. Evidence collected for assessments often includes studies with insufficient statistical power (e.g., because of small sample sizes) to detect any true treatment effects. By combining the results of multiple studies, a meta-analysis may have sufficient power to detect a true treatment effect if one exists, or at least narrow the confidence interval about the mean treatment effect.

Although meta-analysis has been applied primarily for treatments, meta-analytic techniques are being extended to diagnostic technologies. As in other applications of meta-analysis, the usefulness of these techniques for diagnostic test accuracy is subject to publication bias and the quality of primary studies of diagnostic test accuracy. Although meta-analysis is often applied to RCTs, it may be used for observational studies as well.

The basic steps in meta-analysis are the following:

1. Specify the problem of interest.
2. Specify the criteria for inclusion of studies (e.g., type and quality).
3. Identify all studies that meet inclusion criteria.
4. Classify study characteristics and findings according to, e.g.: study characteristics (patient types, practice setting, etc.), methodological characteristics (e.g., sample sizes, measurement process), primary results and type of derived summary statistics.
5. Statistically combine study findings using common units (e.g., by averaging effect sizes); relate these to study characteristics; perform sensitivity analysis.
6. Present results.

Some of the particular techniques used in the statistical combination of study findings in meta-analysis are: pooling, effect size, variance weighting, Mantel-Haenszel, Peto, DerSimonian and Laird, and confidence profile method. The suitability of any of these techniques for a group of studies depends upon the comparability of circumstances of investigation, type of outcome variables used, assumptions about the uniformity of treatment effects and other factors.

The different techniques of meta-analysis have specific rules about whether or not to include certain types of studies and how to combine their results.

Some meta-analytic techniques adjust the results of the individual studies to try to account for differences in study design and related biases to their internal and external validity. Special computational tools (e.g., computer software) may be required to make the appropriate adjustments for the various types of biases in a systematic way.

Meta-analysis can be limited by poor quality of data in primary studies, publication bias, biased selection of available studies, insufficiently comparable studies selected (or available) for a meta-analysis, and biased interpretation of findings. The quality of RCTs used in meta-analyses can bias results. The results of meta-analyses that are based on sets of RCTs with lower methodological quality tend to show greater treatment effects (i.e., greater efficacy of interventions) than those based on sets of RCTs of higher methodological quality (Moher 1998). However, it is not apparent that any individual quality measures are associated with the magnitude of treatment effects in meta-analyses of RCTs (Balk 2002). As is the case for RCTs, there are instruments for assessing the quality of meta-analyses and systematic reviews (Moher 1999).

The shortcomings of meta-analyses, which are shared by unstructured literature reviews and other less rigorous synthesis methods, can be minimized by maintaining a systematic approach to meta-analysis. Performing meta-analyses in the context of systematic reviews, i.e., that have objective means of searching the literature and applying predetermined inclusion and exclusion criteria to the primary studies used, can diminish the impact of these shortcomings on the findings of meta-analyses (Egger 2001). Compared to the less rigorous methods of combining evidence, meta-analysis can be time-consuming and requires greater statistical and methodologic skills. However, meta-analysis is a much more explicit and accurate method.

Even though many assessments still tend to rely on overall subjective judgments and similar less rigorous approaches of integrating evidence, there is a clear trend toward learning about and using more meta-analytic approaches. An assessment group that uses the inclusion/exclusion rules and other stipulations of meta-analysis is likely to conduct a more thorough and credible assessment, even if the group decides not to perform the final statistical consolidation of the results of pertinent studies.

More advanced meta-analytic techniques are being applied to assessing health technologies, e.g., involving multivariate treatment effects, meta-regression, and Bayesian methods. As meta-analysis and other structured literature syntheses are used more widely in evaluating health care interventions, methodological standards for conducting and reporting meta-analyses are rising.

Modeling

Quantitative modeling is used to evaluate the clinical and economic effects of health care interventions. Models are used to answer "What if?" questions. That is, they are used to represent (or simulate) health care processes or decisions and their impacts under conditions of uncertainty, such as in the absence of actual data or when it is not possible to collect data on all potential conditions, decisions, and outcomes. For example, decision analytic modeling is used to represent the sequence of clinical decisions and its health and economic impacts. Economic modeling can be used to estimate the cost-effectiveness of alternative technologies for a given health problem.

By making informed adjustments or projections of existing primary data, modeling can help account for patient conditions, treatment effects, and costs that are not present in primary data. This may include bridging efficacy findings to estimates of effectiveness, and projecting future costs and outcomes.

Among the main types of techniques used in quantitative modeling are decision analysis (described below), Markov model process, Monte Carlo simulation, survival and hazard functions, and fuzzy logic (Tom 1997). A Markov model (or chain) is a way to represent and quantify changes from one state of health to another. A Monte Carlo simulation uses sampling from random number sequences to assign estimates to parameters with multiple possible values, e.g., certain patient characteristics.

Decision analysis uses available quantitative estimates to represent (model or simulate) the sequences of alternative strategies (e.g., of diagnosis and/or treatment) in terms of the probabilities that certain events and outcomes will occur and the values of the outcomes that would result from each strategy. Decision models often are shown in the form of "decision trees" with branching steps and outcomes with their associated probabilities and values. Various software programs may be used in designing and conducting decision analyses, accounting for differing complexity of the strategies, extent of sensitivity analysis, and other quantitative factors.

Decision models can be used in different ways. They can be used to predict the distribution of outcomes for patient populations and associated costs of care. They can be used as a tool to support development of clinical practice guidelines for specific health problems. For individual patients, decision models can be used to relate the likelihood of potential outcomes of alternative clinical strategies, and/or to identify the clinical strategy that has the greatest utility for a patient. Decision models are also used to set priorities for HTA (Sassi 2003).

The basic steps of decision analysis are:

1. Develop a model (e.g., a decision tree) that depicts the set of important choices (or decisions) and potential outcomes of these choices. For treatment choices, the outcomes may be health outcomes (health states); for diagnostic choices, the outcomes may be test results (e.g., positive or negative).
2. Assign estimates (based on available literature) of the probabilities (or magnitudes) of each potential outcome given its antecedent choices.
3. Assign estimates of the value of each outcome to reflect its utility or desirability (e.g., using a HRQL measure or QALYs).
4. Calculate the expected value of the outcomes associated with the particular choice(s) leading to those outcomes. This is typically done by multiplying the set of outcome probabilities by the value of each outcome.
5. Identify the choice(s) associated with the greatest expected value. Based on the assumptions of the decision model, this is the most desirable choice, as it provides the highest expected value given the probability and value of its outcomes.
6. Conduct a sensitivity analysis of the model to determine if plausible variations in the estimates of probabilities

of outcomes or utilities change the relative desirability of the choices.

A limitation of modeling with decision trees is representing recurrent health states (e.g., recurrent complications or stages of a chronic disease). An alternative approach is to use state-transition models that use probabilities of moving from one state of health to another, including remaining in a given state or returning to it after intervening health states. Markov modeling is a commonly used type of state-transition modeling.

The assumptions and estimates of variables used in models should be validated against actual data as it becomes available, and the models should be modified accordingly. Modeling should incorporate sensitivity analyses to quantify the conditional relationships between model inputs and outputs.

Models and their results are only aids to decision-making, not statements of scientific, clinical, or economic fact. The report of any modeling study should carefully explain and document the assumptions, data sources, techniques, and software. Modelers should make clear that the findings of a model are conditional upon these components. The use of decision modeling in cost-effectiveness analysis in particular has advanced in recent years, with development of checklists and standards for these applications.

CONSENSUS DEVELOPMENT

In various forms, group judgment or consensus development is used to set standards, make regulatory recommendations/ decisions, make payment recommendations/policies, make technology acquisition decisions, formulate practice guidelines, define the state-of-the-art, and other purposes. "Consensus development" can refer to discrete group processes or techniques that contribute to an assessment, such as the nominal group technique or Delphi method; it also can refer to particular consensus development approaches (e.g., the consensus development conferences conducted by the NIH).

In contrast to the quantitative synthesis methods of meta-analysis and decision analysis, consensus development is generally qualitative in nature. It may be unstructured and informal, or it may involve formal group methods such as the nominal group technique and Delphi technique. Although these processes typically involve face-to-face interaction, someconsensus development efforts combine remote, iterative interaction of panelists (as in the formal Delphi technique) with face-to-face meetings. Computer conferencing and related telecommunications approaches also are used. There is a modest but growing body of literature on consensus development methods in HTA. For example, one review examined the factors affecting the findings of these processes, including selection of topics and questions, selection of participants, choosing and preparing the scientific evidence, structuring the interaction among participants, and methods for synthesizing individual judgments. Findings and associated support regarding methods of synthesizing individual judgments into consensus are summarize.

Virtually all HTA efforts involve consensus development at some juncture, particularly to formulate findings and recommendations. Consensus development also can be used for ranking, such as to set assessment priorities, and rating. For example, RAND has used a two-stage modified Delphi process (first stage, independent; second stage, panel meeting) in which expert panels rate the appropriateness of a procedure (e.g., tympanostomy tubes for children) for each of many possible patient indications on a scale of 1.0 (extremely inappropriate) to 9.0 (extremely appropriate) (Kleinman 1994).

The opinion of an expert committee concerning, e.g., the effectiveness of a particular intervention, does not in itself constitute strong evidence. Where the results of pertinent, rigorous scientific studies exist, these should take precedence. In the absence of strong evidence, and where practical guidance is needed, expert group opinion can be used to infer or extrapolate from the limited available evidence. Where many assessment efforts are deficient is not making clear where the evidence stops and where the expert group opinion begins.

Consensus development programs typically embrace most of the steps of HTA described here. In these programs, the consensus development conference usually spans at least three of the HTA steps: interpret evidence, integrate evidence, and formulate findings and recommendations. Increasingly, consensus development efforts start with presentations of previously compiled evidence reports.

Many current consensus development programs in the US and around the world are derived from the model of consensus development conference originated at the US NIH in 1977 as part of an effort to improve the translation of NIH biomedical research findings to clinical practice. NIH has modified and experimented with its process over the years. As of late 2003, NIH had held 120 consensus development conferences. (NIH also has conducted about 25 state-of-the-science conferences, using a similar format to its consensus development conferences.) Australia, Canada, Denmark, France, Israel, Japan, The Netherlands, Spain, Sweden and the UK are among the countries that use various forms of consensus development programs to evaluate health technologies. Consensus conferences also are held jointly by pairs of countries and by international health organizations. Although they originally may have been modeled after the US program, these programs have evolved to meet the needs of their respective national environments and sponsoring organizations (McGlynn 1990).

The variety in consensus development programs can be described and compared along several main types of characteristics, as follows.

- Context of the process: e.g., intended audience, topics and impacts addressed, topic selection
- Pre-panel preparation: e.g., responsibility for planning, evidence preparation, prior drafting of questions and/or recommendations
- Panel composition: e.g., panel size, selection, types of expertise/representation, characteristics of chairperson
- Consensus conference attributes: e.g., length of conference, public involvement, private panel sessions, definition of consensus, decision-making procedures (such as voting), process for handling disagreement, format and dissemination of final product.

Among most programs, preparation for conferences takes approximately one year. Some programs prepare assessment questions and draft a consensus statement prior to the consensus conference; other programs do not. Most programs assemble compilations of evidence and share this in advance some form with the panelists; in some instances, this involves providing systematic literature reviews with specific review instructions to panelists weeks in advance of the conference. Programs usually provide for speakers to present the evidence during the consensus conference. Most programs select panels of 9-18 members, including clinicians, scientists and analysts, and lay people, with varying attention to balancing panels for members' known positions on the assessment issues. In most instances, the conference is held over a two-to-three day period, although others have multiple meetings over longer periods of time. Programs generally provide for part or all of the conference to be held in a public forum. Some programs also conduct evaluations of their programs on such matters as impact of conference findings and panelist satisfaction with the process.

In general, the advantages of consensus development processes are that they:

- Provide a focus for assembling experts on an assessment topic
- Provide a means for participation of lay people
- Are relatively inexpensive and less time-consuming compared to new primary data collection
- Provide a good way to call public attention to HTA
- Increase exposure of participants and the public to relevant evidence
- Can prompt face-to-face, evidence-based resolution of opposing viewpoints
- Can apply expert judgment in areas where data are insufficient or inconclusive

In general, the disadvantages of consensus development processes are that they:

- Do not generate new scientific evidence

- May appear to offer veracity to viewpoints that are not supported by evidence
- May over-emphasize or inhibit viewpoints depending upon the stature or personalities of the participants
- May be structured to force or give the appearance of group agreement when it does not exist
- Are difficult to validate.

Consensus development programs are not immune to the economic, political, and social forces that often serve as barriers or threats to evidence-based processes. Organizations that sponsor consensus development conferences may do so because they have certain expectations for the findings of these processes, and may find themselves at odds with evidence-based findings. Other stakeholders, including from industry, biomedical research institutions, health professions, patient groups, and politicians seeking to align themselves with certain groups, may seek to pressure consensus development panelists or even denounce a panel's findings in order to render desired results, the evidence notwithstanding.

An infamous instance of such political reaction occurred in connection with the NIH Consensus Development Conference on Breast Cancer Screening for Women Ages 40 to 49, sponsored by the National Cancer Institute in 1997.

QUESTIONNAIRE DESIGN

No survey can achieve success without a well-designed questionnaire. Unfortunately, questionnaire design has no theoretical base to guide the marketing researcher in developing a flawless questionnaire. All the researcher has to guide him/her is a lengthy list of do's and don'ts born out of the experience of other researchers past and present. Hence, questionnaire design is more of an art than a science.

Structure of the Chapter

A brief account of the key attributes of a sound questionnaire serves as the opening section of the chapter. This is followed by a nine-point framework for developing an effective questionnaire. These are the only two components of this chapter on questionnaire design.

The Qualities of a Good Questionnaire

The design of a questionnaire will depend on whether the researcher wishes to collect exploratory information (i.e. qualitative information for the purposes of better understanding or the generation of hypotheses on a subject) or quantitative information (to test specific hypotheses that have previously been generated). Exploratory questionnaires: If the data to be collected is qualitative or is not to be statistically evaluated, it may be that no formal questionnaire is needed. For example, in interviewing the female head of the household to find out how decisions are made within the family when purchasing breakfast foodstuffs, a formal questionnaire may restrict the discussion and prevent a full exploration of the woman's views and processes. Instead one might prepare a brief guide, listing perhaps ten major open-ended questions, with appropriate probes/prompts listed under each.

Formal standardised questionnaires: If the researcher is looking to test and quantify hypotheses and the data is to be analysed statistically, a formal standardised questionnaire is designed. Such questionnaires are generally characterised by:

- prescribed wording and order of questions, to ensure that each respondent receives the same stimuli
- prescribed definitions or explanations for each question, to ensure interviewers handle questions consistently and can answer respondents' requests for clarification if they occur
- prescribed response format, to enable rapid completion of the questionnaire during the interviewing process.

Given the same task and the same hypotheses, six different people will probably come up with six different questionnaires that differ widely in their choice of questions, line of questioning, use of open-ended questions and length. There are no hard-and-fast rules about how to design a questionnaire, but there are a number of points that can be borne in mind:

1. A well-designed questionnaire should meet the research objectives. This may seem obvious, but many research surveys omit important aspects due to inadequate preparatory work, and do not adequately probe particular issues due to poor understanding. To a certain degree some of this is inevitable. Every survey is bound to leave some questions unanswered and provide a need for further research but the objective of good questionnaire design is to 'minimise' these problems.
2. It should obtain the most complete and accurate information possible. The questionnaire designer needs to ensure that respondents fully understand the questions and are not likely to refuse to answer, lie to the interviewer or try to conceal their attitudes. A good questionnaire is organised and worded to encourage respondents to provide accurate, unbiased and complete information.
3. A well-designed questionnaire should make it easy for respondents to give the necessary information and for the interviewer to record the answer, and it should be arranged so that sound analysis and interpretation are possible.
4. It would keep the interview brief and to the point and be so arranged that the respondent(s) remain interested throughout the interview.

Each of these points will be further discussed throughout the following sections. The questionnaire design fits into the overall process of research design that was described in chapter 1 of this textbook. It emphasises that writing of the questionnaire proper should not begin before an exploratory research phase has been completed.

Even after the exploratory phase, two key steps remain to be completed before the task of designing the questionnaire should commence. The first of these is to articulate the questions that research is intended to address. The second step is to determine the hypotheses around which the questionnaire is to be designed.

It is possible for the piloting exercise to be used to make necessary adjustments to administrative aspects of the study. This would include, for example, an assessment of the length of time an interview actually takes, in comparison to the planned length of the interview; or, in the same way, the time needed to complete questionnaires. Moreover, checks can be made on the appropriateness of the timing of the study in relation to contemporary events such as avoiding farm visits during busy harvesting periods.

Preliminary Decisions in Questionnaire Design

There are nine steps involved in the development of a questionnaire:

1. Decide the information required.
2. Define the target respondents.
3. Choose the method(s) of reaching your target respondents.
4. Decide on question content.
5. Develop the question wording.
6. Put questions into a meaningful order and format.
7. Check the length of the questionnaire.
8. Pre-test the questionnaire.
9. Develop the final survey form.

Deciding on the Information Required

It should be noted that one does not start by writing questions. The first step is to decide 'what are the things one needs to know from the respondent in order to meet the survey's objectives?'

One may already have an idea about the kind of information to be collected, but additional help can be obtained from secondary data, previous rapid rural appraisals and exploratory research. In respect of secondary data, the researcher should be aware of what work has been done on the same or similar problems in the past, what factors have not yet been examined, and how the present survey questionnaire can build on what has already been discovered. Further, a small number of preliminary informal interviews with target respondents will give a glimpse of reality that may help clarify ideas about what information is required.

Define the Target Respondents

At the outset, the researcher must define the population about which he/she wishes to generalise from the sample data to be collected. For example, in marketing research, researchers often have to decide whether they should cover only existing users of the generic product type or whether to also include non-users. Secondly, researchers have to draw up a sampling frame. Thirdly, in designing the questionnaire we must take into account factors such as the age, education, etc. of the target respondents.

Choose the Method(s) of Reaching Target Respondents

It may seem strange to be suggesting that the method of reaching the intended respondents should constitute part of the questionnaire design process. However, a moment's reflection is sufficient to conclude that the method of contact will influence not only the questions the researcher is able to ask but the phrasing of those questions. The main methods available in survey research are:

- personal interviews
- group or focus interviews
- mailed questionnaires
- telephone interviews.

Within this region the first two mentioned are used much more extensively than the second pair. However, each has its advantages and disadvantages. A general rule is that the more sensitive or personal the information, the more personal the form of data collection should be.

Decide on Question Content

Researchers must always be prepared to ask, "Is this question really needed?" The temptation to include questions without critically evaluating their contribution towards the achievement of the research objectives, as they are specified in the research proposal, is surprisingly strong. No question should be included unless the data it gives rise to is directly of use in testing one or more of the hypotheses established during the research design.

There are only two occasions when seemingly "redundant" questions might be included:

- Opening questions that are easy to answer and which are not perceived as being "threatening", and/or are perceived as being interesting, can greatly assist in gaining the respondent's involvement in the survey and help to establish a rapport.
- This, however, should not be an approach that should be overly used. It is almost always the case that questions which are of use in testing hypotheses can also serve the same functions.
- "Dummy" questions can disguise the purpose of the survey and/or the sponsorship of a study. For example, if a manufacturer wanted to find out whether its distributors were giving the consumers or end-users of its products a reasonable level of service, the researcher would want to disguise the fact that the distributors' service level was being investigated. If he/she did not, then rumours would abound that there was something wrong with the distributor.

9

Application of Statistical Tools and Techniques in Social Work Research

MAINTENANCE OF RECORD IN SOCIAL WORK RESEARCH

Record is a storing of data either in written form or in video. It may be written in form or not but has used as prove/ evidence of any incidents.

Definition: Chamber Dictionary defines record as "act of setting down in writing or other permanent form, a formal writing of any fact or proceeding, a book of such writing."

Objective:

- To improve the professional skills & techniques of workers
- To evaluate the work of the agency & to improve upon methods & techniques used therein
- To create satisfaction & keep up the interest of the workers
- To build a body of knowledge of social work administration
- To facilitate supervision & training
- To show the progress of the agency to the board, community, public authorities etc.

- To ensure continuing of work & keep a note thereof
- To do work on a systematic basis

Types of Records:

1. Organizational Records
2. Programme Records
3. Administrative Records
4. Procedural Records
5. Financial Records
6. General Records.

1. Organizational Records:
   - Registration Certificate
   - Copy of the constitution, Bye-laws of the agency
   - Agenda Papers
   - Minute books/register
   - Returns to field with the registrar of society
   - Register of board members with their address
   - Resolutions for formulation of the committees, sub-committees & record of their work.
2. Programme Records:
   - Blue print of the agency's plan of work of the scheme
   - Case histories in case work process
   - Survey report of the community
   - Diary of field work
   - Attendance register for programme staff
   - Register of volunteers
   - Visitor's book.
3. Administrative Records:
   - Personal files of staff members
   - Attendance register
   - Leave record

- Telephone calls register
- Building plan file, sanctioned plan
- File for each branch.

4. Procedural records:
   - Diary
   - Dispatch Register
   - Register of files
   - Reminder register
   - Recording register.
5. Financial Register:
   - Budget File
   - Case book
   - Receipt & bill Books
   - Voucher file
   - Salary register
   - Stock register
   - Property register.
6. General Records:
   - Annual Report
   - File containing material for the annual report
   - For the next year
   - List of address of agency's contacts.

MEASUREMENT

Measurement is the process observing and recording the observations that are collected as part of a research effort. There are two major issues that will be considered here.

Second, you have to understand the different types of measures that you might use in social research. We consider four broad categories of measurements. Survey research includes the design and implementation of interviews and questionnaires. Scaling involves consideration of the major methods of developing and implementing a scale. Qualitative research provides an overview of the broad range of non-numerical measurement approaches. And unobtrusive measures presents a variety of measurement methods that don't intrude on or interfere with the context of the research.

MEASUREMENT VALIDITY TYPES

There's an awful lot of confusion in the methodological literature that stems from the wide variety of labels that are used to describe the validity of measures. I want to make two cases here.

First, it's dumb to limit our scope only to the validity of measures. We really want to talk about the validity of any operationalization. That is, any time you translate a concept or construct into a functioning and operating reality (the operationalization), you need to be concerned about how well you did the translation. This issue is as relevant when we are talking about treatments or programs as it is when we are talking about measures. (In fact, come to think of it, we could also think of sampling in this way. The population of interest in your study is the "construct" and the sample is your operationalization.

If we think of it this way, we are essentially talking about the construct validity of the sampling!). Second, I want to use the term construct validity to refer to the general case of translating any construct into an operationalization. Let's use all of the other validity terms to reflect different ways you can demonstrate different aspects of construct validity.

Face Validity

In face validity, you look at the operationalization and see whether "on its face" it seems like a good translation of the construct. This is probably the weakest way to try to demonstrate construct validity. For instance, you might look at a measure of math ability, read through the questions, and decide that yep, it seems like this is a good measure of math ability (i.e., the label "math ability" seems appropriate for this measure). Or, you might observe a teenage pregnancy prevention program and conclude that, "Yep, this is indeed a teenage pregnancy prevention program." Of course, if this is all you do to assess face validity, it would clearly be weak evidence because it is essentially a subjective judgment call. (Note that just because it is weak evidence doesn't mean that it is wrong. We need to rely on our subjective judgment throughout the research process. It's just that this form of judgment won't be very convincing to others.) We can improve the quality of face validity assessment considerably by making it more systematic. For instance, if you are trying to assess the face validity of a math ability measure, it would be more convincing if you sent the test to a carefully selected sample of experts on math ability testing and they all reported back with the judgment that your measure appears to be a good measure of math ability.

Content Validity

In content validity, you essentially check the operationalization against the relevant content domain for the construct. This approach assumes that you have a good detailed description of the content domain, something that's not always true. For instance, we might lay out all of the criteria that should be met in a program that claims to be a "teenage pregnancy prevention program." We would probably include in this domain specification the definition of the target group, criteria for deciding whether the program is preventive in nature (as opposed to treatment-oriented), and lots of criteria that spell out the content that should be included like basic information on pregnancy, the use of abstinence, birth control methods, and so on. Then, armed with these criteria, we could use them as a type of checklist when examining our program. Only programs that meet the criteria can legitimately be defined as "teenage pregnancy prevention programs." This all sounds fairly straightforward, and for many operationalizations it will be. But for other constructs (e.g., self-esteem, intelligence), it will not be easy to decide on the criteria that constitute the content domain.

Criterion-Related Validity

In criteria-related validity, you check the performance of

your operationalization against some criterion. How is this different from content validity? In content validity, the criteria are the construct definition itself — it is a direct comparison. In criterion-related validity, we usually make a prediction about how the operationalization will *perform* based on our theory of the construct. The differences among the different criterion-related validity types is in the criteria they use as the standard for judgment.

Predictive Validity

In predictive validity, we assess the operationalization's *ability to predict something it should theoretically be able to predict*. For instance, we might theorize that a measure of math ability should be able to predict how well a person will do in an engineering-based profession. We could give our measure to experienced engineers and see if there is a high correlation between scores on the measure and their salaries as engineers. A high correlation would provide evidence for predictive validity — it would show that our measure can correctly predict something that we theoretically think it should be able to predict.

Concurrent Validity

In concurrent validity, we assess the operationalization's *ability to distinguish between groups that it should theoretically be able to distinguish between*. For example, if we come up with a way of assessing manic-depression, our measure should be able to distinguish between people who are diagnosed manic-depression and those diagnosed paranoid schizophrenic. If we want to assess the concurrent validity of a new measure of empowerment, we might give the measure to both migrant farm workers and to the farm owners, theorizing that our measure should show that the farm owners are higher in empowerment. As in any discriminating test, the results are more powerful if you are able to show that you can discriminate between two groups that are very similar.

Convergent Validity

In convergent validity, we examine the degree to which the

operationalization is similar to (converges on) other operationalizations that it theoretically should be similar to. For instance, to show the convergent validity of a Head Start program, we might gather evidence that shows that the program is similar to other Head Start programs. Or, to show the convergent validity of a test of arithmetic skills, we might correlate the scores on our test with scores on other tests that purport to measure basic math ability, where high correlations would be evidence of convergent validity.

Discriminant Validity

In discriminant validity, we examine the degree to which the operationalization is not similar to (diverges from) other operationalizations that it theoretically should be not be similar to. For instance, to show the discriminant validity of a Head Start program, we might gather evidence that shows that the program is *not* similar to other early childhood programs that don't label themselves as Head Start programs. Or, to show the discriminant validity of a test of arithmetic skills, we might correlate the scores on our test with scores on tests that of verbal ability, where *low* correlations would be evidence of discriminant validity.

IDEA OF CONSTRUCT VALIDITY

Construct validity refers to the degree to which inferences can legitimately be made from the operationalizations in your study to the theoretical constructs on which those operationalizations were based. I find that it helps me to divide the issues into two broad territories that I call the "land of theory" and the "land of observation." The land of theory is what goes on inside your mind, and your attempt to explain or articulate this to others.

It is all of the ideas, theories, hunches and hypotheses that you have about the world. In the land of theory you will find your idea of the program or treatment as it should be. You will find the idea or construct of the outcomes or measures that you believe you are trying to affect. The land of observation consists of what you see happening in the world around you and the public manifestations of that world. In the land of observation you will find your actual program or treatment, and your actual measures or observational procedures. Presumably, you have constructed the land of observation based on your theories. You developed the program to reflect the kind of program you had in mind. You created the measures to get at what you wanted to get at.

Construct validity is an assessment of how well you translated your ideas or theories into actual programs or measures. Why is this important? Because when you think about the world or talk about it with others (land of theory) you are using words that represent concepts. If you tell someone that a special type of math tutoring will help their child do better in math, you are communicating at the level of concepts or constructs.

You aren't describing in operational detail the specific things that the tutor will do with their child. You aren't describing the specific questions that will be on the math test that their child will do better on. You are talking in general terms, using constructs. If you based your recommendation on research that showed that the special type of tutoring improved children' math scores, you would want to be sure that the type of tutoring you are referring to is the same as what that study implemented and that the type of outcome you're saying should occur was the type they measured in their study. Otherwise, you would be mislabeling or misrepresenting the research. In this sense, construct validity can be viewed as a "truth in labeling" kind of issue.

There really are two broad ways of looking at the idea of construct validity. I'll call the first the "definitionalist" perspective because it essentially holds that the way to assure construct validity is to define the construct so precisely that you can operationalize it in a straightforward manner. In a definitionalist view, you have either operationalized the construct correctly or you haven't — it's an either/or type of thinking. Either this program is a "Type A Tutoring Program" or it isn't. Either you're measuring self esteem or you aren't.

The other perspective I'd call "relationalist." To a relationalist, things are not either/or or black-and-white —

concepts are more or less related to each other. The meaning of terms or constructs differs relatively, not absolutely. The program in your study might be a "Type A Tutoring Program" in some ways, while in others it is not. It might be more that type of program than another program. Your measure might be capturing a lot of the construct of self esteem, but it may not capture all of it. There may be another measure that is closer to the construct of self esteem than yours is. Relationalism suggests that meaning changes gradually. It rejects the idea that we can rely on operational definitions as the basis for construct definition.

To get a clearer idea of this distinction, you might think about how the law approaches the construct of "truth." Most of you have heard the standard oath that a witness in a U.S. court is expected to swear. They are to tell "*the truth, the whole truth and nothing but the truth.*" What does this mean? If we only had them swear to tell the truth, they might choose to interpret that as "make sure that what you say is true." But that wouldn't guarantee that they would tell everything they knew to be true.

They might leave some important things out. They would still be telling the truth. They just wouldn't be telling everything. On the other hand, they are asked to tell "nothing but the truth." This suggests that we can say simply that Statement X is true and Statement Y is not true.

Now, let's see how this oath translates into a measurement and construct validity context. For instance, we might want our measure to reflect "*the construct, the whole construct, and nothing but the construct.*" What does this mean? Let's assume that we have five distinct concepts that are all conceptually related to each other — self esteem, self worth, self disclosure, self confidence, and openness.

Most people would say that these concepts are similar, although they can be distinguished from each other. If we were trying to develop a measure of self esteem, what would it mean to measure "*self esteem, all of self esteem, and nothing but self esteem?*" If the concept of self esteem overlaps with the others, how could we possibly measure all of it (that would presumably include the part that overlaps with others) *and* nothing but it? We couldn't! If you believe that meaning is relational in nature — that some concepts are "closer" in meaning than others — then the legal model discussed here does not work well as a model for construct validity.

In fact, we will see that most social research methodologists have (whether they've thought about it or not!) rejected the definitionalist perspective in favor of a relationalist one. In order to establish construct validity you have to meet the following conditions:

- You have to set the construct you want to operationalize (e.g., self esteem) within a semantic net (or "net of meaning"). This means that you have to tell us what your construct is more or less similar to in meaning.
- You need to be able to provide direct evidence that you control the operationalization of the construct — that your operationalizations look like what they should theoretically look like. If you are trying to measure self esteem, you have to be able to explain why you operationalized the questions the way you did. If all of your questions are addition problems, how can you argue that your measure reflects self esteem and not adding ability?
- You have to provide evidence that your data support your theoretical view of the relations among constructs. If you believe that self esteem is closer in meaning to self worth than it is to anxiety, you should be able to show that measures of self esteem are more highly correlated with measures of self worth than with ones of anxiety.

CONVERGENT & DISCRIMINANT VALIDITY

Convergent and discriminant validity are both considered subcategories or subtypes of construct validity. The important thing to recognize is that they work together — if you can demonstrate that you have evidence for both convergent and discriminant validity, then you've by definition demonstrated that you have evidence for construct validity. But, neither one alone is sufficient for establishing construct validity. To estimate the degree to which any two measures are related to each other we typically use the correlation coefficient. That is, we look at the patterns of intercorrelations among our measures. Correlations between theoretically similar measures should be "high" while correlations between theoretically dissimilar measures should be "low".

The main problem that I have with this convergent-discrimination idea has to do with my use of the quotations around the terms "high" and "low" in the sentence above. The question is simple — how "high" do correlations need to be to provide evidence for convergence and how "low" do they need to be to provide evidence for discrimination?

And the answer is — we don't know! In general we want convergent correlations to be as high as possible and discriminant ones to be as low as possible, but there is no hard and fast rule. Well, let's not let that stop us. One thing that we *can* say is that the convergent correlations should always be *higher* than the discriminant ones. At least that helps a bit. Before we get too deep into the idea of convergence and discrimination, let's take a look at each one using a simple example.

Convergent Validity

Notice, however, that while the high intercorrelations demonstrate the four items are probably related to the *same* construct, that doesn't automatically mean that the construct is *self esteem*. Maybe there's some other construct that all four items are related to (more about this later). But, at the very least, we can assume from the pattern of correlations that the four items are converging on the same thing, whatever we might call it.

THREATS TO CONSTRUCT VALIDITY

Before we launch into a discussion of the most common threats to construct validity, let's recall what a threat to validity is. In a research study you are likely to reach a conclusion that your program was a good operationalization of what you wanted and that your measures reflected what you wanted them to reflect. Would you be correct? How will you be criticized if you make these types of claims? How might you strengthen your claims. The kinds of questions and issues your critics will raise are what I mean by threats to construct validity.

Inadequate Preoperational Explication of Constructs

This one isn't nearly as ponderous as it sounds. Here, preoperational means *before translating constructs into measures or treatments*, and explication means *explanation* — in other words, you didn't do a good enough job of *defining* (operationally) what you mean by the construct. How is this a threat? Imagine that your program consisted of a new type of approach to rehabilitation. Your critic comes along and claims that, in fact, your program is neither *new* nor a true *rehabilitation* program. You are being accused of doing a poor job of thinking through your constructs. Some possible solutions:

- think through your concepts better
- use methods (e.g., concept mapping) to articulate your concepts
- get experts to critique your operationalizations.

Mono-Operation Bias

Mono-operation bias pertains to the independent variable, cause, program or treatment in your study — it does not pertain to measures or outcomes. If you only use a single version of a program in a single place at a single point in time, you may not be capturing the full breadth of the concept of the program. Every operationalization is flawed relative to the construct on which it is based. If you conclude that your program reflects the construct of the program, your critics are likely to argue that the results of your study only reflect the peculiar version of the program that you implemented, and not the actual construct you had in mind. Solution: try to implement multiple versions of your program.

Mono-Method Bias

Mono-method bias refers to your measures or observations,

not to your programs or causes. Otherwise, it's essentially the same issue as mono-operation bias. With only a single version of a self esteem measure, you can't provide much evidence that you're really measuring self esteem. Your critics will suggest that you aren't measuring self esteem — that you're only measuring part of it, for instance. Solution: try to implement multiple measures of key constructs and try to demonstrate (perhaps through a pilot or side study) that the measures you use behave as you theoretically expect them to.

Interaction of Different Treatments

You give a new program designed to encourage high-risk teenage girls to go to school and not become pregnant. The results of your study show that the girls in your treatment group have higher school attendance and lower birth rates. You're feeling pretty good about your program until your critics point out that the targeted at-risk treatment group in your study is also likely to be involved simultaneously in several other programs designed to have similar effects. Can you really label the program effect as a consequence of your program? The "real" program that the girls received may actually be the *combination* of the separate programs they participated in.

Interaction of Testing and Treatment

Does testing or measurement itself make the groups more sensitive or receptive to the treatment? If it does, then the testing is in effect a part of the treatment, it's inseparable from the effect of the treatment. This is a labeling issue (and, hence, a concern of construct validity) because you want to use the label "program" to refer to the program alone, but in fact it includes the testing.

Restricted Generalizability Across Constructs

This is what I like to refer to as the "unintended consequences" treat to construct validity. You do a study and conclude that Treatment X is effective. In fact, Treatment X does cause a reduction in symptoms, but what you failed to anticipate was the drastic negative consequences of the side effects of the treatment. When you say that Treatment X is effective, you have defined "effective" as only the directly targeted symptom. This threat reminds us that we have to be careful about whether our observed effects (Treatment X is effective) would generalize to other potential outcomes.

Confounding Constructs and Levels of Constructs

Imagine a study to test the effect of a new drug treatment for cancer. A fixed dose of the drug is given to a randomly assigned treatment group and a placebo to the other group. No treatment effects are detected.

Perhaps the result that's observed is only true for that dosage level. Slight increases or decreases of the dosage may radically change the results. In this context, it is not "fair" for you to use the label for the drug as a description for your treatment because you only looked at a narrow range of dose. Like the other construct validity threats, this is essentially a labeling issue — your label is not a good description for what you implemented.

Hypothesis Guessing

Most people don't just participate passively in a research project. They are trying to figure out what the study is about. They are "guessing" at what the real purpose of the study is. And, they are likely to base their behavior on what they guess, not just on your treatment.

In an educational study conducted in a classroom, students might guess that the key dependent variable has to do with class participation levels. If they increase their participation not because of your program but because they think that's what you're studying, then you cannot label the outcome as an effect of the program. It is this labeling issue that makes this a construct validity threat.

Evaluation Apprehension

Many people are anxious about being evaluated. Some are even phobic about testing and measurement situations. If their apprehension makes them perform poorly (and not your program conditions) then you certainly can't label that as a treatment effect. Another form of evaluation apprehension concerns the human tendency to want to "look good" or "look smart" and so on. If, in their desire to look good, participants perform better (and not as a result of your program!) then you would be wrong to label this as a treatment effect. In both cases, the apprehension becomes confounded with the treatment itself and you have to be careful about how you label the outcomes.

Experimenter Expectancies

These days, where we engage in lots of non-laboratory applied social research, we generally don't use the term "experimenter" to describe the person in charge of the research. So, let's relabel this threat "researcher expectancies." The researcher can bias the results of a study in countless ways, both consciously or unconsciously. Sometimes the researcher can communicate what the desired outcome for a study might be (and participant desire to "look good" leads them to react that way). For instance, the researcher might look pleased when participants give a desired answer. If this is what causes the response, it would be wrong to label the response as a treatment effect.

THE NOMOLOGICAL NETWORK

The nomological network is an idea that was developed by Lee Cronbach and Paul Meehl in 1955. Construct validity in psychological tests, *Psychological Bulletin*, 52, 4, 281-302.) as part of the American Psychological Association's efforts to develop standards for psychological testing. The term "nomological" is derived from Greek and means "lawful", so the nomological network can be thought of as the "lawful network." The nomological network was Cronbach and Meehl's view of construct validity.

That is, in order to provide evidence that your measure has construct validity, Cronbach and Meehl argued that you had to develop a nomological network for your measure. This network would include the theoretical framework for what you are trying to measure, an empirical framework for how you are going to measure it, and specification of the linkages among and between these two frameworks.

The nomological network is founded on a number of principles that guide the researcher when trying to establish construct validity. They are:

- Scientifically, to make clear what something is or means, so that laws can be set forth in which that something occurs.
- The laws in a nomological network may relate:
  - o observable properties or quantities to each other
  - o different theoretical constructs to each other
  - o theoretical constructs to observables
- At least some of the laws in the network must involve observables.
- "Learning more about" a theoretical construct is a matter of elaborating the nomological network in which it occurs or of increasing the definiteness of its components.
- The basic rule for adding a new construct or relation to a theory is that it must generate laws (nomologicals) confirmed by observation or reduce the number of nomologicals required to predict some observables.
- Operations which are qualitatively different "overlap" or "measure the same thing" if their positions in the nomological net tie them to the same construct variable.

What Cronbach and Meehl were trying to do is to link the conceptual/theoretical realm with the observable one, because this is the central concern of construct validity. While the nomological network idea may work as a philosophical foundation for construct validity, it does not provide a practical and usable methodology for actually assessing construct validity. The next phase in the evolution of the idea of construct validity — the development of the multitrait-multimethod matrix — moved us a bit further toward a methodological approach to construct validity.

THE DIFFERENCE BETWEEN AN ARITHMETIC MEAN AND A GEOMETRIC MEAN

Understanding the difference between an arithmetic mean

and a geometric mean might sound like something that can be left to statisticians. But now, because of a change proposed in the Budget, it has become crucially important to the great majority of current and prospective pensioners. The difference means that they are all going to be worse off in their retirement.

The change is the Government's proposal to adopt the CPI rather than the RPI for the indexation of benefits, tax credits and public service pensions from April 2011. So the change directly affects every current or future pensioner who is entitled to a State Second Pension (previously SERPS) or to a pension from a public service pension – that means almost everyone who has ever been employed.

The Consumer Prices Index (CPI) and the Retail Prices Index (RPI) are both measures of the cost of living. One important difference between them is the basket of goods and services upon which they are based, with only the RPI including housing costs. So whenever housing costs increase faster than other prices, increases in the RPI will be higher than those in the CPI. But the reverse also applies, like at present, and the CPI can be higher than the RPI. In the long term the effect should be neutral, except to the extent that people consistently spend more (or less) on housing. In the short-term housing costs are expected to increase faster than the average, as interest rates return to more normal levels, so the RPI is likely to be higher for some years to come.

But there is also a significant technical difference in the way that the RPI and the CPI are calculated. The RPI is an arithmetic mean of price changes (the increases are added together and divided by the number of increases), while the CPI is a geometric mean (the increases are multiplied together and the nth root is taken – where n is the number of increases). While this appears abstruse, of interest only to mathematicians, the Treasury have estimated that: "... the CPI annual rate would typically have been about 0.5 percentage points higher if the elementary aggregates had been calculated using arithmetic means as in the RPI."

In other words, pension increases will in future average about 0.5% less each year, simply because of the change in the way the index is calculated. So which index is the right one? This is a topic of much debate among statisticians and, of course, there is no single correct answer. It all depends on what you are trying to measure. But for most people, looking at what they buy themselves at the shops and elsewhere, there is little doubt. They want to know how much more their basket of goods will cost today, compared to what it cost yesterday. And this is shown by an arithmetic mean.

As a very simple example, imagine the basket of goods is a loaf of bread and a kilo of potatoes. Initially they cost 50p each so the total cost is £1.00. But then, over the year, the price of bread increases by 4%, while that for potatoes increases by 8%. So the bread costs 52p and the potatoes cost 54p, which means the basket now costs £1.06, an increase of 6%. It can be seen that this is the weighted average of 4% and 8%.

But the geometric mean of increases of 4% and 8% with equal weights is 5.98%. In this example it makes only a minor difference in the result but, as mentioned above, the Treasury estimate that in practice it means a difference on average of 0.5% per annum, when compounded across a whole basket of goods.

SOCIAL SCIENCES STATISTICS – MEAN, MEDIAN, AND MODE

When conducting and producing research, the researcher may be in a position where he/she will have to employ the use of statistics. However daunting the task may be, integrating statistics into any research project must be conducted appropriately. The use of statistics is vital when presenting work. Properly utilized statistics afford the researcher credibility towards the validity and meaning of the data and results. This article aims to provide the reader with examples and suggestions regarding understanding the usage of mean, median, and modeas measures of central tendency.

Measures of Central Tendency

The term, 'Measures of Central Tendency' basically means how the distribution of scores are going to be presented. The measures mean, median, and mode are employed to represent the scores of the data. Measures of central tendency tell the audience where the scores would most likely be clustered in order to represent the most common score.

Using Statistics in Research – The Mode

Note: statistical symbol for Mode is *Mo*

The most widely used measure of central tendency, the mode, is simply presented by identifying what score is the most common. For example, a data set using the scores of 1,1,2,4,5,6,7,8,9 would have a mode of 1. Because there are (2) 1's and there are only one score represented for the other numbers, then the 1 occurs the most often.

MEASURES OF DISPERSION

Measures of Dispersion are descriptive statistics which provide information about the extent to which the responses from different elements are spread out across the variable's values. These are used to determine the degree of diversity among respondents.

One way to think about dispersion is reflected in two terms which are used frequently among researchers, especially in reference to ordinal and interval data. These terms are:

1. Peaked distributions-which are frequency distributions with less dispersion or variability. There are many people with the same haracteristics. The graphs of these distributions have a "peak."
2. Flat distributions-which have more variability. People are more spread out with respect to different attributes. The graphs are "flat."

Measures of dispersion include:

A. Range-a measure of dispersion which is based on the total distance between the highest and lowest values. This is calculated by subtracting the number which represents the lowest value from the number of the highest value. The more categories which had actual answers from elements, the higher the range. This works for all levels of measurement.

For example, the range for gender is always 0 or 1. A range of zero would mean that all elements are the same gender. A range of one would mean both genders are represented in the sample or population. (2-1=1)

The age range would have a low value for a homogenous sample (20-18=2); a high value for a sample with people who were very different in age (87-14=73).

B. Dispersion (S)-a measure of how far from a even spread the values of a variable are. S varies between 0 and 1, with zero meaning no dispersion; one, a completely even spread. This may be used for all levels of measurement.

C. Standard Deviation(s)-the amount an average score differs from the mean. This is appropriate only for interval or dichotomous variables. The higher the standard deviation, the more diverse the scores. This is a very popular measure of dispersion, is produced by SPSS, and is sometimes abused through its use with ordinal data.

The formula is: s = the square root of the sum of the difference between each score and the mean squared divided by the number of scores.

(You are not required to remember the formula.).

For example, there are two samples of two people. The first sample is composed of one person who makes $1,000,000. and one who makes nothing. The mean income for this sample is $500,000. The standard deviation is: 500,000

The second sample is composed of two people who both make $500,000. The mean is still the same, $500,000., but the standard deviation is zero.

D. Z score-mathematical way to relate a specific score to the mean and standard deviation. This is a way to tell how different an individual score is from the rest of the scores. The formula is:

Z = the specific score minus the mean divided by the standard deviation (You are not required to remember this.)

STANDARD DEVIATION

Standard deviation is a widely used measurement of variability or diversity used in statistics and probability theory. It shows how much variation or "dispersion" there is from the "average" (mean, or expected/budgeted value). A low standard deviation indicates that the data points tend to be very close to the mean, whereas high standard deviation indicates that the data are spread out over a large range of values.

Technically, the standard deviation of a statistical population, data set, or probability distribution is the square root of its variance. It is algebraically simpler though practically less robust than the average absolute deviation. A useful property of standard deviation is that, unlike variance, it is expressed in the same units as the data. Note, however, that for measurements with percentage as unit, the standard deviation will have percentage points as unit. In addition to expressing the variability of a population, standard deviation is commonly used to measure confidence in statistical conclusions. For example, the margin of error in polling data is determined by calculating the expected standard deviation in the results if the same poll were to be conducted multiple times. The reported margin of error is typically about twice the standard deviation -- the radius of a 95 percent confidence interval. In science, researchers commonly report the standard deviation of experimental data, and only effects that fall far outside the range of standard deviation are considered statistically significant – normal random error or variation in the measurements is in this way distinguished from causal variation. Standard deviation is also important in finance, where the standard deviation on the rate of return on an investment is a measure of the volatility of the investment.

PEARSON'S CHI-SQUARE TEST

Pearson's chi-square (χ^2) test is the best-known of several chi-square tests – statistical procedures whose results are evaluated by reference to the chi-square distribution. Its properties were first investigated by Karl Pearson. In contexts where it is important to make a distinction between the test statistic and its distribution, names similar to Pearson ×-squared test or statistic are used.

It tests a null hypothesis stating that the frequency distribution of certain events observed in a sample is consistent with a particular theoretical distribution. The events considered must be mutually exclusive and have total probability 1. A common case for this is where the events each cover an outcome of a categorical variable. A simple example is the hypothesis that an ordinary six-sided die is "fair", i.e., all six outcomes are equally likely to occur.

Definition

Pearson's chi-square is used to assess two types of comparison: tests of goodness of fit and tests of independence. A test of goodness of fit establishes whether or not an observed frequency distribution differs from a theoretical distribution. A test of independence assesses whether paired observations on two variables, expressed in a contingency table, are independent of each other – for example, whether people from different regions differ in the frequency with which they report that they support a political candidate.

The first step in the chi-square test is to calculate the chi-square statistic. In order to avoid ambiguity, the value of the test-statistic is denoted by $\times^2$ rather than χ^2 (i.e. uppercase chi instead of lowercase); this also serves as a reminder that the distribution of the test statistic is not exactly that of a chi-square random variable.

However some authors do use the χ^2 notation for the test statistic. An exact test which does not rely on using the approximate χ^2 distribution is Fisher's exact test: this is significantly more accurate in evaluating the significance level of the test, especially with small numbers of observation.

The chi-square statistic is calculated by finding the difference between each observed and theoretical frequency for each possible outcome, squaring them, dividing each by the theoretical frequency, and taking the sum of the results. A second important part of determining the test statistic is to define the degrees of freedom of the test: this is essentially the number of observed frequencies adjusted for the effect of using some of those observations to define the "theoretical frequencies".

CHI-SQUARE DISTRIBUTION

In probability theory and statistics, the chi-square distribution (also chi-squared or ÷²-distribution) with *k* degrees of freedom is the distribution of a sum of the squares of *k* independent standard normal random variables. It is one of the most widely used probability distributions in inferential statistics, e.g. in hypothesis testing or in construction of confidence intervals. When there is a need to contrast it with the noncentral chi-square distribution, this distribution is sometimes called the central chi-square distribution.

The chi-square distribution is used in the common chi-square tests for goodness of fit of an observed distribution to a theoretical one, the independence of two criteria of classification of qualitative data, and in confidence interval estimation for a population standard deviation of a normal distribution from a sample standard deviation. Many other statistical tests also use this distribution, like Friedman's analysis of variance by ranks.

The chi-square distribution is a special case of the gamma distribution.

CHI-SQUARE TEST

A chi-square test (also chi squared test or ÷² test) is any statistical hypothesis test in which the sampling distribution of the test statistic is a chi-square distribution when the null hypothesis is true, or any in which this is *asymptotically* true, meaning that the sampling distribution (if the null hypothesis is true) can be made to approximate a chi-square distribution as closely as desired by making the sample size large enough.

Some examples of chi-squared tests where the chi-square distribution is only approximately valid:

- Pearson's chi-square test, also known as the chi-square goodness-of-fit test or chi-square test for independence. When mentioned without any modifiers or without other precluding context, this test is usually understood (for an exact test used in place of ÷², see Fisher's exact test).

- Yates' chi-square test, also known as Yates' correction for continuity
- Mantel–Haenszel chi-square test.
- Linear-by-linear association chi-square test.
- The portmanteau test in time-series analysis, testing for the presence of autocorrelation
- Likelihood-ratio tests in general statistical modelling, for testing whether there is evidence of the need to move from a simple model to a more complicated one (where the simple model is nested within the complicated one).

One case where the distribution of the test statistic is an exact chi-square distribution is the test that the variance of a normally-distributed population has a given value based on a sample variance. Such a test is uncommon in practice because values of variances to test against are seldom known exactly.

Chi-square Test for Variance in a Normal Population

If a sample of size n is taken from a population having a normal distribution, then there is a well-known result which allows a test to be made of whether the variance of the population has a pre-determined value. For example, a manufacturing process might have been in stable condition for a long period, allowing a value for the variance to be determined essentially without error.

Suppose that a variant of the process is being tested, giving rise to a small sample of product items whose variation is to be tested. The test statistic T in this instance could be set to be the sum of squares about the sample mean, divided by the nominal value for the variance (i.e. the value to be tested as holding). Then T has a chi-square distribution with n–1 degrees of freedom. For example if the sample size is 21, the acceptance region for T for a significance level of 5% is the interval 9.59 to 34.17.

SPEARMAN'S RANK CORRELATION COEFFICIENT

In statistics, Spearman's rank correlation coefficient or Spearman's rho, named after Charles Spearman and often denoted by the Greek letter ñ (rho) or as r_s, is a non-parametric measure of statistical dependence between two variables. It assesses how well the relationship between two variables can be described using a monotonic function. If there are no repeated data values, a perfect Spearman correlation of +1 or "1 occurs when each of the variables is a perfect monotone function of the other.

Definition and Calculation

The Spearman correlation coefficient is often thought of as being the Pearson correlation coefficient between the ranked variables. In practice, however, a simpler procedure is normally used to calculate ñ. The n raw scores X_i, Y_i are converted to ranks x_i, y_i, and the differences $d_i = x_i$ " y_i between the ranks of each observation on the two variables are calculated.

Bibliography

Arora, Chandralekha: *Advances in Science Research*, Oxford Book Company, 2009.

Azhar Iqbal : *Principles and Practices of Social Work*, Sublime, Delhi, 2005.

Babbie, E.R.: *Survey Research Methods*. Belmont, CA: Wadsworth, 1973.

Bailey, Kenneth, D.: *Methods of Social Research*, New York, The Free Press, 1987.

Bajpai, R B : *Research Methodology : Data Presentation*, APH, 2007.

Bhaskaran, Vanila : *Research Methods for Social Work,* Rawat, Delhi 2008.

Brannen, J.: *Mixing Methods: Qualitative and Quantitative Research.* London: Avebury, 1992.

Bryman, A.: *Quality and Quantity in Social Research.* London: Unwin Hyman, 1992.

Das, D.K. Lal : *Practice of Social Research : Social Work* Perspective, Rawat, 2000.

Dasgupta, Manas: *Research Methodology in Economics : Problems and Issues*, Deep and Deep, 2007.

Denzin, N.: *The Research Act: A Theoretical Introduction to Sociological Methods*. Chicago: Aldine Press, 1967.

Diwan, Jagmohan: *Fundamentals of Rural Sociology*, Cyber Tech Pub, Delhi, 2009.

Fowler, Floyd J., : *Survey Research Methods*, Newbury Park, CA: Sage, 1993.

Fox, J. & Tracy, P.: *Randomized Response: A Method for Sensitive Surveys*. Beverly Hills, CA: Sage, 1986.

Frederic G. Reamer : *Social Work Values and Ethics,* Rawat, Delhi, 2005.

Goode, W.J. and Hat: *Methods in Social Research*, New York, McGraw-Hill, 1962.

Gupta, Sudhir: *Workshop on Research Methodology*, Centrum Press, 2011.

Kalton, Graham: *Introduction to Survey Sampling.* Beverly Hills, CA: Sage, 1983.

Kanti Bagchi: *Research Methodology in Social Sciences: A Practical Guide*, Abhijeet Pub, 2007.

Krishnaswamy, O.R.: *Methodology of Research in Social Sciences*, Mumbai: Himalaya Publishing House, 1993.

Kumar, Ajit : *Social Work Concerns and Challenges in the 21 Century*, APH, Delhi, 2009.

Maxwell, J. A.: *Qualitative Research Design: An interactive approach.* Thousand Oaks, CA: Sage Publishing, 1996.

Milton Reimer : *Christian Perspectives on Sociology,* Grand Rapids, Mich., Zondervan, 1982.

Mittal, Kapila: *Research Methodology in Social Sciences*, Vista International, 2006.

Mujawar, W.R. : *Research Methodology in Social Work*, Manglam Publications, 2010.

Neelam, Sandhya: *Research Methodology in Sociological Research*, Manglam Pub, Delhi, 2008.

Polansky, N.A.: *Social Work Research* Chicago: University of Chicago, 1960.

Pratima Chaturvedi : *Social Work : Theories and Practices,* Book Enclave, Delhi, 2005.

Ramachandran, S.P. : *Social Work for Minorities*, Sumit Enterprises, Delhi, 2008.

Sen, S K : *Social Work Practices*, Book Enclave, Delhi, 2007.

Subhedar, I.S. : *Social Work Perspectives,* Om Pub, Delhi, 2006.

Trochim, W.: *The Research Methods Knowledge Base.* Ithaca, NY: Cornell Custom Publishing, 1999.

Index

F

G

I

L

M

N

O

P

R

□□□